The Authority and Importance of the Sunnah

حجية وأهمية السنة

Jamaal al-Din M. Zarabozo

2000

The Authority and Importance of the Sunnah
By Jamaal al-Din M. Zarabozo

Published by:
Al-Basheer Company for Publications and Translations
10515 E. 40th Ave. Suite #108
Denver, CO   80239-3264
U.S.A.
www.al-basheer.com

(Note: Not affiliated with Basheer Publications)

Printed in U.S.A.

Cover Design by Ahmed Ali Ansari, Al-Basheer Graphics

ISBN 1-891540-09-2 $16.00 softcover

Preface

In the name of Allah, Most Compassionate, Most Merciful. All praises are due to Allah; we praise Him; we seek His help; we seek His forgiveness; and we seek His guidance. We seek refuge in Allah from the evil in our souls and the badness of our deeds. For whomever Allah guides, there is none to lead him astray. And for whomever He allows to go astray, there is none to guide him. I bear witness that there is none worthy of worship except Allah, for whom there is no partner. And I bear witness that Muhammad is His servant and Messenger. O believers, have *taqwa* [fear] of Allah according to His right and die not save as Muslims. O mankind, have *taqwa* of your Lord, the One who created you from one soul and created from it its mate and from them spread forth many men and women. And fear Allah from whom you demand your mutual rights and [do not cut] familial ties. Surely, Allah is ever an All-Watcher over you. O believers, have *taqwa* of Allah and always speak the truth. He will direct you to do righteous deeds and will forgive you your sins. And whosoever obeys Allah and His Messenger has indeed achieved a great achievement.

To proceed: Verily, the truest speech is the Book of Allah. The best guidance is the guidance of Muhammad. The worst affairs are the innovated ones. Every innovated matter is a heresy. And every heresy is a going astray. And every astray act is in the Hell-fire.

I praise and thank Allah for giving me the ability to complete this book. I pray that He accepts this work from me and forgives me for any mistakes and errors that have occurred herein.

As always, there are many people whom I would like to thank for their help in this particular work. First, I would like to express my thanks to brothers Zulfiqar Muhammad Ali and Khalil Kramer for editing and proofreading portions of the book. I must also express my appreciation to those who have helped me in so many various ways: Nahar al-Rashid, Said Lahrichi, Muhammad al-Osimi, Fahd al-Yahya, Ahmad al-Teraiqi, Muhammad Tahlawi and Abdul Azeez al-Khurayif. Of course, my beloved wife deserves special mention for all of her years of encouragement, help and patience. Special thanks must also go to Br. Homaidan al-Turki, President, al-Basheer Company, for his continual encouragement and support. May Allah reward all of these people greatly.

Finally, I pray that this work is beneficial to those who read it. If anyone has any comments, corrections or suggestions for this work, they should feel free to contact me through the publisher.

Jamaal Zarabozo
Boulder, CO
U.S.A.
December 20, 1999

Table of Contents

Introduction:
The Need for Such a Book

It is generally understood that the Quran and the Prophet Muhammad's (peace be upon him) sunnah[1] form the cornerstones of Islam. However, some phenomena have occurred that make it a necessity to write about the sunnah and to once again emphasize its place in Islam. These phenomena include the following:

(1) There is a misunderstanding concerning the place of the sunnah vis-a-vis the Quran. It is not uncommon to hear some Muslims make statements such as, "What the Quran states you must follow. What is found in the sunnah is good to follow." One can also hear, "Something cannot be made obligatory unless it is in the Quran. If it is only in the sunnah, then it can only be considered recommended and one is not required to follow it." This misunderstanding is usually due to the fact that the relevant information and usage of the word sunnah has reached the person in a confusing manner.[2]

(2) There has also appeared some groups who claim that Muslims are not obliged to follow the sunnah. These people claim that they are following the Quran and only the Quran. They try to give elaborate arguments to support their views. Unfortunately, they have been able to fool some people. In particular, in the West, they try to approach new converts to Islam whose understanding or experience in Islam is still

---

[1] The word "sunnah" is defined in the following chapter. Here, it can be taken to mean, "the way of life of the Prophet Muhammad (peace be upon him)."
[2] This particular problem shall be dealt with in the following chapter.

rather rudimentary. When studied in detail, however, one finds that their arguments are not completely unacceptable.[1]

(3) There has been influence from some movements among the Muslims who seem to downplay the role of the sunnah in order to make Islam more "viable" with the modern age and, in particular, Western civilization.[2] The arguments of these people are usually more intricate and detailed than those who reject the sunnah as a whole. Often times, they show an acceptance for the authority of the sunnah as a whole but a refusal to accept particular hadith that they find troublesome. Furthermore, they have a tendency to delve into matters involving terminology that the listener may not be completely

---

[1] The first appearance of such a group seems to have been in the Indo-Pak subcontinent. The idea then spread to Egypt and other areas, although it never gained strong support in the Arab world. Unfortunately, groups with such thoughts have appeared in the West. For more details of their history and a refutation of their views, see Khaadim Husain Ilaahi Bakhsh, *Al-Quraaniyoon wa Shubahaatuhum Haul al-Sunnah* (Al-Taif, Saudi Arabia: Maktabah al-Sideeq, 1989), *passim*.

[2] The attacks of the modernists upon the sunnah are well-known. The goal is to strip Islam of all of its practical aspects and make it a sedentary religion like that of most of modern-day Christianity. S. M. Yusuf offered an explanation of why they attack the sunnah in particular. Yusuf wrote, "In our own day the so-called modernity, the protagonists of which keep a sinister silence on its full and proper definition, is but the same old challenge to the Sunnah in a new garb with the difference that this time it is accompanied by a fanfare of scientific achievement and industrial and technological power... In the circumstances it would appear to be a generous concession indeed that religion is allowed to survive: only it is called upon to adjust itself to the new demands of the age. The method suggested for such adjustment is none other than sloughing off the old forms and revaluing the values arbitrarily according to the exigencies of modernity itself. No surprise that the brunt of the attack is directed at the Sunnah—the repository of forms and institutions. It makes little difference if the allegiance to the Sunnah is retained so long as it is regarded as a mere carton package for graded values... Modernity is at war with the dimensional Islam—its practices and institutions." S. M. Yusuf, *An Essay on the Sunnah: Its Importance, Transmission, Development and Revision* (Lahore, Pakistan: Institute of Islamic Culture, 1966), pp. 9-10.

2

familiar with, such as the argument over *mutawaatir* hadith versus *ahaad* hadith.[1]

(4) Lastly, Orientalists, missionaries and the like are still continuing their attacks on the sunnah of the Messenger of Allah (peace be upon him). These people fully realize the importance of the sunnah to Islam. Due to a general and overall lack of knowledge among Muslims regarding the sunnah and hadith, they have found this to be an opening through which they may attack Islam. In some cases, their arguments are the most drawn out and intricate, sometimes presented in the form of dissertations and scholarly articles. In other cases, especially among some of the evangelists, their arguments amount to not much more than blatant deception and falsehood.[2]

This particular work is mostly concerned with issues (1) and (2) above. Categories (3) and (4) require discussions that involve great detail concerning the sciences of hadith, their preservation and so on. Allah willing, they will be dealt with in a future work. The purpose of this present work is simply to present in clear and unquestionable fashion the place and importance of the sunnah and hadith in Islam.

---

[1] *Mutawaatir* refers to any report that has been narrated through so many people and in such a way that it is inconceivable that they have all committed the same mistake or all agreed upon the same forgery. An *ahaad* report is, in essence, any report that does not meet the conditions to be *mutawaatir*. Note that there are a number of topics related to the sunnah of the Prophet (peace be upon him) that will not be covered in this work. Those topics include the authority of *ahaad* vis-a-vis *mutaawatir* hadith, abrogation of the Quran by the sunnah, analysis of the actions of the Prophet (peace be upon him) and so forth. The author hopes to discuss those topics in another work entitled, *The Sunnah: An Islamic Legal Theory Perspective*. May Allah grant that hope fruition.

[2] A detailed defense of the sunnah against the claims made against it is also beyond the scope of this work. By the grace and mercy of Allah, Professor Mustafa al-Azami has refuted a number of the claims of the Orientalists and their followers. See Muhammad Mustafa al-Azami, *On Schacht's Origins of Muhammadan Jurisprudence* (New York: John Wiley and Sons, Inc. 1985), *passim*; Muhammad Mustafa al-Azami, *Studies in Early Hadith Literature* (Indianapolis, IN: American Trust Publications, 1978), *passim*.

For those who are not affected by any of the above influences or misconceptions, this work may still serve very important purposes. First, it may be a reminder as to the importance and need to adhere to the sunnah of the Messenger of Allah (peace be upon him). One may be very much aware of the obligation of following the sunnah, yet at times one may forget the extreme emphasis placed by Allah and His Messenger (peace be upon him) on obeying the commands and following the example of the Prophet (peace be upon him). Hence, a reminder and another reading of the relevant verses and hadith may serve to rejuvenate the person and make his commitment to follow the sunnah even stronger. As Allah says in the Quran,

$$وَذَكِّرْ فَإِنَّ الذِّكْرَى تَنفَعُ الْمُؤْمِنِينَ$$

"But remind for, indeed, reminding benefits the believers" (*al-Dhaariyaat* 55).

Second, it may serve as an encouragement to learn more of the sunnah and to study hadith in greater detail. Again, one may realize the place of the sunnah in a general sense, but when rereading the words of Allah concerning obeying and following the Messenger of Allah (peace be upon him) this may spark the desire to learn more of the sunnah and hadith; the motivated person may then learn hadith not just at a superficial level but in detail, to try to receive as much guidance as he can from this important form of revelation from Allah.

Third, such works can help to increase one's faith. Certainly by following the sunnah of the Prophet (peace be upon him), the Muslim is definitely following the way that is pleasing to Allah and that will lead, Allah willing, to His pleasure and Paradise in the Hereafter.

Fourth, although a person may recognize the importance of the sunnah and he may not be confused by the types of misconceptions referred to earlier, he may still have some "lesser misconceptions" concerning the sunnah of the

Prophet (peace be upon him). It has been this author's experience that even among those who believe in adhering to the sunnah, there are still some issues that are not completely clear in their minds. This is understandable, as one can easily become confused given the plethora of opinions that one hears. Hence, this work may help make those sometimes confusing issues clear, so that the person may worship Allah based on a true and correct understanding of His religion.

Chapter One:
The Meanings of the Words
"Sunnah" and "Hadith"

The first step that must be taken is to define the terms "sunnah" and "hadith" in a very clear manner. This is particularly important with respect to the word "sunnah." Indeed, one of the first sources of confusion concerning the sunnah and its importance is the different usages of the word "sunnah." The word "sunnah" is used in different ways by scholars of different disciplines. Each discipline defines and uses the word in the manner that is most appropriate for its needs and purposes. As shall be noted, not realizing this fact can be quite disastrous for one's overall perception of the place of the sunnah in Islam.

The Meanings of the Word "Sunnah"

When used in its most general and common sense, the word sunnah is a reference to the overall teachings and way of life of the Prophet Muhammad (peace be upon him). However, to be more precise, the word sunnah is used by different types of scholars to connote very different concepts.[1] This is because the purpose and goals of the various disciplines are

---

[1] The different usages of the word "sunnah" are discussed in a number of works, including: Mustafa al-Sibaa'ee, *Al-Sunnah wa Makaanatuhaa fi al-Tashree al-Islaami* (Beirut: al-Maktab al-Islaami, 1982), pp. 47-49; Muhammad Luqmaan al-Salafi, *Al-Sunnah: Hujiyyatuhaa wa Makaanatuhaa fi-l-Islaam wa al-Radd ala Munkireehaa* (Madinah: Maktabah al-Imaan, 1989), pp. 11-18; Al-Husain Shawaat, *Hujiyyat al-Sunnah* (Falls Church, VA: American Open University, n.d.), pp. 14-25.

different. In particular, one needs to differentiate the meaning of the word as it is used in general parlance and how it is used as a technical term by specialists in *aqeedah* (creed and beliefs), jurisprudence, Islamic legal theory and scholars of hadith.

Lexical Definition of the Word *Sunnah*

Lane gives the lexical definition for the word "sunnah" (سنة) (whose plural is *sunan* سنن) as , "A way, course, rule or manner, of acting or conduct of life or the like... whether good or bad; approved or disapproved... a way that has been instituted or pursued by former people and has become one pursued by those after them."[1] As Lane noted, a conduct of life may be a praiseworthy way of life or a blameworthy way of life. Lexically, the word "sunnah" could be used for either one. However, in parlance it is usually used for a praiseworthy way of life; in fact, when used in a negative sense, that is customarily made explicit by the context or an additional adjective.

It is not surprising to find this lexical usage of the word in the Prophet's own speech. In fact, in the following hadith, the word "sunnah" is used in this sense:

عَنْ جَرِيرِ بْنِ عَبْدِ اللَّهِ قَالَ جَاءَ نَاسٌ مِنَ الْأَعْرَابِ إِلَى رَسُولِ اللَّهِ صَلَّى اللَّهُمَّ عَلَيْهِ وَسَلَّمَ عَلَيْهِمُ الصُّوفُ فَرَأَى سُوءَ حَالِهِمْ قَدْ أَصَابَتْهُمْ حَاجَةٌ فَحَثَّ النَّاسَ عَلَى الصَّدَقَةِ فَأَبْطَئُوا عَنْهُ

---

[1] E. W. Lane, *Arabic-English Lexicon* (Cambridge, England: Islamic Texts Society, 1984), vol. 1, p. 1438. The word "sunnah" has other lexical meanings that shall not be discussed here. As Shawaat notes, all of the other meanings have some integral relationship with the term as defined above. Cf., Lane, vol. 1, p. 1438; Shawaat, p. 17.

حَتَّى رُئِيَ ذَلِكَ فِي وَجْهِهِ قَالَ ثُمَّ إِنَّ رَجُلاً مِنَ الأَنْصَارِ جَاءَ

بِصُرَّةٍ مِنْ وَرِقٍ ثُمَّ جَاءَ آخَرُ ثُمَّ تَتَابَعُوا حَتَّى عُرِفَ السُّرُورُ

فِي وَجْهِهِ فَقَالَ رَسُولُ اللَّهِ صَلَّى اللَّهم عَلَيْهِ وَسَلَّمَ مَنْ سَنَّ

فِي الإِسْلَامِ سُنَّةً حَسَنَةً فَعُمِلَ بِهَا بَعْدَهُ كُتِبَ لَهُ مِثْلُ أَجْرِ مَنْ

عَمِلَ بِهَا وَلَا يَنْقُصُ مِنْ أُجُورِهِمْ شَيْءٌ وَمَنْ سَنَّ فِي الإِسْلَامِ

سُنَّةً سَيِّئَةً فَعُمِلَ بِهَا بَعْدَهُ كُتِبَ عَلَيْهِ مِثْلُ وِزْرِ مَنْ عَمِلَ بِهَا

وَلَا يَنْقُصُ مِنْ أَوْزَارِهِمْ شَيْءٌ

On the authority of Jaabir ibn Abdullah who said: "A group of bedouins came to the Messenger of Allah (peace be upon him) wearing woolen clothing. The Prophet (peace be upon him) noticed their harsh situation and that they had been afflicted with need. He then exhorted the people to give charity but they were slow in doing so, until they saw the signs on anger on his face. Then a man from the Ansaar came with a container of silver. Then another came. These were followed by others until the signs of happiness could be seen on his [the Prophet's] face. The Messenger of Allah (peace be upon him) then said, 'Whoever introduces a good practice (sunnah) in Islam that is acted upon after him shall have written for him a reward similar to the one who acted upon it without the reward of either of them being lessened in any way. And whoever introduces an evil practice (sunnah) into Islam that is acted upon after him shall have the burden of the ones who acted upon it recorded for him without the burden of either of them being reduced in any way.'" (Recorded by Muslim.[1])

---

[1] Note that this particular hadith could be misunderstood to imply that there is such a thing as "good innovations." From the Shareeah point of view, all innovations and heresies are definitely acts taking one away from the straight

Before discussing the definition of the word "sunnah" as used by different scholars, it should be noted that the Quran speaks about "the sunnah of Allah." For example, Allah says,

سُنَّةَ اللَّهِ فِي الَّذِينَ خَلَوْا مِنْ قَبْلُ وَلَنْ تَجِدَ لِسُنَّةِ اللَّهِ تَبْدِيلاً

"The sunnah of Allah among those who passed before. And you will not find in the sunnah of Allah any change" (*al-Ahzaab* 62; see also *al-Fath* 23 and *al-Israa* 77). "Sunnah of Allah" refers to the decisions, laws, commands and decrees of Allah that are unchanging and apply to all peoples and times, such as the sunnah to destroy those beforehand when they persistently refused to adhere to the revelations that Allah sent.

A common usage that stretches across the different disciplines is the use of the word sunnah in juxtaposition to the Quran. In other words, one speaks about "the Quran and sunnah," or "the Book of Allah and the sunnah of the Messenger of Allah (peace be upon him)." In this sense, it refers to the guidance received via the Prophet (peace be upon him) other than what he conveyed from the Quran.

Definition of the Word *Sunnah* As Used by the Jurists

Among all the different disciplines discussed here, the way the jurists use the word *sunnah* is closest to its lexical definition. This usage, meaning "a praiseworthy way of action," has actually turned out to be a source of confusion concerning the status and importance of the sunnah.[1]

---

path. The action that the Prophet (peace be upon him) was referring to in this particular hadith is an action sanctioned by the Shareeah and followed by others—the action of giving for the sake of those in need. This type of deed is not considered an innovation because it is directly based on explicit evidences of the Quran or sunnah.

[1] The jurists definitely also use the term "sunnah" as a reference to one of the sources of Islamic law. When doing so, though, they are in essence borrowing the legal theorists' definition of the term. The above discussion is concentrating on their use of the term sunnah as a technical term specific to them as jurists.

Jurists, for the most part, are concerned with the rulings of particular actions. In general, an act may be classified into one of five categories: obligatory, recommended, permissible, reprehensible or forbidden. In addition, an act may be sound and valid or it may be void and non-effective. The scholars use a myriad of terms to describe the category of recommended acts. These terms include *mandoob* (مندوب), *mustahabb* (مستحب) and so on. In some cases, each term has a slightly different connotation.[1] However, without a doubt, one of the most common terms used for that category is the word "sunnah." Therefore, for example, the jurists will say that that two *rakat*s of prayer before the obligatory *Fajr* (Dawn) Prayer are "sunnah." This means that they are not obligatory. Yet they carry a certain status or reward for them such that they are definitely more than merely permissible.[2]

---

[1] Cf., Abdul Ghani Abdul Khaaliq, *Hujjiyah al-Sunnah* (Beirut: Daar al-Quran al-Kareem, 1986), pp. 51-68. The most detailed discussion of this topic (recommended acts, the terms used for them and their different implications) available in English is Ahmad Hasan, *Principles of Islamic Jurisprudence* (Islamabad, Pakistan: Islamic Research Institute, 1993), vol. 1, pp. 78-109.

[2] Some books try to give an example of this usage in the Prophet's own words. Unfortunately, the hadith most often quoted (such as by Hasan, p. 82) is, "Allah has obligated upon you fasting Ramadhaan. And I have established (*sanantu*) for you (as a virtuous act) its night prayers [known as *taraweeh*]. Whoever fasts it and prays [those prayers during] it, with faith and hoping for a reward, will have his sins removed from him like the day on which his mother gave birth to him." This hadith was recorded by al-Nasaai, ibn Maajah and others. Unfortunately, this hadith is reported through a weak chain and is declared weak by scholars such as ibn al-Qattaan, al-Albaani and Shuaib al-Arnaoot. Abdul Qaadir al-Arnaoot considers it *hasan* due to its corroborating evidence; however, he may have been referring only to the concept that whoever prays the nights of Ramadhaan shall have his previous sins forgiven, which is recorded in authentic hadith. Cf., Ali ibn Muhammad ibn al-Qattaan, *Bayaan al-Wahm wa al-Eehaam al-Waqi'een fi Kitaab al-Ahkaam* (Riyadh: Daar Taibah, 1997), vol. 3, pp. 55-58 and 444-445; Muhammad Naasir al-Deen al-Albaani, *Dhaeef Sunan al-Nasaai* (Beirut: al-Maktab al-Islaami, 1990), p. 76; Shuaib al-Arnaoot, et al., footnotes to Ahmad ibn Hanbal, *Musnad al-Imaam Ahmad ibn Hanbal* (Beirut: Muassasat al-Risaalah, 1997), vol. 3, p. 199 and 217; Abdul Qaadir al-Arnaoot, footnotes to al-Mubaarak

11

In general, the jurists define this category of acts, that they call "recommended" or "sunnah," in a number of ways:[1]

(1) A sunnah act is one whose performance is indicated or encouraged by the law; however, the law falls short of declaring it to be obligatory or required.

(2) A sunnah act is one that when performed a person is rewarded for it, but for which he is not punished if he fails to perform it; or, in other words, it is an act that a person is praised for doing and, on the other hand, he is not to be blamed or censured if he does not perform the act. This is a common definition among the Malikis of North Africa and the Hanbalis.

(3) A sunnah act is an action that one is requested to perform but not in a strict sense. This is a common definition among the Malikis of the Eastern regions (non-North Africans) and among the Shaafi'ees.

(4) A sunnah act is what the Prophet (peace be upon him) performed on a continual basis, although he would sometimes not perform it with no particular apparent reason for not performing it. This is a definition given by the Hanafis.[2]

In such definitions, it seems that the jurists were trying to present the most concise "legalese" definition. As a general concept, one may need to go beyond such a strict legal definition. Perhaps it would be better to consider "recommended" acts as those acts that are becoming of a Muslim and anyone who desires to complete his Islam and his faith would be best served to perform those acts as much as he feasibly can—without them taking on the position of obligatory acts. Furthermore, it should never be forgotten that "sunnah" acts are definitely pleasing to Allah and they are a means of getting closer to Allah.

---

ibn al-Atheer, *Jaami al-Usool fi Ahaadeeth al-Rasool* (Maktabah al-Hilwaani, et al., 1972), vol. 9, p. 441.

[1] Cf., Shawaat, p. 22; Hasan, *Principles*, vol. 1, pp. 78-80.

[2] Technically speaking, this is a Hanafi definition for what is known as "non-emphasized sunnah."

There is also another important point to keep in mind concerning the overall category of those acts considered only recommended or sunnah. Dhumairiyyah notes,

Some people are lax with respect to what has been established as sunnah in the usage of the jurists. [They are lax] based on the claim that sunnah acts are those for which one is rewarded for doing them but is not punished for not doing them. But that is in general. At the same time, the scholars have stated, based on numerous hadith that encourage one to follow and adhere to the sunnah, that one who customarily leaves the sunnah acts is to be punished or castigated. He is doing wrong and committing a sin. The Companions would eagerly perform those acts in a manner similar to how they would perform the obligatory deeds,[1] al-Laknawi has quoted many texts to that effect in his book *Tuhfah al-Akhyaar*. As for the jurists' distinction between obligatory and sunnah, that is concerning individual instances and not with respect to leaving the sunnah acts completely.[2]

---

[1] It may be an exaggeration to claim that they performed them in a manner similar to their adherence to the obligatory deeds. Indeed, to treat a recommended deed like an obligatory deed and to insist on it for oneself and others would, in itself, be a type of innovation. The statement in the quote must be understood to mean that they gretaly disliked missing the recommended deeds, although they recognized that they were not obligatory.

[2] Uthmaan ibn Jumuah Dhumairiyyah, *Madkhal li-Diraasah al-Aqeedah al-Islaamiyyah* (Jeddah: Maktabah al-Suwaari, 1993), p. 93. Furthermore, among the sunnah acts, there are some which are described as "emphasized sunnah." For the Hanafis, in particular, an emphasized sunnah takes on almost the same status as an obligatory act. For example, ibn Abideen, a leading Hanafi jurist, wrote, "The strongest opinion is that it is a sin to leave an emphasized sunnah like it is a sin to leave an obligatory act." For more details on this point, see Muhammad Abu al-Fath al-Bayaanooni, *Al-Hukum al-Takleefi fi al-Shareeah al-Islaamiyyah* (Damascus: Dar al-Qalam, 1988), pp. 171-178.

Another common usage of the word sunnah among the jurists is anything which is juxtaposed with an innovation or heresy (Ar., *bidah* بدعة). In this sense, the word sunnah may refer to anything that is sanctioned by the shareeah. That would include whatever is derived from the Quran, practice of the Prophet (peace be upon him) or even the collective action of the Companions.[1] For example, the jurists may refer to a divorce which is done according to the sunnah (*talaaq al-sunnah*) vis-a-vis a divorced that is done not completely in accord with the sunnah (*talaaq al-bidah*). Sometimes, even though the act is not done completely in accord with the sunnah, the act may still have legal effect and implications but the person has done wrong for performing the act in that fashion. Hence, they make this distinction.

Definition of the Word *Sunnah* as Used by the Scholars of Hadith

The topic of study for the scholars of hadith is everything that has been narrated or reported concerning the Prophet (peace be upon him). They desire to gather all of that information to determine what of it is sound and acceptable and to distinguish that from what has been narrated through untrustworthy or unacceptable means. Hence, first and foremost, they concentrate on anything narrated about or from the Prophet (peace be upon him). All of the information about the Prophet (peace be upon him) that one could imagine was passed on and recorded in detail, the extent of which is not comparable to anyone in the history of mankind.

The purpose of study or goal of the scholars of hadith has greatly affected their technical definition of the word "sunnah." Indeed, their definition of the word "sunnah" is the broadest of all definitions, trying to encompass everything that

---

[1] Al-Sibaa'ee, p. 48.

14

was passed on concerning the Prophet (peace be upon him). In general, the definition of "sunnah" from the scholars of hadith perspective is: "What has been passed down from the Prophet (peace be upon him) of his statements, actions, tacit approvals, manners, physical characteristics or biography, regardless of whether it was before he was sent as a prophet or afterwards."[1]

To make this definition clearer, examples of each category shall be given:

An example of one of his statements is the hadith narrated by Umar ibn al-Khataab that the Messenger of Allah (peace be upon him) said,

$$ إِنَّمَا الأَعْمَالُ بِالنِّيَّاتِ وَإِنَّمَا لِكُلِّ امْرِئٍ مَا نَوَى فَمَنْ كَانَتْ $$

$$ هِجْرَتُهُ إِلَى اللَّهِ وَرَسُولِهِ فَهِجْرَتُهُ إِلَى اللَّهِ وَرَسُولِهِ فَمَنْ كَانَتْ $$

$$ هِجْرَتُهُ لِدُنْيَا يُصِيبُهَا أَوْ إِلَى امْرَأَةٍ يَنْكِحُهَا فَهِجْرَتُهُ إِلَى مَا $$

$$ هَاجَرَ إِلَيْهِ $$

"Surely, all actions are but driven by intentions and, verily, every man shall have but that which he intended. Thus, he whose migration was for Allah and His Messenger, [then] his migration was for Allah and His Messenger; and he whose migration was to achieve some worldly benefit or to take a woman in marriage, his migration was for that which he migrated." (Recorded by al-Bukhari and Muslim.)

An example of one his actions is the following report recorded on the authority of Aishah:

$$ كَانَ إِذَا صَلَّى رَكْعَتَيِ الْفَجْرِ فِي بَيْتِهِ اضْطَجَعَ عَلَى يَمِينِهِ $$

---

[1] Al-Salafi, p. 15; Shawaat, p. 20.

15

"When he [the Prophet (peace be upon him)] would perform the two [non-obligatory] *rakats* of *Fajr* in his house, he would then lie on his right side."[1]

An example of the Prophet's tacit approval is found in the hadith from *Sahih Muslim* in which Anas was asked if the Prophet (peace be upon him) ever performed the two *rakats* of prayer before the *Maghrib* (Sunset) Prayer. He replied, "He used to see us performing them and he would neither order us to do them or forbid us from performing them."

An example of a report describing the Prophet's manner or behavior is:

$$كَانَ النَّبِيُّ صَلَّى اللَّهم عَلَيْهِ وَسَلَّمَ أَشَدَّ حَيَاءً مِنَ الْعَذْرَاءِ فِي خِدْرِهَا فَإِذَا رَأَى شَيْئًا يَكْرَهُهُ عَرَفْنَاهُ فِي وَجْهِهِ$$

"The Prophet (peace be upon him) was more bashful than the virgin girls kept in their private compartments. If he saw anything he did not like, we would recognize it by [the expression on] his face." (Recorded by al-Bukhari and Muslim.)

Reports describing the Prophet's physical characteristics are numerous. They are reports about his height and physical appearance. For example, ibn Umar narrated that the Messenger of Allah (peace be upon him) had approximately twenty gray hairs.[2] Another example is the report from Jaabir ibn Saumurah that the Prophet (peace be upon him) had a full beard. (Recorded by Muslim.)

---

[1] With this wording, this is recorded by al-Tirmidhi. According to al-Albaani, it is *sahih*. See Muhammad Naasir al-Deen al-Albaani, *Saheeh Sunan al-Tirmidhi* (Riyadh: Maktab al-Tarbiyyah al-Arabi Li-Duwal al-Khaleej, 1988), vol. 1, p. 132.

[2] Recorded by al-Tirmidhi in *al-Shamaail*. According to al-Albaani, this report is *sahih*. See Muhammad Naasir al-Deen al-Albaani, *Saheeh al-Jaami al-Sagheer* (Beirut: al-Maktab al-Islaami, 1986), vol. 2, p. 873. These kinds of reports demonstrate the amount of information that has been preserved and passed on concerning the final prophet and Messenger of Allah (peace be upon him).

Reports concerning his biography include the report that he married Khadeejah when he was twenty-five years old while they were living in Makkah and before he had received his first revelation. Also included in this category would be the reports that he lived in Makkah for thirteen years after receiving revelation and then migrated to Madinah.

Again, these types of reports all fall under the hadith specialists' definition of the word "sunnah," even though some of them may have no direct bearing on Islamic law. For the hadith specialists they are important because those scholars are concerned with everything that has been narrated from or about the Prophet (peace be upon him).

Definition of the Word *Sunnah* as Used in Islamic Legal Theory

One of the goals of the Islamic legal theorists is to determine what is or is not an authority in Islamic law. They are not concerned with the details of the actual law but they are concerned with the sources and methodology of that law. When they define the word *sunnah*, they are defining it from that perspective. Therefore, when it comes to the reports that have been narrated about or from the Prophet (peace be upon him), they try to distinguish what is an authority and what is an example for the Muslims to follow from that which does not fall into that category. Their definition will definitely differ from that of the scholars of hadith, being much less broad in scope.

Perhaps the most common definition given for the sunnah from Islamic legal theory perspective is: Whatever comes from the Prophet (peace be upon him), other than the Quran itself, in the form of his speech, actions or tacit approvals. His speech includes what he commanded, recommended, permitted, disapproved or forbade. The Prophet's actions are considered an authority in Islamic law because the Muslims have been ordered to take him as their example. His tacit approvals are considered an authority in Islamic law because it would not be right for the Prophet (peace be upon him) to remain silent in the presence of something wrong; hence, his silence implies his approval while his approval implies that the act is correct according to the Shareeah.

In this definition, the legal theorists have obviously excluded the Quran from part of the definition—but the definition is inclusive of *hadith qudsi*.[1] By referring to him as "the Prophet (peace be upon him)" they are thereby excluding what the Prophet (peace be upon him) said, did or approved of before he received revelation. Such would not be considered an authority in Islamic law.

Although "actions" of the Prophet (peace be upon him) is mentioned in the definition given above, in reality, the scholars of Islamic legal theory mean "selected actions" of the Prophet (peace be upon him). That is, there are certain actions that are not considered as examples for others to follow. For example, it is narrated that the Prophet (peace be upon him) used to snore lightly. Note that the definition of the word "sunnah" as given by the scholars of hadith would encompass this report as part of the sunnah. However, since this act has no legal bearing—in the sense that no Muslim is requested to follow that act—it would not fall under the Islamic legal definition of the word sunnah.[2] Furthermore, there were some

---

[1] *Hadith qudsi* are statements that the Prophet (peace be upon him) attributed to Allah yet they do not form part of the Quran. For example, they would include any hadith in which the Prophet (peace be upon him) said, "The Lord, Exalted and Perfect, said..."

[2] The above is not meant to imply that there are some acts of the Prophet (peace be upon him) that have no bearing whatsoever upon the *shareeah*. Except for those laws specific to the Prophet (peace be upon him) alone, anything he did indicates, at the very least, that said act is permissible. There are some who try to divide the Prophet's sunnah into what is meant to be part of the *shareeah* and what is not meant to be part of the *shareeah*. Unfortunately, many times this is done as a way to remove much of the sunnah from the *shareeah*. For a complete

laws that were special for the Prophet (peace be upon him) only and that are not to be followed by the Muslims. An example of this type would be his marrying more than four wives. That was allowed for the Prophet (peace be upon him) and not for anyone after him. By the hadith scholars' definition, these would fall under the term "sunnah," while, strictly speaking, it would not be a "sunnah" in the legal theorists' point of view since no one is allowed to follow him in that action.

Examples Illustrating the Difference Between the Jurists' and the Legal Theorists' Usage Of the Term "Sunnah"

In this author's experience, one of the major reasons for confusion about the status of the sunnah is a failure to distinguish between the word sunnah as used in its different contexts and disciplines. In particular, the usage of the jurists has led many to believe that, as some have explicitly said, "Whatever comes from the Quran must be applied. If one also applies the sunnah, that is good but is not mandatory." Some have also expressed that only the Quran can establish something as obligatory and the sunnah can only establish something as recommended. It is important, therefore, to give some examples that may remove this misunderstanding.

The first example deals with Allah's statement in the Quran,

$$\text{يَاأَيُّهَا الَّذِينَ آمَنُوا إِذَا تَدَايَنتُم بِدَيْنٍ إِلَى أَجَلٍ مُسَمًّى فَاكْتُبُوهُ}$$

"O you who believe! When you deal with each other in transactions involving future obligations in a fixed period of time reduce them to writing" (*al-Baqarah* 283). According to the majority of the scholars, the command here to record the

---

discussion and refutation of those claims, see Fathi Abdul Kareem, *Al-Sunnah: Tashree Laazim... Wa Daaim* (Maktabah Wahbah, 1985), *passim*.

transaction is one of recommendation and not obligation. Hence, the recording of such a transaction is considered, in the jargon of the jurists, a "sunnah" or non-obligatory but recommended act, even though the source for the act is found in the Quran.[1]

Another example comes from later in the same verse, *al-Baqarah* 283:

$$\text{وَأَشْهِدُوا إِذَا تَبَايَعْتُمْ}$$

"Take witnesses whenever you make a business dealing" (*al-Baqarah* 283).This command from the Quran is, once again, for an act that is recommended and not obligatory. Hence, even though the source for the act is a Quranic verse, that does not necessarily imply that the act is obligatory.[2]

On the other hand, one can note the example of the beard. There is no explicit verse in the Quran referring to the beard. Yet it is covered in the sunnah or statements of the Prophet (peace be upon him). The Prophet (peace be upon him) said, for example,

$$\text{انْهَكُوا الشَّوَارِبَ وَأَعْفُوا اللِّحَى}$$

"Trim the mustache down and leave the beard." (Recorded by al-Bukhari.) Based on this statement and many others of the Prophet (peace be upon him), the majority of scholars consider the beard to be obligatory. In this case, therefore, one finds

---

[1] For the ruling concerning the recording of debts and future obligations, see Kuwaiti Ministry of Religious Endowments and Religious Affairs, *Al-Mausooah al-Fiqhiyyah* (Kuwait: 1992), vol. 21, p. 123. It is true that al-Tabari, ibn Hazm and some others interpret the command to mean one of obligation. Their conclusion does not affect the point above: the scholars understood that simply because something is found in the Quran, that does not automatically make that act obligatory; it could possibly be only recommended or "sunnah".

[2] The evidence for the non-obligatory nature of taking witnesses for business transactions is in the practice of the Prophet (peace be upon him) himself. Cf., Mustafa Salaamah, *Al-Tasees fi Usool al-Fiqh ala Dhau al-Kitaab wa al-Sunnah* (Cairo: Maktabah al-Haramain li-l-Uloom al-Naafiah, 1415 A.H.), p. 42.

something only in the sunnah or statements of the Prophet (peace be upon him) but the ruling for that act is not "sunnah" in the jurists' use of the word. Instead, the ruling is that the act is obligatory or, in the terminology of the jurists, *waajib*.[1] Another example of this nature is *zakaat al-fitr* or the *zakaat* that is paid at the end of the month of Ramadhaan. Al-Bukhari and Muslim record from ibn Umar that the Prophet (peace be upon him) obligated the Muslims to pay the *zakaat al-fitr* at the end of Ramadhaan. Based on this narration and others similar to it, there is a consensus that *zakaat al-fitr* is obligatory (*waajib*). There is absolutely no reference to *zakaat al-fitr* in the Quran but there is still a consensus that it is obligatory.[2]

In essence, the source or text for an act is irrelevant with respect to the ruling of the act—whether it be obligatory or recommended ("sunnah" in the usage of the jurists). A verse in the Quran may describe a specific act and that act may only be considered "sunnah." On the other hand, a statement of the Prophet (peace be upon him), which one could call a "sunnah," could determine that an act is obligatory. The source of the common confusion on this point is that the word "sunnah" is being used with two implications or according to two different technical definitions.

---

[1] For a discussion of the ruling concerning the beard, see Umar al-Ashqar, *Thalaath Sha'aair* (Kuwait: al-Daar al-Salafiyyah, 1985), pp. 33-46. He notes (p. 45) that Ali Mahfoodh stated (and quoted his sources) that the four schools of fiqh all agree that it is forbidden to shave the beard.

[2] Saadi Abu Jaib, after stating that there is a consensus on the obligation of *zakaat al-fitr*, notes a couple of scholars who considered it to be an abrogated practice. Abu Jaib notes that their evidence is weak, to say the least. Hence, their opinions on this issue are considered anomalies. See Saadi Abu Jaib, *Mausooah al-Ijmaa fi al-fiqh al-Islaami* (Beirut: Daar al-Arabiyyah, n.d.), vol. 1, p. 519.

Definition of the Word *Sunnah* As Used by the Specialists in *Aqeedah*

By the third Hijri century, the specialists in the field of *aqeedah* (dogma, creed and faith) use the term *sunnah* to refer to the foundations of the faith, the well-established obligatory deeds, the matters of creed and the definitive rulings of Islam. This terminology became popular as more and more sects appeared.[1] Some scholars would use the term "sunnah" to refer to the established articles of faith and to distinguish them from the beliefs of the newly-formed heretical groups.[2] Ibn Rajab noted, "Many of the later scholars [meaning after the first couple of generations] used the word 'sunnah' to specifically refer to what is related to creed, because that forms the foundation of the religion and the one who contradicts it is in a very dangerous situation."[3]

Some used the word "sunnah" in a very comprehensive sense to basically include everything that forms the essential parts of the faith—this is acceptable because everything that forms part of the faith was either believed in, practiced or preached by the Prophet (peace be

---

[1] Naasir al-Aql, *Mafhoom Ahl al-Sunnah wa al-Jamaah Ind Ahl al-Sunnah wa al-Jamaah* (Riyadh: Daar al-Watan, n.d.), p. 42.
[2] As noted, this was a very common usage of the term by the third century. Many of the scholars wrote works on the beliefs and foundations of the faith and entitled their works, *The Sunnah*. There are from ten to twenty works of such nature. For example, there was *al-Sunnah* by Ahmad ibn Hanbal (d. 241 A.H.), *al-Sunnah* by ibn Abi Asim (d. 287 A.H.), *al-Sunnah* by Ahmad ibn Muhammad al-Khalaal (d. 311 A.H.), *al-Sunnah* by Abu Bakr ibn al-Athram (d. 273 A.H.), *al-Sunnah* by Abdullah ibn Ahmad ibn Hanbal (d. 290 A.H.), *al-Sunnah* by Muhammad ibn Nasr al-Marwazi (d. 292), *al-Sunnah* by al-Asaal (d. 349), *Sharh al-Sunnah* by ibn Abi Zamanain and *Sareeh al-Sunnah* by Abu Jafar al-Tabari. Again, these works are not collections of hadith but are all works dedicated to the discussion of beliefs and fundamental issues of creed. Cf., Dhumairiyyah, pp. 96-99; Uthmaan ibn Hasan, *Minhaj al-Istidlaal ala Masaail al-Itiqaad Ind Ahl al-Sunnah wa al-Jamaah* (Riyadh: Maktabah al-Rushd, 1992), vol. 1, pp. 31-32; Muhammad al-Hamad, *Aqeedah Ahl al-Sunnah wa al-Jamaah: Mafhoomuhaa, Khasaaisuhaa, Khasaais Ahluhaa* (Riyadh: Dar al-Watan, 1416 A.H.), p. 16.
[3] Quoted in al-Aql, p. 46.

upon him) himself. For example, sunnah is defined by some as, "The guidance upon which the Prophet (peace be upon him) and his Companions were, [encompassing all aspects of] knowledge, belief, statement and deeds."[1] In this definition, the practices and beliefs of the Companions are considered part of the sunnah because they followed the same methodology as that taught by the Prophet (peace be upon him)—as opposed to some members of later generations who devised their own methodologies contrary to that of the Prophet (peace be upon him).

For the specialists in the field of *aqeedah*, sunnah is also used as the opposite of heresy (Ar., *bidah* بدعة). In this respect, one says, "So and so is upon the sunnah (or following the sunnah)." This means that with respect to his beliefs, overall methodology and behavior, he is following the way established by the Prophet (peace be upon him) and passed on to his Companions and those who followed in their path. Again, it is important to note that in this sense, the word "sunnah" also encompasses that way of life and belief that the Companions followed as a continuation of what they learned directly from the Prophet (peace be upon him). If a person refuses to follow the way of the Companions in their understanding and practice of the religion, they are, in essence, turning away from the sunnah itself.

On the other hand, one says, "So and so is upon an innovation," if he has some beliefs or methodology that contradicts with the pure teachings of Islam. Those who follow the way of the Prophet (peace be upon him) are known as *ahl al-sunnah* or the people of the sunnah. Those who follow any

---

[1] Cf., Naasir al-Aql, *Mabaahith fi Aqeedah Ahl al-Sunnah wa al-Jamaah wa Muwaqif al-Harakaat al-Islaamiyyah al-Muaasirah Minha* (Riyadh: Daar al-Watan, n.d.), p. 13. This usage mostly started after the time of the Companions and Followers. However, some quotes exist to imply that the earliest generations also used the term in this sense. For example, ibn Umar is quoted as saying, "Whoever leaves the sunnah has committed a blasphemy." See al-Aql, *Mafhoom*, pp. 42-43.

of the myriad of differing ways are known as *ahl al-bidah* or people of heresy. Hence, sunnah means the correct belief and understanding of the religion.[1] Abu al-Qaasim al-Asbahaani said, "So and so is upon the sunnah or from the people of the sunnah means that he is in accord with what has been revealed and also what has been passed on [from the Companions and others] with respect to his actions and belief. This is so because the sunnah cannot possibly [be present] when one is in contradiction to Allah and contradiction to His Messenger."[2]

Shawaat notes that it is in this sense of the word that hadith such as the following are to be understood:[3] The Prophet (peace be upon him) said,

$$\text{فَمَنْ رَغِبَ عَنْ سُنَّتِي فَلَيْسَ مِنِّي}$$

"Whoever turns away from my sunnah [my way] is not from me." (Recorded by al-Bukhari and Muslim.) The Prophet (peace be upon him) also said,

---

[1] This distinction was, obviously, not made until heretical beliefs and groups appeared in Islam. In particular, it was used after the killing of the third caliph and companion Uthmaan ibn Affaan (may Allah be pleased with him), during which time the Muslim community started to divide into sects. Muhammad ibn Seereen's statement is well-known, "They did not use to ask for the chain of authorities [for reports]. But when the *fitnah* [the killing of Uthmaan and the subsequent civil war] occurred, they would say, 'State the names of your men [meaning sources].' They would look for the people of the sunnah and take their hadith. They would look for the people of heresy and not take their hadith." Ibn Seereen's statement is found with its complete chain in Muslim's introduction to his *Sahih*. Cf., Yahya al-Nawawi, *Sharh Saheeh Muslim* (Beirut: Daar al-Marifah, 1996), vol. 2, p. 44.

[2] Abu al-Qaasim Ismaaeel al-Asbahaani, *al-Hujjah fi Bayaan al-Muhijjah wa Sharh Aqeedah Ahl al-Sunnah* (Riyadh: Daar al-Raayah, 1990), vol. 2, pp. 384-5.

[3] Shawaat, p. 23.

24

مَنْ يَعِشْ مِنْكُمْ فَسَيَرَى اخْتِلافًا كَثِيرًا فَعَلَيْكُمْ بِسُنَّتِي وَسُنَّةِ
الْخُلَفَاءِ الرَّاشِدِينَ الْمَهْدِيِّينَ عَضُّوا عَلَيْهَا بِالنَّوَاجِذِ وَإِيَّاكُمْ
وَمُحْدَثَاتِ الْأُمُورِ فَإِنَّ كُلَّ بِدْعَةٍ ضَلالَةٌ

"Certainly, the one who will live among you will see lots of differences. So stick to my sunnah and the sunnah of the right-principled and rightly-guided successors. Bite onto that with your molar teeth. And avoid newly-introduced matters. Verily, every heresy is a going astray."[1]

This meaning is also apparent in many of the statements of the early scholars. For example, Abdullah ibn Masood said, "For one to be moderate in practicing the sunnah is better than for him to exert himself in heresies."[2] Muhammad ibn Shihaab al-Zuhri said, "Our scholars who have passed on would say, 'Adhering to the sunnah is salvation.'"[3]

Some of the earlier scholars take this definition even further and use the word "sunnah" to apply to all of the guidance that the Prophet (peace be upon him) brought and passed on to his Companions and them to their followers, whether related to the foundations of the religion or specific issues. This is a very broad definition. Sunnah is the straight path, with all of its general aspects and detailed points. In fact, in this usage, the word "sunnah" becomes equivalent to Islam itself. According to al-Aql, this is the meaning of the word "sunnah" as found in quotes from many of the early scholars.

---

[1] This hadith is *sahih*. It was recorded, with slightly different wordings, by Ahmad, Abu Daawood, al-Tirmidhi, ibn Hibbaan, ibn Abi Aasim, al-Baihaqi, al-Haakim and a number of others from al-Waleed ibn Muslim from Thaur ibn Yazeed from Khaalid ibn Madaan from both Abdul Rahmaan ibn Amr al-Sulami and Hujr ibn Hujr al-Kalaai from al-Irbaad. This chain is of *sahih* quality as all of the narrators are well-known trustworthy narrators.
[2] Quoted in Shawaat, p. 24.
[3] Quoted in Shawaat, p. 24.

For example, Abu Bakr is quoted to have said, "The sunnah is the firm handhold of Allah."[1]

The Meaning of the Word Hadith

Lexically speaking, the word "*hadith*"[2] (حديث, whose plural is *ahaadeeth* أحاديث) is,

> New, recent... existing newly, for the first time, not having been before... Information, a piece of information, intelligence, an announcement... a thing, or matter, that is talked of, told, or narrated...[3]

In both the Quran and hadith, the word has been used in reference to a religious communication, a story of a general nature, a historical story and a current story or conversation.[4]

As a technical term, a hadith is basically any report of the Messenger of Allah's (peace be upon him) saying, action, tacit approval, manners, physical characteristic or biographical data. In other words, it is any report about the "sunnah," as defined by the scholars of hadith.[5]

---

[1] Al-Aql, *Mafhoom*, p. 26.

[2] A strict transliteration of the word would actually be *hadeeth*. However, it has become well-known and pronounced correctly as hadith; hence, this author leaves the word as hadith in all of his writings, except in the transliteration of Arabic titles. Furthermore, this author prefers to use the word hadith for both the singular and the plural, like the word deer in English, rather than the Arabic plural *ahaadeeth*.

[3] Lane, vol. 1, p. 529.

[4] Cf., Mustafa Muhammad Azami, *Studies in Hadith Methodology and Literature* (Indianapolis, IN: American Trust Publications, 1977), pp. 1-2.

[5] There are two other important terms that are closely related. One is *khabar* (خبر) and the other is *athar* (أثر). The word *khabar* literally means "a report, news." It is used by some scholars of hadith as a synonym for hadith. However, others use the word hadith for what is attributed to the Prophet (peace be upon him) and what is attributed to other than the Prophet (peace be upon him) would be called *khabar*. Hence, a person specializing in the sunnah is called a *muhaddith* while someone concerned with history and other narrations is called *ikhbaari*. Al-Suyooti notes that when the word "hadith" is used by itself, without

Every hadith is composed of two parts: (a) *isnaad* (إسناد), or chain of authorities, and (b) *matn* (متن), or the actual text of the hadith. Both of these parts have to meet stringent requirements for the hadith to be accepted and considered true.

In general, one can divide all hadith into five basic categories: (a) *sahih* (صحيح) or authentic hadith; (b) *hasan* (حسن) or "good" hadith; (c) *dhaeef* (ضعيف) or weak hadith; (d) *dhaeef jiddan* (ضعيف جدا) or very weak hadith and (e) *maudhoo* (موضوع) or fabricated, forged hadith.[1] Actually, these can be broken down into two even more basic categories: accepted hadith (*sahih* or *hasan*) and rejected hadith (*dhaeef*, *dhaeef jiddan* and *maudhoo*).

To be a source or authority of Islamic law, a hadith must be from the categories of *sahih* or *hasan*. In order for a hadith to be *sahih* or *hasan* on its own merit, it must meet the following five criteria:[2]

(1) The chain or *isnaad* must be unbroken. In other words, each source must have received the hadith directly from the one on whose authority he is relating it all the way back to the Prophet (peace be upon him). If there are any missing

---

any additional adjective describing its source, it should only be used in reference to hadith of the Prophet (peace be upon him). *Athar* literally means the remnants or remains of something. Technically, it is used for what is narrated from the Prophet (peace be upon him), his Companions, their followers and other early scholars. A person who studies these reports and follows them is referred to as *athari*. Al-Suyooti says that *athar* should be used only for what is narrated from the Companions and the Followers and not for what comes from the Prophet (peace be upon him), which should be termed hadith. Cf., Muhammad Dhiyaa al-Rahmaan al-Adhami, *Mujam Mustalahaat al-Hadeeth wa Lataaif al-Asaaneed* (Riyadh: Adhwaa al-Salaf, 1999), pp. 8 (for *athar*) and 148 (for *khabar*); Muhammad al-Manshaawi, *Qaamoos Mustalahaat al-Hadeeth al-Nabawi* (Cairo: Daar al-Fadheelah, n.d.), pp. 16 (for *athar*) and 56 (for *khabar*).

[1] A fabricated or forged hadith is one which can be traced to an actual fabricator of hadith. When discussing hadith, many scholars do not even consider it a type of hadith.

[2] This brief introduction is not meant to be extensive or detailed. The interested reader should consult this author's "Sahih Hadith," *al-Basheer* (Vol. 3, No. 4, Nov.-Dec. 1989).

authorities, the chain would be considered broken and unacceptable.

(2) Every narrator in the chain must be of acceptable righteousness and character; in other words, each narrator must be morally fit. Impious people are not accepted for their impiety is a sign that they do not fear Allah and, hence, they cannot be trusted to take extreme care in narrating the statements of the Prophet (peace be upon him). If just one narrator in the chain does not meet this criterion, the hadith will have to be rejected.

(3) Moral characteristics are not sufficient. Each narrator must also be proficient and exact when it comes to narrating hadith. If a person is known to make lots of mistakes when narrating hadith, either from his memory or from his writings, his hadith will not be accepted.

(4) Both the chain and the text of the hadith must be such that they do not contradict what has been narrated through stronger means.

(5) Upon inspection of the different ways a hadith is narrated, it must be the case that no mistake or defect is spotted in either the chain or the text of the hadith.

If any of these conditions are not met, the hadith will be rejected as either weak (*dhaeef*) or very weak (*dhaeef jiddan*), depending on the magnitude of the weakness. Hadith which are graded *dhaeef* or weak may be raised to the level of *hasan* if sufficient corroborating evidence is found for them. Hadith which are *dhaeef jiddan* may never be raised because the nature of their weakness prevents them from being considered as supporting evidence or as being supported by other similar evidence. Of course, fabricated hadith are in a different category completely and would never, under any circumstances, be considered an authority or acceptable in Islamic law.

The Relationship Between Sunnah and Hadith

Now that the terms sunnah and hadith have been defined and discussed, the relationship between sunnah and hadith can be given. The sunnah is the reality or the actual statement, act or tacit approval of the Prophet (peace be upon him)—what he actually did, said or approved of. There is no such thing as a "weak sunnah" or a "rejected sunnah." However, that actual sunnah is captured in the reports that have come down from the Prophet (peace be upon him), which constitute the hadith literature. As just noted, not every report is correct and substantiated—indeed, some reports are even blatant fabrications. In other words, the entire hadith literature does not represent the sunnah of the Prophet (peace be upon him). Only the acceptable hadith represent and portray the real sunnah of the Messenger of Allah (peace be upon him).[1]

---

[1] Sulaimaan al-Nadwi has, to this author, an unacceptable and unprecedented differentiation between sunnah and hadith. In his work, *Tahqeeq Mana al-Sunnah wa Bayaan al-Haajah Ilaihaa*, he wrote (pp. 52-53), "Hadith is every incident ascribed to the Prophet (peace be upon him), even if he just did it once in his noble life or if it is narrated by just one person from him. Sunnah, on the other hand, is, in reality, the name for the deeds passed on in *mutawaatir* fashion. In other words, it is how the Prophet (peace be upon him) performed his deeds, passed on to us through a continuous transmission of practice—as the Prophet (peace be upon him) performed it, then the Companions after him performed it, and then the Followers and so forth. It is not necessary that it be *mutawaatir* with respect to its wording [in its text; it is sufficient to be *mutawaatir* with respect to its meaning]... This *mutawaatir* practice and transmission is what is called the sunnah. And this is what is mentioned in conjunction with the Book in the Prophet's saying, 'I have left among you two matters that, if you adhere to them, you will never go astray: the Book of Allah and the sunnah of His Messenger.'" Later (p. 60), he writes after quoting the same hadith, "The meaning of that sunnah mentioned in conjunction with the Book is the *mutawaatir* practice of the Messenger (peace be upon him) and his path and guided way that is the correct, practical interpretation of the Quran. It does not mean every narration of speech that is narrated by so and so on the authority of so and so." What he seems to be implying is that portions of the sunnah that have been transmitted via non-*mutawaatir* means, and which maybe were only known to some Companions and not all, are not part of that sunnah that is referred to in the above hadith. This implies that if someone does

29

Ibn Taimiyah wrote, for example,

The sunnah that is a must to be followed, for which one is praised upon following it and blamed for going against it, is the sunnah of the Messenger of Allah (peace be upon him) in matters of beliefs, matters of worship and the rest of the affairs of the religion. And that is known only by knowledge of the hadith of the Prophet (peace be upon him) that are confirmed on his authority.[1]

Al-Albaani also wrote,

The sunnah that has such importance in the law is the confirmed sunnah from the Prophet (peace be upon him) via methodological means and well-known sound chains according to the people of knowledge of hadith and its narrators. It is not the one that is found in the various books of Quranic commentary, books of fiqh, books of exhortation and admonishing,

---

not abide by those sunnah, he will still be rightly guided and his religion is not affected in any negative sense because they are not what are actually meant by the sunnah. This implies that it is perfectly acceptable to refuse to abide by a hadith simply because it is not *mutawaatir* or because its implications were not practiced by the Muslims in a *mutawaatir* sense. What al-Nadwi claims to be the definition of the sunnah was not the conception of the Companions and those who followed them. It is known and established, even with respect to the earliest caliphs, that sometimes they would be ignorant of some portion of the sunnah. Once they heard the appropriate hadith, they immediately applied that hadith, regardless of whether it was known on a wide scale or not. (Examples of that nature will be given in the section entitled, "The Companions' View of the Sunnah.") What is very perplexing to this author is that the referred to work by al-Nadwi was annotated by all of Muhammad Rasheed Ridha, Muhib al-Deen al-Khateeb, Muhammad Naasir al-Deen al-Albaani and Zuhair al-Shaweesh and none of them commented on the obvious errant implication of what al-Nadwi was saying (while this author is certain that they do not agree with such an implication). Allah alone is the true source of guidance. Cf., Sulaimaan al-Nadwi, *Tahqeeq Mana al-Sunnah wa Bayaan al-Haajah Ilaihaa* (Beirut: al-Maktab al-Islaami, 1994), pp. 52-60.

[1] Ahmad ibn Taimiyyah, *Majmoo Fataawa Shaikh al-Islaam ibn Taimiyyah* (Riyadh: Daar al-Ifta, n.d.), vol. 3, p. 387.

books of stories to make the heart soft and admonitions and so forth. In those books are many weak, rejected and fabricated hadith, some of them that Islam has absolutely nothing to do with... It is incumbent upon the people of knowledge, especially those whose opinions and statements are spread among the masses, to not be so bold as to argue by hadith until after they certify its truthfulness.[1]

Once the role and the importance of the sunnah in Islam is made clear, as it hopefully will be in the remainder of this book, the importance of the hadith should be very obvious. One needs to know what the sunnah of the Prophet (peace be upon him) was. One also needs to know where to look to find the statements of the Prophet (peace be upon him). By the grace of Allah, unlike the messengers who preceded the Prophet Muhammad (peace be upon him), Allah has preserved for Muslims the actual statements and actions of His last Prophet (peace be upon him). The Prophet's statements, actions and even his physical appearance are all captured in the body of literature known as the hadith literature. Virtually nothing has been lost from his noble life. A Muslim can know exactly how he prayed, fasted, and participated in daily matters with his fellow companions or with his wives. He can visualize how he ate, drank and sat. Such a miraculous and complete record cannot be found for any other historical figure since the creation of man.[2]

---

[1] Muhammad Naasir al-Deen al-Albaani, *Manzilah al-Sunnah fi al-Islaam* (Kuwait: al-Daar al-Salafiyyah, 1980), pp. 13-14.
[2] This is actually another sign of the truth of the prophethood of Muhammad, peace be upon him, and of the fact that he is the final prophet, after whom no prophet is needed.

The Meaning of the Words "Authority" and "Sunnah" in the Expression: The Authority of the Sunnah

According to Islamic legal theory, Allah is the only lawgiver. This right rests solely with Him and none of the creation has the right to lay down any legislation over other humans—unless it be something sanctioned or permitted within the bounds of what Allah has revealed. Allah says,

إِنِ الْحُكْمُ إِلَّا لِلَّهِ

"The command [and rule] is only for Allah" (*Yoosuf* 40 and 67). However, Allah's law and rule is known by different means or indicators. Among them is the Quran or Allah's speech. Among them also is the sunnah of the Messenger of Allah (peace be upon him).

In Arabic, the word *hujjah* (حجة, "authority") means "an indication, definitive proof." As a technical term in the expression, "the authority of the sunnah," it means that the sunnah is a legitimate evidence in Islamic law that leads one to the ruling of Allah. It also means that it is part of the worship of Allah to fulfill what the sunnah commands and refrain from what the sunnah prohibits. Furthermore, it means that one must believe in what the sunnah comprises and one must act upon what it requires in all realms of one's life.[1]

The exact meaning of the word "sunnah" used in this expression also needs to be specifically identified. Table 1 reviews the different definitions discussed earlier. Basically, the word sunnah here is the definition of the Islamic legal theorists (which is, more or less, inclusive of the definition given by the *aqeedah* specialists). However, it is conditional upon the fact that the report of that sunnah be an acceptable

---

[1] Shawaat, p. 236.

hadith. In other words, it refers to the Prophet's statements, selected actions, tacit approvals and general guidance that the Prophet (peace be upon him) passed on to his Companions and which is captured in the authentic (*sahih* and *hasan*) hadith literature.

Type of Scholar	Main Concern of the Discipline	Definition of Sunnah	Comments
Jurist (*Faqeeh* فقيه)	The value of deeds or actions, whether they be obligatory, recommended and so forth	An act which is between obligatory and permissible; a recommended act; an act for which one is rewarded for performing and not punished for not performing	This definition is irrelevant to the discussion of the authority of the sunnah
Scholar of hadith (*muhaddith* محدّث)	Any report concerning any aspect of the Prophet's life; goal is to judge which of those reports are authentic and which are not	What has been passed down from the Prophet (peace be upon him) of his statements, actions, tacit approvals, manners, physical characteristics or biography, regardless of whether it was before he was sent as a prophet or afterwards.	This definition is too broad and includes some matters that do not fit into the concept of "authority"
Legal theorist (*usooli* أصولي)	Determination of what is an authority in Islamic law and how that authority is used to derive laws	What comes from the Prophet (peace be upon him) in the form of speech, action or tacit approval, other than the Quran itself.	This is the exact meaning of the word "sunnah" in the expression "the authority of the sunnah"
Specialists in Aqeedah (Questions related to faith and creed)	What a Muslim is supposed to belief and related matters	The foundations of the faith, the obligatory deeds, the matters of creed and the definitive rulings of Islam.	Too restricted a definition, leaves out many facets that are necessary to be part of the definition

Table 1. Review of the Different Definitions for the Word "Sunnah"

Conclusions

In this chapter, the term "sunnah" has been defined. Among the most important points to note is that the jurists' usage of the word should never be confused with the meaning of the word in the phrase, "the authority of the sunnah." Their usage of the word implies that a specific act lies somewhere between obligatory and permissible; that is, it is recommended. That usage is much closer to the lexical meaning of the word "sunnah" and it essentially has nothing to do with the meaning of the word "sunnah" in the expression, "the authority of the sunnah."

The definition of the word "sunnah" as used by the scholars of hadith is too broad to be considered the meaning of the word "sunnah" in the expression, "the authority of the sunnah." This is because they include in their definition aspects of the "sunnah" that have no legal authority or bearing, such as acts that the Prophet (peace be upon him) performed before receiving revelation.

The definition of the word "sunnah" as used by the legal theorists is: the statements, actions and tacit approvals of the Messenger of Allah (peace be upon him). This definition is, in essence, inclusive of the definition given by the specialists in *aqeedah*. It is the definition that is meant when speaking about the authority and importance of the sunnah.

The sunnah is captured in the authentic hadith literature. Hence, in order to know what the sunnah is, one must turn to the authentic hadith literature. Thus, "the authority and importance of the sunnah" directly means, "the authority and importance of the authentic hadith."

Chapter Two:
Proofs Establishing the Authority and Importance of the Sunnah

Introduction

The proofs concerning the importance of the sunnah may be divided into four categories: proofs from the Quran, proofs from the sunnah itself, corroborating evidence in the statements of the Companions of the Prophet, and conclusions of the leading scholars of Islam.[1]

Obviously, if somebody denies the importance of the sunnah *in toto*, hadith cannot be used as arguments to prove the importance of the sunnah. Instead, one must derive some proof from the Quran itself concerning the position of the sunnah in Islam. There exist many verses in the Quran that point to the importance of the sunnah. In fact, many verses give a clear indication that it is obligatory for a person who believes in Allah to follow the sunnah.[2] Many of these verses

---

[1] Of course, these last two are not stand alone proofs—unless they reach the level of a consensus. Herein, they are first quoted as supporting arguments and then to note that they do reach the level of consensus. (Actually, the authority of a statement of a Companion is a disputed issue among legal theorists.) Yet other proofs establishing the authority and indispensability of the sunnah shall be noted throughout this work.

[2] Ibn Taimiyyah stated that the position of the sunnah has been confirmed in over forty places in the Quran. Cf., Ibn Taimiyyah, *Majmooat al-Fataawa ibn Taimiyyah*, vol. 19, pp. 93f. A study of the appendix will demonstrate that what he stated is not an exaggeration.

are so emphatic that no conscientious person can deny their implications concerning the authority and importance of the sunnah. The first section of this chapter shall be a discussion of only some of the relevant Quranic verses.

The Quranic Verses Related to the Sunnah of the Prophet (peace be upon him)

The Quran points to the importance and necessity of the sunnah of the Prophet (peace be upon him) in numerous places.[1] Indeed, they are so numerous that they can be easily broken down into separate categories or types of commands for following the sunnah. These different verses, therefore, will be discussed under their appropriate subheadings.

Obedience to the Prophet (peace be upon him) is Obedience to Allah

Allah revealed to His Prophet (peace be upon him),

مَنْ يُطِعِ الرَّسُولَ فَقَدْ أَطَاعَ اللَّهَ وَمَنْ تَوَلَّى فَمَا أَرْسَلْنَاكَ عَلَيْهِمْ حَفِيظًا

"Whoever obeys the Messenger verily obeys Allah; but if any turn away, We have not sent you to watch over their (evil deeds)" (*al-Nisaa* 80). In this verse, Allah clearly states that obedience to the Messenger (peace be upon him) is nothing less than obedience to Allah. The verse is so clear it cannot be construed in any other manner.

---

[1] The verses of the Quran pointing to the importance and place of the sunnah are actually sprinkled throughout this work and not all contained in the following section. Hence, in order to have a complete listing that the reader may reference and research, an appendix has been added which includes all of the relevant verses referred to in this work.

In the *Sahihs* of al-Bukhari and Muslim it is recorded that the Messenger of Allah (peace be upon him) said,

مَنْ أَطَاعَنِي فَقَدْ أَطَاعَ اللَّهَ وَمَنْ عَصَانِي فَقَدْ عَصَى اللَّهَ

"Whoever obeys me, obeys Allah. Whoever disobeys me, disobeys Allah." Not following the sunnah or the commands of the Prophet (peace be upon him) is exactly the same as not following the commands of Allah. Ibn Katheer noted that it is the Prophet's job only to convey the message and it is up to each person to accept or to reject his message. The one who follows his message will be saved. Hence, whoever obeys Allah and His Messenger is guided; whoever disobeys Allah and His Messenger harms no one except himself.[1] Al-Shaukaani points out that this verse proves that anything that comes from the Messenger (peace be upon him) actually originated with Allah.[2]

In another verse, Allah describes the swearing of allegiance to the Prophet (peace be upon him) as swearing allegiance to Himself in the following verse,

إِنَّ الَّذِينَ يُبَايِعُونَكَ إِنَّمَا يُبَايِعُونَ اللَّهَ يَدُ اللَّهِ فَوْقَ أَيْدِيهِمْ فَمَنْ نَكَثَ فَإِنَّمَا يَنْكُثُ عَلَى نَفْسِهِ وَمَنْ أَوْفَى بِمَا عَاهَدَ عَلَيْهُ اللَّهَ فَسَيُؤْتِيهِ أَجْرًا عَظِيمًا

"Lo those who swear allegiance to you (Muhammad), swear allegiance only unto Allah. The Hand of Allah is above their hands. So whosoever breaks his oath, breaks it only to his soul's hurt; while whosoever keeps his covenant with Allah, on him will He bestow immense reward" (*al-Fath* 10). Here

---

[1] Ismaaeel Ibn Katheer, *Tafseer al-Quran al-Adheem al-Maroof bi Tafseer ibn Katheer* (Riyadh: Maktabah Daar al-Salaam, 1998), p. 345.

[2] Muhammad ibn Ali al-Shaukaani, *Fath al-Qadeer* (Mustafa al-Babi al-Halabi, 1964), vol. 1, p. 489.

Allah describes the making of an oath of allegiance to the Messenger of Allah (peace be upon him) as being the same as swearing allegiance to Allah. This clearly implies that obeying the Messenger (peace be upon him) is the same as obeying Allah.

Allah Orders Obedience to the Prophet (peace be upon him) and Warns Against Disobeying Him

Allah says in the Quran,

يَاأَيُّهَا الَّذِينَ آمَنُوا أَطِيعُوا اللَّهَ وَأَطِيعُوا الرَّسُولَ وَأُوْلِي الأَمْرِ مِنْكُمْ فَإِنْ تَنَازَعْتُمْ فِي شَيْءٍ فَرُدُّوهُ إِلَى اللَّهِ وَالرَّسُولِ إِنْ كُنْتُمْ تُؤْمِنُونَ بِاللَّهِ وَالْيَوْمِ الآخِرِ ذَلِكَ خَيْرٌ وَأَحْسَنُ تَأْوِيلاً

"O you who believe, obey Allah and obey the Messenger and those in authority among you. And if you are in dispute over any matter, refer it to Allah and His Messenger if you are actually believers in Allah and the Last Day. That is better for you and more seemly in the end" (*al-Nisaa* 59). Many important points may be deduced from this one verse of the Quran. First, it must be noted that Allah explicitly uses the command "to obey" (Ar., *ateeu*) not only for Himself but also for the Messenger (peace be upon him), that is, "*obey* Allah and *obey* the Messenger." (The same verb or command does not directly precede "those in authority among you."[1]) This establishes the Messenger of Allah (peace be upon him) as an independent object of obedience while obedience to anyone else is conditional upon consistency with the Quran or sunnah.

---

[1] Of course, this is not proper according to English syntax which requires that the items in the position following *obey* be the objects of *obey*. But in Arabic, such a construction can be done to emphasize the obedience to those stated directly after the command.

Second, this implies that obedience to the Messenger (peace be upon him) is, in sense, something different than obedience to Allah. It is true that obedience to the Messenger of Allah (peace be upon him) is obedience to Allah. What is meant here is that obedience to the Messenger (peace be upon him) differs from simply obeying the Messenger (peace be upon him) in what he has conveyed from the word of Allah or the Quran. (This closes the door to the argument that some have tried to use which claims that obeying the Messenger only means obeying him in what he has conveyed from Allah as part of the Quran.)

Third, Muslims are commanded to take any dispute that they may have to only two arbiters: Allah and His Messenger (peace be upon him). The Companions of the Prophet (peace be upon him) and later scholars have understood "refer it to Allah" to mean "to refer it to the Book of Allah." And referring the matter to the Messenger of Allah (peace be upon him) means to refer it directly to him during his lifetime and to his sunnah after his death. Note also that the two, the Book of Allah and the sunnah of the Messenger (peace be upon him), are placed together here and the verse does not say, "refer the matter to Allah and then to the Messenger of Allah," nor does it say, "refer the matter to Allah and if you do not find the answer there, refer the matter to the Messenger."

Fourth, Allah states that the true believers are the ones who refer their disputes not only to Allah but to Allah and His Messenger (peace be upon him).

Fifth, the believer knows that the important life is that of the Hereafter. It is better in the end (that is, in the Hereafter), when the person must face Allah, for the believer to refer any dispute to both Allah and His Messenger (peace be upon him) and to not deny the position of the sunnah of the Prophet (peace be upon him).

Sixth, one should realize that this verse refers to all types of disputes, whether concerning matters of worship, business or other worldly affairs. Some scholars mention that this verse was revealed with respect to some of the deputies of the Messenger of Allah (peace be upon him). Before the time of the Prophet (peace be upon him), the Arabs had no real idea of governmental authority and, hence, this led to disputes concerning which, Allah states, the solution was to refer the matter to Allah and His Messenger (peace be upon him).

Ibn al-Qayyim noted about the phrase, "if you dispute about anything," that the Arabic phrase is a word in the indefinite, "anything," being used as part of a condition. This implies generality. In other words, it refers to anything that the Muslims may dispute about concerning their religion, whether it be a small matter or a large matter. They must refer that matter to the Book and the sunnah. This implies that the solution for that matter—any matter—must be found in the Quran and sunnah. It would be an impossibility for Allah to order the Muslims to refer the matter to these two sources while the resolution to their dispute is not found therein.[1]

Finally, ibn al-Qayyim also noted that Allah says in this verse, "refer it to Allah and His Messenger," and He did not say, "refer it to Allah and to His Messenger." (In other words, the word إلى "to" is used only once.) He says that such is the case because whatever Allah decides is exactly the decision of the Messenger of Allah (peace be upon him). And whatever the Messenger of Allah (peace be upon him) decides is exactly the decision of Allah. Hence, when Musims dispute over a matter and take it back to Allah (His book), they are in essence taking it back to the Messenger (peace be upon him). And when they take it back to the Messenger (peace be upon him), they have in fact taken it back to Allah. This is one of the very subtle and intricate points that one can find in the Quran.[2]

Allah says in another verse,

---

[1] Ibn al-Qayyim was quoted in Abdul Khaaliq, p. 301.
[2] Cf., Ali al-Saalihi, *Al-Dhau al-Muneer ala al-Tafseer* (Riyadh: Maktabah Daar al-Salaam, n.d.), vol. 2, p. 235. It was quoted from ibn al-Qayyim's *al-Risaalah al-Tabookiyyah.*

وَأَطِيعُوا اللَّهَ وَالرَّسُولَ لَعَلَّكُمْ تُرْحَمُونَ

"Obey Allah and the Messenger that you may attain mercy" (*ali-Imraan* 132). In this verse, Allah states that the Mercy in the next life will be showered upon those who obeyed Allah and His Messenger (peace be upon him).

It should be noted that the same words, "obey Allah and the Messenger," also occur in *ali-Imraan* 32. Furthermore, the phrase, "obey Allah and His Messenger," occurs four times in the Quran (*al-Anfaal* 1, *al-Anfaal* 20, *al-Anfaal* 46 and *al-Mujaadalah* 13). For example, Allah says,

يَاأَيُّهَا الَّذِينَ آمَنُوا أَطِيعُوا اللَّهَ وَرَسُولَهُ وَلَا تَوَلَّوْا عَنْهُ وَأَنْتُمْ تَسْمَعُونَ

"O you who believe! Obey Allah and His Messenger, and turn not away from him while you hear (what he spoke)" (*al-Anfaal* 20). Ibn Katheer said that the last part of that verse means, "That is, after you know what it is the he is calling you to."[1] In other words, once a Muslim knows what the Prophet (peace be upon him) has said, it is not acceptable for him to turn away from it or to ignore it.

Finally, the phrase, "obey Allah and obey the Messenger" occur an additional five times in the Quran (*al-Nisaa* 59, *al-Maaidah* 92, *al-Noor* 54, *Muhammad* 33 and *al-Taghaabun* 12). An example using this phrase is found in the verse,

قُلْ أَطِيعُوا اللَّهَ وَأَطِيعُوا الرَّسُولَ فَإِنْ تَوَلَّوْا فَإِنَّمَا عَلَيْهِ مَا حُمِّلَ وَعَلَيْكُمْ مَا حُمِّلْتُمْ وَإِنْ تُطِيعُوهُ تَهْتَدُوا وَمَا عَلَى الرَّسُولِ إِلَّا الْبَلاغُ الْمُبِينُ

"Say: Obey Allah, and obey the Messenger. But if you turn away, he is only responsible for the duty placed on him and

---
[1] Ibn Katheer, p. 574.

43

you for that placed on you. If you obey him, you shall be on right guidance. The Messenger's duty is only to preach the clear (Message)" (*al-Noor* 54).

Another example using this expression is,

يَاأَيُّهَا الَّذِينَ آمَنُوا أَطِيعُوا اللَّهَ وَأَطِيعُوا الرَّسُولَ وَلَا تُبْطِلُوا أَعْمَالَكُمْ

"O you who believe, obey Allah and obey the Messenger and do not make your deeds vain" (*Muhammad* 33). Al-Qurtubi quotes Muqaatil as explaining this verse by saying, "If you disobey the Messenger, you have rendered your deeds vain."[1]

Hence, in nine verses of the Quran, Allah clearly commands obedience not only to Himself but also to His Messenger (peace be upon him). Many of these verses are explicitly addressed to the believers, "O you who believe." This means that the command to obey and follow the Messenger (peace be upon him) was not just restricted to the Prophet's lifetime and to his Companions. Instead, the command is addressed to everyone who claims to be a believer. If a person today says that he does not have to follow the Prophet (peace be upon him) because obedience to the Prophet (peace be upon him) was only required while he was alive, in essence, he is saying about himself that he is not from "those who believe," whom Allah is addressing in these verses. If he is not from "those who believe," he must be from the disbelievers.[2]

Al-Salafi and Usmani note that there is no place in the Quran in which Allah orders obedience to Himself except that

---

[1] Abu Abdullah Al-Qurtubi, *al-Jaami li-Ahkaam al-Quran* (Beirut: Daar Ihyaa al-Turaath al-Arabi), vol. 16, p. 255.
[2] There is also other evidence that proves that the sunnah of the Prophet (peace be upon him) must be followed even after his death. For example, in a hadith to be discussed later, the Messenger of Allah (peace be upon him) said, "I have left among you two matters—you will not stray as long as you adhere to them: the Book of Allah and my sunnah."

obedience to the Messenger (peace be upon him) is explicitly
mentioned in conjunction with obedience to Allah. Similarly,
Allah does not warn about disobeying Himself without also
mentioning a warning about disobedience to the Messenger
(peace be upon him).[1] What this implies is that there can
be no real obedience to Allah unless it is via obedience to the
Messenger (peace be upon him)—in other words, via the path
and guidance that Allah revealed to the Prophet (peace be upon
him). In fact, this is the only way by which one knows how to
worship and obey Allah.

Although there is no verse in which Allah commands
obedience to Himself without also mentioning obedience to the
Messenger (peace be upon him), one can find verses in which
Allah obliges obedience to the Messenger (peace be upon him)
without mentioning obedience to Himself. Thus, the door is
closed to any possible confusion of whether the Messenger
(peace be upon him) himself must be obeyed. For example,
one finds in *soorah al-Noor*:

وَأَقِيمُوا الصَّلَاةَ وَآتُوا الزَّكَاةَ وَأَطِيعُوا الرَّسُولَ لَعَلَّكُمْ تُرْحَمُونَ

"So establish regular prayer and give the zakaat; and obey the
Messenger; that you may receive mercy" (*al-Noor* 56). Allah
also says,

وَمَنْ يُشَاقِقِ الرَّسُولَ مِنْ بَعْدِ مَا تَبَيَّنَ لَهُ الْهُدَى وَيَتَّبِعْ غَيْرَ سَبِيلِ
الْمُؤْمِنِينَ نُوَلِّهِ مَا تَوَلَّى وَنُصْلِهِ جَهَنَّمَ وَسَاءَتْ مَصِيرًا

"If anyone contends with the Messenger even after guidance
has been plainly conveyed to him, and follows a path other
than that of the believers, We shall leave him in the path he has

---

[1] Al Salafi, p. 34; Muhammad Taqi Usmani, *The Authority of Sunnah* (New Delhi,
India: Kitab Bhavan, 1991), p. 15. Usmani's work is an excellent work on the
authority of the sunnah and goes into some topics that are beyond the scope of
this present work, such as refuting some of the claims of those who refuse to
adhere to the sunnah of the Prophet (peace be upon him).

chosen, and land him in Hell, what an evil refuge" (*al-Nisaa* 115).

Usmani explains this phenomenon of always mentioning obedience to the Messenger (peace be upon him) while only sometimes mentioning obedience to Allah:

> The reason for so much stress upon "the obedience of the Prophet" is that "obedience to Allah" cannot be carried out except through "obedience of the Prophet." Allah does not address each and every individual to tell him what He requires from him... [T]he obedience of the Prophet (peace be upon him) represents the obedience of Allah and the reference to the former always includes the latter. That is why the Holy Quran [*sic*] in some verses deemed it sufficient to refer to the obedience of the Messenger only, for the practical way to obey Allah is only to obey the Prophet. On the contrary, the Holy Quran [*sic*] did not deem it sufficient to refer to the "obedience of Allah" without referring to the "obedience of the Messenger," to remove even the remotest excuse for ignoring the "obedience of the Prophet" and to leave no doubt whatsoever in the fact that the "obedience of Allah" is not complete unless the "obedience of the Prophet" is fully observed with all its implications.[1]

The emphasis that Allah has given to this command is clear from its repetitions. No Muslim should have any doubt in his mind that it is obligatory upon him to obey and follow the Prophet (peace be upon him). This aspect is further emphasized by the numerous verses (*al-Nisaa* 13, *al-Nisaa* 69, *al-Noor* 52, *al-Ahzaab* 71, *al-Fath* 17) in which Allah describes the reward that will come to those who obey both

---

[1] Usmani, pp. 16-17.

Allah and the Messenger (peace be upon him). For example, Allah says,

وَمَنْ يُطِعْ اللَّهَ وَرَسُولَهُ يُدْخِلْهُ جَنَّاتٍ تَجْرِي مِنْ تَحْتِهَا الأَنْهَارُ خَالِدِينَ فِيهَا وَذَلِكَ الْفَوْزُ الْعَظِيمُ

"Those who obey Allah and His Messenger will be admitted to Gardens with rivers flowing beneath, to abide therein (forever) and that will be the supreme achievement" (*al-Nisaa* 13). Allah also says,

وَمَنْ يُطِعْ اللَّهَ وَالرَّسُولَ فَأُوْلَئِكَ مَعَ الَّذِينَ أَنْعَمَ اللَّهُ عَلَيْهِمْ مِنْ النَّبِيِّينَ وَالصِّدِّيقِينَ وَالشُّهَدَاءِ وَالصَّالِحِينَ وَحَسُنَ أُوْلَئِكَ رَفِيقًا

"All who obey Allah and the Messenger are in the company of those on whom is the Grace of Allah, of the Prophets, the sincere, the martyrs, and the righteous. Ah! What a beautiful fellowship" (*al-Nisaa* 69).

Furthermore, part of the description of the true believers is that they obey Allah and His Messenger (peace be upon him). These are the people who can look forward to Allah's mercy. The Lord says,

وَالْمُؤْمِنُونَ وَالْمُؤْمِنَاتُ بَعْضُهُمْ أَوْلِيَاءُ بَعْضٍ يَأْمُرُونَ بِالْمَعْرُوف وَيَنْهَوْنَ عَنْ الْمُنكَرِ وَيُقِيمُونَ الصَّلاةَ وَيُؤْتُونَ الزَّكَاةَ وَيُطِيعُونَ اللَّهَ وَرَسُولَهُ أُوْلَئِكَ سَيَرْحَمُهُمْ اللَّهُ إِنَّ اللَّهَ عَزِيزٌ حَكِيمٌ

"The believers, men and women, are protectors one of another. They enjoin what is right and forbid what is evil. They establish the prayers, give the zakaat, and obey Allah and His Messenger. On them will Allah pour His Mercy, for Allah is Exalted in power, Wise" (*al-Taubah* 71).

However, in addition to that, in three places in the Quran (*al-Nisaa* 14, *al-Ahzaab* 36 and *al-Jinn* 23), Allah describes the negative and fatal results of deciding to disobey

Allah or His Messenger (peace be upon him). Al-Salafi notes that specifically mentioning the negative results of disobeying the Prophet (peace be upon him) leaves a stronger impact then what is simply understood from the command to obey the Prophet (peace be upon him).[1] Among such verses is,

وَمَنْ يَعْصِ اللَّهَ وَرَسُولَهُ فَإِنَّ لَهُ نَارَ جَهَنَّمَ خَالِدِينَ فِيهَا أَبَدًا

"For any who disobeys Allah and His Messenger, for them is Hell: they shall dwell therein forever" (*al-Jinn* 23).

One also finds verses specifically describing the plight and remorse of those who refused to follow and obey the Messenger of Allah (peace be upon him). Allah says,

يَوْمَ تُقَلَّبُ وُجُوهُهُمْ فِي النَّارِ يَقُولُونَ يَالَيْتَنَا أَطَعْنَا اللَّهَ وَأَطَعْنَا الرَّسُولَ

"The Day that their faces will be turned upside down in the Fire, they will say: 'Woe to us! Would that we had obeyed Allah and obeyed the Messenger'" (*al-Ahzaab* 66). Another verse reads,

يَوْمَئِذٍ يَوَدُّ الَّذِينَ كَفَرُوا وَعَصَوْا الرَّسُولَ لَوْ تُسَوَّى بِهِمُ الأَرْضُ وَلَا يَكْتُمُونَ اللَّهَ حَدِيثًا

"On that day those who reject faith and disobey the Messenger will wish that the earth were made one with them [so they may escape punishment]. But never will they hide a single fact from Allah" (*al-Nisaa* 42). Just conspiring or discussing intentional disobedience of the Messenger of Allah (peace be upon him) is forbidden and a sin:

يَاأَيُّهَا الَّذِينَ آمَنُوا إِذَا تَنَاجَيْتُمْ فَلَا تَتَنَاجَوْا بِالإِثْمِ وَالْعُدْوَانِ وَمَعْصِيَةِ الرَّسُولِ وَتَنَاجَوْا بِالْبِرِّ وَالتَّقْوَى وَاتَّقُوا اللَّهَ الَّذِي إِلَيْهِ تُحْشَرُونَ

---

[1] Al-Salafi, p. 34.

"O you who believe! When you hold secret counsel, do it not for iniquity and hostility, and disobedience to the Messenger; but do it for righteousness and self-restraint; and fear Allah, to whom you shall be brought back" (*al-Mujaadalah* 9).

After all of the above, it seems a logical conclusion that only a hypocrite or one whose faith is truly diseased would turn away from what the Messenger of Allah (peace be upon him) said, commanded or instituted. Indeed, Allah describes the turning away from what Allah has revealed and what the Messenger of Allah (peace be upon him) has presented to be a characteristic of the hypocrites. *Soorah al-Nisaa*, verse 61 reads:

$$\text{وَإِذَا قِيلَ لَهُمْ تَعَالَوْا إِلَى مَا أَنزَلَ اللَّهُ وَإِلَى الرَّسُولِ رَأَيْتَ الْمُنَافِقِينَ}$$
$$\text{يَصُدُّونَ عَنكَ صُدُودًا}$$

"When it is said to them, 'Come to what Allah has revealed, and to the Messenger,' you see the hypocrites avert their faces from you in disgust."

Allah has also stated another warning for those who insist on going against the orders and commands that come from His Messenger (peace be upon him):

$$\text{فَلْيَحْذَرِ الَّذِينَ يُخَالِفُونَ عَنْ أَمْرِهِ أَنْ تُصِيبَهُمْ فِتْنَةٌ أَوْ يُصِيبَهُمْ}$$
$$\text{عَذَابٌ أَلِيمٌ}$$

"Let those who oppose his orders beware lest a calamity or painful punishment should befall them" (*al-Noor* 63). Al-Qurtubi said that jurists point to this verse as a proof that it is obligatory to follow the commands and orders that come from Allah and His Messenger (peace be upon him). In this verse Allah has given a warning to anyone who decides not to follow His Prophet's commands that a punishment shall befall them.[1]

---

[1] Al-Qurtubi, vol. 12, p. 322.

49

In yet other verses, Allah says,

إِذْ يُوحِي رَبُّكَ إِلَى الْمَلَائِكَةِ أَنِّي مَعَكُمْ فَثَبِّتُوا الَّذِينَ آمَنُوا سَأُلْقِي

فِي قُلُوبِ الَّذِينَ كَفَرُوا الرُّعْبَ فَاضْرِبُوا فَوْقَ الْأَعْنَاقِ وَاضْرِبُوا

مِنْهُمْ كُلَّ بَنَانٍ ذَلِكَ بِأَنَّهُمْ شَاقُّوا اللَّهَ وَرَسُولَهُ وَمَنْ يُشَاقِقْ اللَّهَ

وَرَسُولَهُ فَإِنَّ اللَّهَ شَدِيدُ الْعِقَابِ

"Remember your Lord inspired the angels (with the message), 'I am with you. Give firmness to the believers. I will strike terror into the hearts of the unbelievers. Smite above their necks and smite all their fingertips off them.' This because they defied and disobeyed Allah and His Messenger: if any defy and disobey Allah and His Messenger, Allah is strict in punishment" (*al-Anfaal* 12-13).

Accepting the Prophet's Decisions and Rulings Is Part of Faith

Allah also states in the Quran,

فَلَا وَرَبِّكَ لَا يُؤْمِنُونَ حَتَّى يُحَكِّمُوكَ فِيمَا شَجَرَ بَيْنَهُمْ ثُمَّ لَا يَجِدُوا

فِي أَنفُسِهِمْ حَرَجًا مِمَّا قَضَيْتَ وَيُسَلِّمُوا تَسْلِيمًا

"But no, by your Lord, they will not actually believe until they make you the judge of what is in dispute between them and find within themselves no dislike of that which you decide and they submit with full submission" (*al-Nisaa* 65). The occasion for the revelation of this verse—or, at least, a case that it explicitly applies to—is recorded in *Sahih al-Bukhari* as:

Al-Zubair quarreled with a man from the Ansaar because of a natural mountain stream at al-Harra. The Prophet (peace be upon him) said, "O Zubair, irrigate your land and then let the water flow to your neighbor." The Ansaar said, "O Allah's Apostle, (is this because) he is your cousin?" At that the Prophet's face became red (with anger) and he said, "Zubair, irrigate your land and then withhold the water until it fills the land up to the walls and then let if flow to your neighbor." So the Prophet (peace be upon him) enabled al-Zubair to take his full right after the Ansaari had provoked his anger. The Prophet (peace be upon him) had previously given an order that was in favor of both of them. Al-Zubair said, "I do not think that this verse, 'No, by your Lord... [al-Nisaa 65, quoted above]', was revealed except on this occasion."

Al-Shaukaani points out that one's belief is not perfected until one completely accepts the Messenger of Allah (peace be upon him) as the decider of affairs. By the word *haraj* (translated above as "dislike") is meant, according to some authorities, doubt concerning any decision made by the Prophet (peace be upon him); others say that it means "sin"— by finding in their hearts the desire to reject the decision of the Prophet (peace be upon him). The last part of the verse means that the true Muslim will have no doubt concerning what the Messenger of Allah (peace be upon him) said or ordered and will submit and accept his authority without any hesitation, rationalization or false excuses. In conclusion, a Muslim cannot truthfully call himself a believer until, in his heart, he completely accepts the decisions of the Messenger of Allah (peace be upon him) and his way of life, his sunnah.[1]

Another point that deserves attention is that Allah begins this verse by swearing. This is fairly common in the Quran, but in this particular instance Allah swears by the Lord of the Prophet (peace be upon him). This swearing is much greater than any other found in the Quran, and it is after this

---

[1] al-Shaukaani, *Fath*, vol. 1, p. 483.

great swearing that Allah informs the believers that it is necessary for them to completely accept the authority of the Prophet (peace be upon him). In commenting on this verse, Ibn Katheer quotes a hadith of the Prophet (peace be upon him) which further emphasizes what this verse implies, "None of you truly believes until his desires are subservient to what I have come with."[1]

Allah also revealed,

وَمَا كَانَ لِمُؤْمِنٍ وَلَا مُؤْمِنَةٍ إِذَا قَضَى اللَّهُ وَرَسُولُهُ أَمْرًا أَنْ يَكُونَ لَهُمُ الْخِيَرَةُ مِنْ أَمْرِهِمْ وَمَنْ يَعْصِ اللَّهَ وَرَسُولَهُ فَقَدْ ضَلَّ ضَلَالًا مُبِينًا

"It does not become a believing man or believing woman, when Allah and His Messenger have decided a matter that they should (after that) claim any say in their affair; and whoever is disobedient to Allah and His Messenger has certainly gone astray in manifest error" (*al-Ahzaab* 36). If Allah or His Messenger has made a decision on any matter, then the believer has no choice but to submit himself to the decrees of Allah and His Messenger (peace be upon him).

Al-Suyooti has recorded the occasion for the revelation of this verse: Qataadah narrated that the Messenger of Allah (peace be upon him) asked Zainab to marry Zaid, but instead she wished to marry the Prophet (peace be upon him) himself. Therefore, she refused to accept the Prophet's choice. This verse was then revealed, and she became pleased and submitted to the Prophet's decision. This was also narrated

---

[1] Ibn Katheer, p. 339. Unfortunately, there is a difference of opinion concerning this hadith. Some of the scholars, for example, al-Albaani, consider it weak while others, such as al-Nawawi, consider it *hasan*. This author has concluded that it is weak. Cf., Jamaal al-Din Zarabozo, *Commentary on the Forty Hadith of al-Nawawi* (Boulder, CO: Al-Basheer Company for Publications and Translations, 1999), vol. 3, pp. 1564-1570.

through a couple of chains on the authority of ibn Abbaas.[1] Ibn Katheer stated a number of authorities who mentioned this incident as the occasion behind the revelation of this verse. If these narrations are correct, a couple of points should be noted with respect to this verse. First, it was revealed in connection with a decision made by the Prophet (peace be upon him). No Quranic commandment had been revealed about this request of the Prophet (peace be upon him); yet Allah describes the Prophet's decision as coming from both Allah and His Messenger, "when Allah and His Messenger have decided a matter." This clearly proves that the Prophet's commands were not from himself but were inspired by Allah. Second, and even more profound, is that this verse was revealed with respect to marriage and the personal desires of the heart. Allah states that even in these delicate matters one must completely submit to the commands of Allah and His Messenger (peace be upon him). Thus the obedience to the Messenger (peace be upon him) must permeate even the most private aspects of our lives.

Allah calls people to be judged by Himself and by His Messenger (peace be upon him). It is one of the signs of a diseased heart for one not to accept what Allah or His Messenger (peace be upon him) have ordered or decided. Allah says,

وَإِذَا دُعُوا إِلَى اللَّهِ وَرَسُولِهِ لِيَحْكُمَ بَيْنَهُمْ إِذَا فَرِيقٌ مِنْهُمْ مُعْرِضُونَ وَإِنْ يَكُنْ لَهُمُ الْحَقُّ يَأْتُوا إِلَيْهِ مُذْعِنِينَ أَفِي قُلُوبِهِمْ مَرَضٌ أَمِ ارْتَابُوا أَمْ يَخَافُونَ أَنْ يَحِيفَ اللَّهُ عَلَيْهِمْ وَرَسُولُهُ بَلْ أُولَئِكَ هُمُ الظَّالِمُونَ

---

[1] Jalaal al-Deen al-Suyooti, *Lubaab al-Naqool fi Asbaab al-Nuzool* (Beirut: Daar Ihyaa al-Uloom, 1980), p. 174. The incident was recorded by al-Tabaraani with a *sahih* chain back to Qataadah. Qataadah, however, was not a Companion of the Prophet (peace be upon him) and, hence, that chain is broken back to the Prophet (peace be upon him). The narrations from ibn Abbaas all have some weakness to them. Other narrations state that it was revealed with respect to a different woman; however, the gist of that story is the same as the one presented above and would not affect the conclusions made above.

إِنَّمَا كَانَ قَوْلَ الْمُؤْمِنِينَ إِذَا دُعُوا إِلَى اللَّهِ وَرَسُولِهِ لِيَحْكُمَ بَيْنَهُمْ أَنْ يَقُولُوا سَمِعْنَا وَأَطَعْنَا وَأُولَئِكَ هُمُ الْمُفْلِحُونَ وَمَنْ يُطِعْ اللَّهَ وَرَسُولَهُ وَيَخْشَ اللَّهَ وَيَتَّقِيهِ فَأُولَئِكَ هُمُ الْفَائِزُونَ

"When they are summoned to Allah and His Messenger, in order that he [the Prophet (peace be upon him)] may judge between them, behold, some of them decline (to come). But if the right is on their side, they come to him with all submission. Is it that there is a disease in their hearts? Or do they doubt, or are they in fear, that Allah and His Messenger will deal unjustly with them? Nay, it is they themselves who do wrong. The answer of the believers, when summoned to Allah and His Messenger, in order that he may judge between them, is no other than this: they say, 'We hear and we obey.' It is such as these who will attain felicity. It is such as obey Allah and His Messenger, and fear Allah and do right, who will win (in the end)" (*al-Noor* 48-52).

Verse seven of *soorah al-Hashr* states,

وَمَا آتَاكُمُ الرَّسُولُ فَخُذُوهُ وَمَا نَهَاكُمْ عَنْهُ فَانْتَهُوا وَاتَّقُوا اللَّهَ إِنَّ اللَّهَ شَدِيدُ الْعِقَابِ

"Whatsoever the Messenger gives you, take it; and whatsoever he forbids for you, abstain from it. And be aware of Allah. Verily, Allah is severe in punishment." This verse was revealed specifically with respect to the spoils of war. In other words, "what the Messenger gives you of the spoils, take it; and what he does not give you of the spoils, abstain from it." No scholar has argued that this verse pertains only to the spoils of war. Ibn Juraij said that its meaning is general, that whatever the Messenger (peace be upon him) orders you to do, you must do; and whatever he shuns for you, you must also shun. Al-Shaukaani said that the wording of the verse is general and the occasion behind the revelation does not confine the ruling of the verse. He said that the verse has a general application and applies to all of the regulations, commands or prohibitions that come from the Prophet (peace be upon him).[1] This verse contains a warning, "And be aware of Allah." This is a clear warning to those who do not respect the limits laid down by the Prophet (peace be upon him). And Allah ends this verse with, "And Allah is certainly severe in punishment." This, notes Shawaat, is an implication that the one who does not abide by what the Prophet (peace be upon him) says becomes a disbeliever because such a threatened punishment could only be for disbelievers.[2]

Following the Messenger (peace be upon him) Is a Key to Allah's Love, Real Life and Guidance

Another verse in the Quran states,

$$\text{قُلْ إِنْ كُنْتُمْ تُحِبُّونَ اللَّهَ فَاتَّبِعُونِي يُحْبِبْكُمُ اللَّهُ وَيَغْفِرْ لَكُمْ ذُنُوبَكُمْ وَاللَّهُ غَفُورٌ رَحِيمٌ}$$

"Say (O Muhammad): If you truly love Allah then follow me and Allah will love you and forgive your sins. Allah is the Forgiving, the Merciful" (*ali-Imraan* 31). The one who truly loves Allah will seek to find the actions that will lead Allah to love him. According to this verse, in order to gain Allah's love one need only follow and obey the Messenger (peace be upon him) and then Allah will love him and forgive his sins. Al-Shaukaani wrote that "to love Allah" implies to desire to obey Allah completely and to do anything that Allah orders. He quoted al-Azhaari, who said, "The love of Allah and His Messenger (peace be upon him) by a human (lit., slave) means (that the human) obeys the two completely and follows them in

---

[1] Al-Shaukaani, *Fath*, vol. 5, p. 198.
[2] Shawaat, p. 283.

his actions."[1] Ibn Katheer adds that this verse makes it a fact that anyone who claims to love Allah yet refuses to obey or follow the Messenger (peace be upon him) is a liar.[2]

One can also find the following verse in the Quran,

يَاأَيُّهَا الَّذِينَ آمَنُوا اسْتَجِيبُوا لِلَّهِ وَلِلرَّسُولِ إِذَا دَعَاكُمْ لِمَا يُحْيِيكُمْ

"O you who believe, respond to Allah and His Messenger when they call you to that which gives you life" (*al-Anfaal* 24). Al-Shaukaani commented that "to respond to" means "to obey" Allah and His Messenger (peace be upon him) when they make a command. The *Shareeah*, which is embodied in the Quran and sunnah, are the proclamations of Allah and His Messenger (peace be upon him). It is this *Shareeah* that gives true meaning and true life to this worldly existence. Ignoring or not responding to this call and guidance is, in fact, a type of death. Al-Shaukaani pointed out that this verse proves that it is obligatory for every Muslim to obey any command (that is, call) that he hears from Allah or His Messenger (peace be upon him), even if the command should go against his own desires, opinion or against popular opinion. The manner in which one should respond to the commands of Allah or His Prophet (peace be upon him) has been exemplified in the story of Abu Saeed ibn Mualla, as recorded by al-Bukhari. While Abu Saeed was praying, the Prophet (peace be upon him) summoned him, but he did not respond until he had finished the prayer. Upon finally coming to the Prophet (peace be upon him), the Messenger of Allah (peace be upon him) recited the above verse to him showing his behavior towards the call of the Prophet (peace be upon him) was incorrect.[3]

Furthermore, it is by truly believing in the Prophet (peace be upon him) and by following him that one can hope to be guided. Allah makes this point in the verse,

---

[1] Al-Shaukaani, *Fath al-Qadeer*, vol. 1, p. 338.
[2] Ibn Katheer, p. 236.
[3] Al-Shaukaani, *Fath*, vol. 2, p. 299-300.

قُلْ يَاأَيُّهَا النَّاسُ إِنِّي رَسُولُ اللَّهِ إِلَيْكُمْ جَمِيعًا الَّذِي لَهُ مُلْكُ
السَّمَاوَاتِ وَالأَرْضِ لا إِلَهَ إِلاَّ هُوَ يُحْيِي وَيُمِيتُ فَآمِنُوا بِاللَّهِ
وَرَسُولِهِ النَّبِيِّ الأُمِّيِّ الَّذِي يُؤْمِنُ بِاللَّهِ وَكَلِمَاتِهِ وَاتَّبِعُوهُ لَعَلَّكُمْ
تَهْتَدُونَ

"Say: O mankind! I am sent unto you all, as the Messenger of
Allah, to Whom belongs the dominion of the heavens and the
earth: there is no god but He. It is He who gives both life and
death. So believe in Allah and His Messenger, the unlettered
Prophet, who believed in Allah and His Words. Follow him
that you may be guided" (*al-Araaf* 158). Note that in this verse
there is an indication as to why the Prophet (peace be upon
him) should be followed. Allah describes him as "the
unlettered prophet." In other words, the wonderful guidance
that he was conveying was not from his own study and
research. On the contrary, it could have only come from Allah
as an inspiration to him (peace be upon him).

The Revealing of the *Hikmah*

Allah has stated,

لَقَدْ مَنَّ اللَّهُ عَلَى الْمُؤْمِنِينَ إِذْ بَعَثَ فِيهِمْ رَسُولاً مِنْ أَنْفُسِهِمْ يَتْلُوا
عَلَيْهِمْ آيَاتِهِ وَيُزَكِّيهِمْ وَيُعَلِّمُهُمُ الْكِتَابَ وَالْحِكْمَةَ وَإِنْ كَانُوا مِنْ
قَبْلُ لَفِي ضَلالٍ مُبِينٍ

"Allah has clearly shown grace to the believers by sending
unto them a Messenger of their own who recites unto them His
revelations, and causes them to grow and teaches them the

57

Book and the *Hikmah*,[1] although before they were in flagrant error" (*ali-Imraan* 164). This is a beautiful verse from which may be derived many important points,[2] but, unfortunately, the discussion here will have to be quite brief. One important phrase of this verse is, "he teaches them the Book and the *Hikmah*." What, in addition to the Book or the Quran, was also revealed to the Prophet Muhammad (peace be upon him)? Allah says,

وَأَنزَلَ اللَّهُ عَلَيْكَ الْكِتَابَ وَالْحِكْمَةَ وَعَلَّمَكَ مَا لَمْ تَكُنْ تَعْلَمُ وَكَانَ فَضْلُ اللَّهِ عَلَيْكَ عَظِيمًا

"Allah has revealed to you the Book and the *Hikmah* and taught you what you knew not (before): and great is the Grace of Allah unto you" (*al-Nisaa* 113). Allah also says,

وَاذْكُرُوا نِعْمَةَ اللَّهِ عَلَيْكُمْ وَمَا أَنزَلَ عَلَيْكُمْ مِنْ الْكِتَابِ وَالْحِكْمَةِ يَعِظُكُمْ بِهِ وَاتَّقُوا اللَّهَ وَاعْلَمُوا أَنَّ اللَّهَ بِكُلِّ شَيْءٍ عَلِيمٌ

"Solemnly recall Allah's favors on you, and the fact that He sent down to you the Book and the *Hikmah* for your instruction. And fear Allah, and know that Allah is well-acquainted with all things" (*al-Baqarah* 231).

Al-Salafi notes that at no time is the word *hikmah* used for the Book or the word Book used for the *hikmah*. They are two separate and distinct entities.[3] Again, the question that flows directly from these verses and this fact is: What else was

---

[1] The word *hikmah* literally means wisdom. However, in these verses it refers to what was revealed along with the Book. It is understood to refer to the Sunnah of the Prophet (peace be upon him) and, therefore, it has been left untranslated as *hikmah*.

[2] This verse is an answer to Abraham's prayer that is recorded in *soorah al-Baqarah* verse 129. The words "of their own" refer to the fact that the Prophet (peace be upon him) was a human being and could, therefore, be a perfect example for the rest of mankind. Cf., ibn Katheer, p. 127. For example, according to the Christian doctrine of trinity, it would be ridiculous to consider Jesus (peace be upon him) as a perfect example for the humans to follow.

[3] Al-Salafi, p. 53.

revealed to the Prophet (peace be upon him)? The answer can only be the sunnah. It is part of the blessing upon the believers that the Prophet taught them both the book (the Quran) and the *Hikmah* (the sunnah).

Commenting on the place of the sunnah, Imam al-Shaafi'ee recorded the following verses:

رَبَّنَا وَابْعَثْ فِيهِمْ رَسُولاً مِنْهُمْ يَتْلُو عَلَيْهِمْ آيَاتِكَ وَيُعَلِّمُهُمُ الْكِتَابَ وَالْحِكْمَةَ وَيُزَكِّيهِمْ

"[Abraham said,] 'O our Lord! Raise up in their midst a Messenger from among them who shall recite unto them Your revelations and shall instruct them in the scripture and in the *Hikmah* and shall make them grow in purity'" (*al-Baqarah* 129).

كَمَا أَرْسَلْنَا فِيكُمْ رَسُولاً مِنْكُمْ يَتْلُو عَلَيْكُمْ آيَاتِنَا وَيُزَكِّيكُمْ وَيُعَلِّمُكُمُ الْكِتَابَ وَالْحِكْمَةَ وَيُعَلِّمُكُمْ مَا لَمْ تَكُونُوا تَعْلَمُونَ

"Even as We have sent unto you a messenger from among you, who recites to you Our revelations and causes you to grow, and teaches you the scripture and the *Hikmah* and teaches you what which you knew not" (*al-Baqarah* 151).

هُوَ الَّذِي بَعَثَ فِي الأُمِّيِّينَ رَسُولاً مِنْهُمْ يَتْلُو عَلَيْهِمْ آيَاتِهِ وَيُزَكِّيهِمْ وَيُعَلِّمُهُمُ الْكِتَابَ وَالْحِكْمَةَ وَإِنْ كَانُوا مِنْ قَبْلُ لَفِي ضَلَالٍ مُبِينٍ

"He it is who has sent among the unlettered ones a messenger of their own to recite to them His revelations and to make them grow. And to teach them the Book and the *Hikmah*, though heretofore they were indeed in error manifest" (*al-Jumuah* 2).

وَاذْكُرُوا نِعْمَةَ اللَّهِ عَلَيْكُمْ وَمَا أَنْزَلَ عَلَيْكُمْ مِنَ الْكِتَابِ وَالْحِكْمَةِ يَعِظُكُمْ بِهِ

"Remember Allah's grace upon you and that which He has revealed unto you of the Book and the *Hikmah*, whereby he does exhort you" (*al-Baqarah* 231).

واذكرن ما يتلى في بيوتكن من آيات الله والحكمة

"And recite that which is rehearsed in your houses of the revelations of Allah and the *Hikmah*" (*al-Ahzaab* 34).

After quoting these verses, al-Shaafi'ee wrote,

> So God mentioned His Book—which is the Quran—and *Hikmah*, and I have heard that those who are learned in the Quran—whom I approve—hold that *Hikmah* is the sunnah of the Apostle of God. This is like what [God Himself] said; but God knows best! For the Quran is mentioned [first], followed by *Hikmah*; [then] God mentioned His favor to mankind by teaching them the Quran and *Hikmah*. So it is not permissible for *Hikmah* to be called here [anything] save the sunnah of the Apostle of God. For [*Hikmah*] is closely linked to the Book of God, and God has imposed the duty of obedience to His Apostle, and imposed on men the obligation to obey his orders. So it is not permissible to regard anything as a duty save that set forth in the Quran and the sunnah of His Apostle. For [God], as we have [just] stated, prescribed that the belief in His Apostle shall be associated with belief in Him.[1]

---

[1] Majid Khadduri, *Islamic Jurisprudence: Shafi'i's Risala* (Baltimore: Johns Hopkins Press, 1961), pp. 111-112. Heretofore referred to al-Shaafi'ee. Note that Khadduri had translated the word *hikmah* into wisdom in the above passage but it has been changed here for the sake of consistency.

Proper Etiquette for the Prophet (peace be upon him) Indicative of His Position and Authority

In *soorah al-Hujuraat*, Allah says,

يَاأَيُّهَا الَّذِينَ آمَنُوا لَا تُقَدِّمُوا بَيْنَ يَدَيِ اللَّهِ وَرَسُولِهِ وَاتَّقُوا اللَّهَ إِنَّ اللَّهَ سَمِيعٌ عَلِيمٌ يَاأَيُّهَا الَّذِينَ آمَنُوا لَا تَرْفَعُوا أَصْوَاتَكُمْ فَوْقَ صَوْتِ النَّبِيِّ وَلَا تَجْهَرُوا لَهُ بِالْقَوْلِ كَجَهْرِ بَعْضِكُمْ لِبَعْضٍ أَنْ تَحْبَطَ أَعْمَالُكُمْ وَأَنْتُمْ لَا تَشْعُرُونَ

"O you who believe, be not forward in the presence of Allah and His Messenger. O you who believe, lift not up your voices above the voice of the Prophet, nor speak aloud to him in talk as you speak loudly one to another, lest your deeds be rendered vain while you perceive not" (*al-Hujuraat* 1-2). Al-Qurtubi stated in his commentary to this verse,

> Do not be forward with any statement or action in the presence of Allah or the statements of His Messenger and his actions in those things that you should take from him regarding your religion or worldly life. Whoever prefers his speech or actions over that of the Messenger (peace be upon him) also puts his speech over that of Allah as the Messenger (peace be upon him) is only ordering what Allah has ordered.[1]

The latter part of these two verses states that just raising one's voice above the Prophet's voice may lead to the destruction of one's deeds. If that is the case with just raising one's voice above the Prophet's voice, what might be the case of the person who turns away from the Prophet's words, refuses to listen to the commands of the Prophet (peace be

---

[1] Al-Qurtubi, vol. 16, p. 300.

upon him) or puts his opinion above the statement of the Messenger of Allah (peace be upon him)?

In another verse, Allah says,

إِنَّمَا الْمُؤْمِنُونَ الَّذِينَ آمَنُوا بِاللَّهِ وَرَسُولِهِ وَإِذَا كَانُوا مَعَهُ عَلَى أَمْرٍ جَامِعٍ لَمْ يَذْهَبُوا حَتَّى يَسْتَأْذِنُوهُ

"Only those are believers who believe in Allah and His Messenger and when they are with him on some common matter, they do not depart until they have asked for his permission" (*al-Noor* 62). Commenting on this verse, ibn al-Qayyim stated,

> Allah has made it a requirement of faith that they do not leave if they are with him except with his permission. Therefore, first and foremost, this requires that they do not follow any statement or view except with his permission—and his permission is recognized by it being indicated in [the teachings] that he brought. [If something is consistent with what he (peace be upon him) taught, it means] that he approves.[1]

Allah's Guidance of the Prophet (peace be upon him)

Mention has already been made of the *Hikmah* as being the sunnah of the Prophet (peace be upon him) and as being a type of revelation from Allah. There is ample evidence in the Quran itself that the Prophet (peace be upon him) was receiving revelation and guidance from Allah, other than the Quran. It was obligatory upon him (peace be upon him) to follow that guidance and he also conveyed that guidance to his followers. For example, Allah says,

---

[1] Muhammad Ibn al-Qayyim, *Ilaam al-Muwaqqieen an Rabb al-Alameen* (Beirut: al-Maktabah al-Asriyyah, 1987), vol. 1, pp. 51-52.

وَمَا جَعَلْنَا الْقِبْلَةَ الَّتِي كُنتَ عَلَيْهَا إِلاَّ لِنَعْلَمَ مَنْ يَتَّبِعُ الرَّسُولَ مِمَّنْ

يَنقَلِبُ عَلَى عَقِبَيْهِ وَإِنْ كَانَتْ لَكَبِيرَةً إِلاَّ عَلَى الَّذِينَ هَدَى اللَّهُ وَمَا

كَانَ اللَّهُ لِيُضِيعَ إِيمَانَكُمْ إِنَّ اللَّهَ بِالنَّاسِ لَرَءُوفٌ رَحِيمٌ قَدْ نَرَى

تَقَلُّبَ وَجْهِكَ فِي السَّمَاءِ فَلَنُوَلِّيَنَّكَ قِبْلَةً تَرْضَاهَا فَوَلِّ وَجْهَكَ

شَطْرَ الْمَسْجِدِ الْحَرَامِ

"We appointed the *qiblah* [direction] to which you used to
follow only to test those who followed the Messenger from
those who would turn on their heels (from the faith). Indeed it
was (a change) momentous, except for those guided by Allah.
And never would Allah make your faith [that is, your prayers]
of no effect. For Allah is to all people most surely full of
Kindness, Most Merciful. We see the turning of your face (for
guidance) to the heavens. Now shall We turn you to a *qiblah*
that shall please you. Turn then your face in the direction of
the Sacred Mosque..." (*al-Baqarah* 143-144). These words are
in reference to the Muslims facing toward Jerusalem before the
direction of the prayer was changed to Makkah. Allah
explicitly states that it was He who had appointed that original
direction of prayer. However, this inspiration and command to
the Prophet (peace be upon him) to face Jerusalem never
formed a portion of the Quran. Hence, the Prophet (peace be
upon him) must have received another type of revelation from
Allah that was binding upon him and his followers.[1]

A set of verses usually used as a proof that the sunnah
is divinely inspired are,

---

[1] Cf., Abdul Khaaliq (pp. 334-339), al-Salafi (pp. 55-61) and Usmani (pp. 23-29)
for more examples and a more in depth discussion of this concept. In particular,
Usmani gives sixteen examples of this nature.

مَا ضَلَّ صَاحِبُكُمْ وَمَا غَوَى وَمَا يَنْطِقُ عَنِ الْهَوَى إِنْ هُوَ إِلاَّ وَحْيٌ يُوحَى

"Your companion errs not nor is he deceived. Nor does he speak out of his own desires. It is only an inspiration that is being revealed to him" (*al-Najm* 2-4). However, this author is not completely convinced that these verses may be used as an evidence for the importance of the sunnah because there is a difference of opinion over whether they refer to everything the Prophet (peace be upon him) said or specifically to only the Quran. Concerning these verses from *al-Najm*, Al-Saadi said, "This [verse] points out that the sunnah is a revelation of Allah to His Messenger (peace be upon him)... And he is protected [from making a mistake] in what he relates about Allah and His law as his speech is not derived from his own desires but it is derived from what is being revealed to him." Al-Saadi, whose Quranic commentary is meant to be brief, never mentions that other scholars do not agree with this interpretation. Al-Qaasimi mentions both opinions—the opinion that the pronoun "it" in "It is only an inspiration..." refers only to the Quran and the opinion that "it" refers to everything the Prophet (peace be upon him) stated. He concludes that the stronger opinion is that the pronoun (*huwa*, "it") refers only to the Quran, "The object is the Quran, as can be understood from the context as the people who were rejecting [the mission] were referring to the Quran." Al-Raazi has the longest discussion on this point, and he also concludes that the verses refer to the Quran.[1] Note that these verses are not needed to prove that sunnah is also divinely inspired; the

---

[1] Cf., Abdul Rahmaan al-Saadi, *Taiseer al-Kareem al-Rahmaan fi Tafseer Kalaam al-Mannaan* (Riyadh: Al-Muasassah al-Saeediyyah), vol. 7, p. 204; Jamaal al-Deen al-Qaasimi, *Mahaasan al-Ta'weel* (Beirut: Daar al-Fikr, 1978), vol. 15, pp. 222-23; Fakhr al-Deen al-Raazi, *Tafseer al-Kabeer* (Beirut: Daar Ihyaa al-Turaath al-Arabi), vol. 28, pp. 282-83.

verses quoted earlier concerning the revelation of the *Hikmah*, for example, are sufficient to prove this point.

Conclusions from the Quranic Verses

Through numerous means, Allah has clearly established and emphasized the importance of following the sunnah of the Prophet (peace be upon him). Allah has done this by ordering obedience to the Messenger of Allah (peace be upon him) and prohibiting disobedience to him.[1] He has also done so by giving tidings of the positive results of obeying the Messenger (peace be upon him), while at the same time intimidating and warning those who would consider disobeying the Prophet (peace be upon him).

Before continuing on to discuss some of the hadith of the Prophet (peace be upon him), what one must conclude from the above verses should be stated. Based solely on the texts of the Quran, one may conclude:[2]

a. It is Allah Himself who has ordered the Muslims to follow and to obey the Prophet Muhammad (peace be upon him). This notion was not an innovation of later jurists, nor is it something open to debate or discussion.

b. If anyone claims to follow the Quran, then he must also follow the sunnah of the Prophet (peace be upon him), as

---

[1] Among the verses of the Quran indicating the obligation to follow the sunnah, some scholars also mention all of the verses that require one to believe in the Prophet Muhammad (peace be upon him). They include these verses because they say that *imaan* (belief) means "to submit, affirm and follow." Furthermore, the Prophet (peace be upon him) was ordered to convey everything that he had received from Allah, implying both the Quran and the sunnah (note verses *al-Maaidah* 67 and *al-Anaam* 106). This command to convey implies a command for the one to whom it is conveyed to follow and obey what has been conveyed. Hence, a number of other verses indicating the importance of the sunnah could be added to those discussed above.

[2] There are yet other verses of the Quran that touch upon the place of the sunnah. Some of them are found in Chapter Three, "The Roles of the Messenger of Allah (peace be upon him)" and in the Appendix.

it is the Quran itself that orders the Muslims to follow the Prophet (peace be upon him). Therefore, it is inconsistent to claim to follow the Quran while denying one's obligation to follow the sunnah.

    c. Allah has stated severe warnings for anyone who refuses to follow the Messenger (peace be upon him); on the other hand, Allah has promised guidance, mercy and forgiveness for those who do follow the way of the Prophet (peace be upon him).

Verses Used As Arguments Against the Authority of the Sunnah

    Before concluding this section discussing the importance of the sunnah in the light of the Quran, it is imperative to discuss those verses that are quoted as Quranic evidence against the authority of the sunnah.[1] From the above, it should already be clear to the reader that the place of the sunnah is definitively established by numerous verses of the Quran. The only thing that could possibly stand up to those verses would be something that is as clearly definitive in its repudiation of the importance of the sunnah. Subjective conclusions from some verses certainly would not be sufficient to deny what all of the above verses have established. Those who argue against the sunnah cannot offer any such clear cut verses of the Quran. Instead, they can only refer to a couple of verses that could possibly support their position. The only verses that they can offer in support of their contention are the following:

---

[1] Some opponents of the sunnah even have the audacity to quote some hadith to support their claim that the sunnah and hadith are not to be followed. However, this demonstrates a logical error since one cannot use something that is not an authority, as they claim, to prove that it is not an authority. Furthermore, they usually rely on fabricating hadith to prove their allegation.

One verse quoted as an argument against the authority of the sunnah is:

$$\text{مَا فَرَّطْنَا فِي الْكِتَابِ مِنْ شَيْءٍ}$$

"Nothing have We omitted from the book" (*al-Anaam* 38); a second verse quoted is:

$$\text{وَنَزَّلْنَا عَلَيْكَ الْكِتَابَ تِبْيَانًا لِكُلِّ شَيْءٍ}$$

"We have sent down to you a book explaining all things" (*al-Nahl* 89).

The argument from these verses is that all necessary guidance is contained in the book, the Quran, itself. In fact, everything has been explained with clarity and detail. There is no need to turn to any other source, as that would imply that something is missing from the Quran—thus, contradicting what these verses state. Anything other than the Quran must, therefore, be superfluous, not meant to be followed by the Muslims and certainly not a source in Islamic law.[1]

The response to this argument is rather straightforward. For example, the verse from *soorah al-Anaam* has to be read in its entirety to get a better understanding of what exactly the verse is referring to. The entire verse reads,

$$\text{وَمَا مِنْ دَابَّةٍ فِي الْأَرْضِ وَلَا طَائِرٍ يَطِيرُ بِجَنَاحَيْهِ إِلَّا أُمَمٌ أَمْثَالُكُمْ مَا}$$
$$\text{فَرَّطْنَا فِي الْكِتَابِ مِنْ شَيْءٍ ثُمَّ إِلَى رَبِّهِمْ يُحْشَرُونَ}$$

"There is not an animal (that lives) on the earth, nor a being that flies with its wings, but (forms part of) communities like you. Nothing have We omitted from the book, and they (all) shall be gathered to their Lord in the end." One interpretation of this verse is that the mentioned "book" is not in reference to the Quran, but it refers to the preserved tablet that has recorded

---

[1] These verses were offered as arguments against the sunnah by Muhammad Taufeeq Sidqi in his article *"Al-Islaam huwa al-Quraan Wahdahu"* in the famed journal *al-Manaar.* Cf., Abdul Khaaliq, p. 383.

on it everything that will occur until the Day of Judgment.[1] In other words, that tablet has all of the lives and sustenance of all of the creatures recorded on it, and nothing has been left out of that book. According to this interpretation, the meaning of this verse is very much similar to another verse which states,

$$وَمَا مِنْ دَابَّةٍ فِي الأَرْضِ إِلاَّ عَلَى اللَّهِ رِزْقُهَا وَيَعْلَمُ مُسْتَقَرَّهَا وَمُسْتَوْدَعَهَا كُلٌّ فِي كِتَابٍ مُبِينٍ$$

"There is no moving creature on earth but its sustenance depends on Allah: He knows the time and place of its definite abode and its temporary deposit: all is in a clear book" (*Hood* 6).

However, a second, although less plausible, interpretation given for this verse is that "the book" refers to the Quran.[2] Even if this interpretation is accepted, it does not necessarily imply that the sunnah is not an authority and obligatory upon Muslims to follow. As shall be demonstrated in the next chapter, it must be admitted that the details concerning the prayer, zakat, fasts and other acts of the *shareeah* are not all spelled out in the Quran. Hence, in order for this interpretation to be accurate given the reality of the situation, it must mean the following, as ibn al-Jauzi explained it, "It is a general statement that has a particular intent behind it. The meaning therefore is: We have not omitted anything which you would be in need of except that it has been made clear in the book, either by clear text, undetailed statement or indication."[3] In other words, everything is mentioned in the

---

[1] This interpretation has been recorded by ibn Abi Talha on the authority of ibn Abbaas. It was also the understanding of Qataadah and ibn Zaid. In addition, it is the only interpretation mentioned by al-Baghawi as the meaning of the verse. Cf., Abdul Rahmaan ibn al-Jauzi, *Zaad al-Maseer fi Ilm al-Tafseer* (Beirut: Daar al-Fikr, 1987), vol. 3, p. 26; Al-Husain al-Baghawi, *Tafseer al-Baghawi: Maalim al-Tanzeel* (Riyadh: Daar Taibah, 1989), vol. 3, p. 142.

[2] This has been narrated by Ataa on the authority of ibn Abbaas. Cf., ibn al-Jauzi, vol. 3, p. 26.

[3] Ibn al-Jauzi, vol. 3, p. 26.

Book in either direct detail or by reference to the source where the necessary detail can be found. Hence, the book itself does not contain the details of the prayers, fasts and so forth, but the book points the believer to where those details can be found: the sunnah of the Prophet (peace be upon him). When understood in this manner, this verse is not an argument against the authority of the sunnah but it is another verse indicating the indispensability of the sunnah itself.

As noted, a second verse quoted as an argument against the authority of the sunnah is:

$$ \text{وَنَزَّلْنَا عَلَيْكَ الْكِتَابَ تِبْيَانًا لِكُلِّ شَيْءٍ} $$

"We have sent down to you a book explaining all things" (*al-Nahl* 89). Commenting on this verse, ibn Katheer noted that the Quran contains all of the beneficial knowledge of what has passed and what will occur, what is lawful and what is unlawful, and what humans need for their well-being in both this life and the Hereafter.[1] There is no question that such is the case. The question is only related to the manner by which Allah does so in the Quran. It is obvious that Allah does not do that by spelling out all of the details of worship, law and life in the Quran itself. Instead, the Quran points the believer to all that is needed to be truly guided. Included in this is the sunnah itself as well as other aspects, such as contemplating creation and so forth. Again, this verse cannot be used as an argument against the authority of the sunnah because its implication is that the Quran clarifies all that one needs in one's life and part of what is needed in one's life is adherence to the sunnah of the Messenger of Allah (peace be upon him). As was demonstrated earlier in this chapter, it is the Book itself that makes this fact abundantly clear.

---

[1] Ibn Katheer, p. 751.

The Prophet's Own Statements Concerning the Importance of the Sunnah

Besides the above verses that point to the necessity of obeying the Messenger of Allah (peace be upon him) and the importance of his sunnah, the Prophet (peace be upon him) himself clearly stated the importance of his own sunnah and warned about abandoning his sunnah. Now that it has been established that the Quran itself tells Muslims to follow the sunnah, it will be acceptable to use the statements of the Prophet (peace be upon him) himself as further proof of the importance of the sunnah in Islam and of the obligation to follow the sunnah. What follows are some examples from the hadith of the Prophet (peace be upon him).

The Messenger of Allah (peace be upon him) said,

لَا أُلْفِيَنَّ أَحَدَكُمْ مُتَّكِئًا عَلَى أَرِيكَتِهِ يَأْتِيهِ أَمْرٌ مِمَّا أَمَرْتُ بِهِ أَوْ نَهَيْتُ عَنْهُ فَيَقُولُ لَا أَدْرِي مَا وَجَدْنَا فِي كِتَابِ اللَّهِ اتَّبَعْنَاهُ

"I had better not find anyone of you reclining on his bed and there comes to him one of my commandments or one of my prohibitions and he says about it, 'I do not know, what we find in the book of Allah (only) do we follow.'"[1]

In a similar hadith, the Messenger of Allah (peace be upon him) is reported to have prohibited the flesh of domestic donkeys and said,

---

[1] Recorded by al-Baihaqi, al-Shaafi'ee, al-Humaidi, Ahmad, Abu Daawood, al-Tirmidhi, Ibn Maajah, Ibn Hibbaan and al-Haakim with a *sahih* chain. According to al-Albaani, it is *sahih*. See Muhammad Naasir al-Deen al-Albaani, *Saheeh al-Jaami al-Sagheer* (Beirut: al-Maktab al-Islaami, 1986), vol. 2, p. 1204.

يُوشِكُ الرَّجُلُ مُتَّكِئًا عَلَى أَرِيكَتِهِ يُحَدَّثُ بِحَدِيثٍ مِنْ حَدِيثِي

فَيَقُولُ بَيْنَنَا وَبَيْنَكُمْ كِتَابُ اللَّهِ عَزَّ وَجَلَّ مَا وَجَدْنَا فِيهِ مِنْ

حَلَالٍ اسْتَحْلَلْنَاهُ وَمَا وَجَدْنَا فِيهِ مِنْ حَرَامٍ حَرَّمْنَاهُ أَلَا وَإِنَّ مَا

حَرَّمَ رَسُولُ اللَّهِ صَلَّى اللَّهم عَلَيْهِ وَسَلَّمَ مِثْلُ مَا حَرَّمَ اللَّهُ

"Soon it will be that a man will recline on his couch and will be told a hadith of my hadith[1] and will say, 'Between us and you is the Book of Allah. What we find allowed therein, we allow. What we find prohibited therein, we prohibit.' But truly, what the Messenger of Allah has forbidden is similar to what Allah has forbidden."[2]

In these two hadith, the Messenger of Allah (peace be upon him) has warned Muslims about people who will neglect the sunnah of the Prophet (peace be upon him) and claim that they need only live by the injunctions of the Quran. In the second hadith, he has stated that what he pronounces as illegal should be treated in the same way as that which Allah has declared illegal. In the latter hadith, the Messenger of Allah (peace be upon him) prohibited the eating of donkey flesh as an example of the type of legislation that comes from only him and which must be obeyed by all Muslims. Nowhere in the Quran is such a prohibition found. But, from the Quran itself, it is known that it is sufficient for the Prophet (peace be upon him) to declare it illegal; no one may consider it legal simply because it is not mentioned as illegal in the Quran.

In these two hadith, one should take note of how the Prophet (peace be upon him) described those who refused to follow his sunnah. The implication as given by the scholars of

---

[1] Here the meaning of the word "hadith" is actually its linguistic meaning, implying, a statement or communique of the Prophet (peace be upon him).

[2] Recorded by al-Baihaqi, Ahmad, al-Tirmidhi and ibn Maajah. According to al-Albaani, it is authentic. See al-Albaani, *Saheeh al-Jaami*, vol. 2, p. 1360.

the words, "one who is reclining on his bed or couch," is one who is "interested in luxuries and heresies in the religion, who stays at home and remains away from seeking knowledge and hadith," or it is one "who is arrogant and wanting to be in charge."[1] There is no doubt that the Prophet (peace be upon him) meant a certain impression by those specific words. The impression is not a positive one. It is a characteristic of those who refuse to submit to the obligation of following the sunnah and who—undoubtedly falsely—claim that they are following the Quran. In fact, it might even give another clue as to why some people refuse to follow the sunnah: out of laziness and desire for ease and luxury. The sunnah makes specific requirements upon a person which one could avoid by claiming to just follow the general teachings of the Quran. Due to their unwillingness to sacrifice, learn and exert efforts, they flee from the sunnah.

The Messenger of Allah (peace be upon him) said,

أَلا إِنِّي أُوتِيتُ الْكِتَابَ وَمِثْلَهُ مَعَهُ

"Verily I have been given the Book and something similar to it with it..."[2] Badr al-Badr said,

> There can be two meanings for this [hadith]: (a) The meaning is that the Messenger of Allah has been given a *batin* (hidden) revelation that is not recited, in the same way that he has been given an apparent [revelation] that is recited. (b) Another meaning it carries is that he has been given the Book which is a revelation that is recited and he has been given its explanation. That is, he has been given the permission to explain what is in the Book, what has

---

[1] Al-Husain al-Teeby, *Sharh al-Teebi ala Mishkaat al-Masaabeeh* (Makkah: Maktaba Nazaar Mustafa al-Baaz, 1997), vol. 2, p. 629.
[2] Recorded by Abu Daawood with a *sahih* chain. The rest of the hadith is similar to the first hadith mentioned above.

general and specific application, and he can increase upon its legislation in matters not mentioned by the Quran. In that manner lies his duty to order and for others to obey his orders in exactly the same manner in which [it is obligatory] to follow the clear recitation of the Quran.[1]

This hadith can be read together with the verses recorded above concerning the *Hikmah*. This hadith supports the view of al-Shaafi'ee that the Prophet (peace be upon him) was not only given the Book but he was also given along with it another type of revelation: the *Hikmah* or sunnah. Hasaan ibn Attiyah said, "Jibreel would reveal the sunnah to the Messenger of Allah (peace be upon him) like he would reveal the Quran to him. He would teach him it like he would teach him the Quran."[2] Ibn Hazm also recorded Imam Malik as saying, "If the Prophet (peace be upon him) were asked about something, he would not respond until he received revelation from heaven."[3]

---

[1] Commentary by Badr al-Badr in Jalaal al-Deen al-Suyooti, *Miftaah al-Jannah fi al-Ihtijaaj bi al-Sunnah* (Kuwait: Daar al-Huda al-Nubuwwa, no date), p. 22, fn. 47. Most of the hadith and other statements found in this chapter may be found in this excellent work by al-Suyooti. Note, however, that many of the reports he uses have weak chains; those have not been used in this work.

[2] Recorded by al-Daarimi and al-Baihaqi. According to ibn Hajr, the chain for this report is *sahih* back to Hasaan. [Ahmad ibn Hajr, *Fath al-Baari Sharh Saheeh al-Bukhaari* (Makkah: Maktabah Daar al-Baaz, 1989), vol. 13, p. 361.] Hasaan was a trustworthy narrator who learned from many of the Followers, including Saeed ibn al-Musayyab (the son-in-law of Abu Huraira) and Naafi (the freed slave of ibn Umar). See Ahmad ibn Hajr, *Tahdheeb al-Tahdheeb* (Beirut: Muassasat al-Risaalah, 1996), vol. 1, p. 382. Unfortunately, the chain between him and the Prophet (peace be upon him) is obviously broken. Hence, it is not known if this was Hasaan's own personal reasoning (*ijtihaad*) or something that he had learned from his teachers among the Followers. Many scholars quote this report. It seems that they believe that such a statement could not be the result of his own personal reasoning. Therefore, he must have learned it from his teachers who must have received it from a Companion who learned that fact from the Prophet (peace be upon him) himself. Allah knows best.

[3] Ali ibn Hazm, *Al-Ihkaam fi Usool al-Ahkaam* (Zakariyyah Ali Yoosuf publisher, n.d.), vol. 1, p. 176.

The Messenger of Allah (peace be upon him) said, during the farewell pilgrimage,

$$\text{تَرَكْتُ فِيكُمْ أَمْرَيْنِ لَنْ تَضِلُّوا مَا تَمَسَّكْتُمْ بِهِمَا كِتَابَ اللَّهِ وَسُنَّةَ نَبِيِّهِ}$$

"I have left among you two matters that if you adhere to them you will never be misguided: the Book of Allah and the sunnah of His prophet."[1] In another version he stated, "O mankind, listen to what I say and live by it."[2] These hadith and other similar hadith have been narrated by a large number of Companions, and there is, therefore, no doubt about their authenticity. In this hadith the Messenger of Allah (peace be upon him) gave Muslims clear advice: if they wish never to be misguided they need only follow the Book of Allah and the sunnah of the Prophet (peace be upon him). Note that he gave this advice during his final pilgrimage when he knew that his death was near and it was a farewell advice to the thousands who thronged around him. (Note also that if his sunnah was only to be followed during his lifetime it would have been his duty to tell that to his followers. Otherwise, he would not be fulfilling his mission of conveying the message. Instead, at a time when he knew his death was near he reiterated that Muslims must cling to both the Book of Allah and the sunnah of His Prophet.)

The Messenger of Allah (peace be upon him) said,

$$\text{لكل عمل شرة ولكل شرة فترة فمن كانت فترته إلى سنتي}$$
$$\text{فقد اهتدى ومن كانت فترته إلى غير ذلك فقد هلك}$$

---

[1] Recorded by Maalik, al-Haakim and al-Baihaqi. It is *sahih*. Cf., al-Albaani, *Saheeh al-Jaami*, vol. 1, p. 566.

[2] Recorded by al-Baihaqi with a *hasan* chain.

74

"Every action has its period of extreme activity and every action has its period of inactivity. Whosoever keeps his period of inactivity within the limits of my sunnah has been guided aright; whoever goes beyond this limit will, in fact, be destroyed."[1] In this hadith, the Messenger of Allah (peace be upon him) has pointed to the fact that the ones who are truly guided and who will be saved in the Hereafter are those whose periods of inactivity—in doing good deeds, voluntary work and so on—are within the limits of the sunnah of the Prophet (peace be upon him). It is often the case that some people are very active for a period of time and then experience a lack of enthusiasm, and their deeds begin to diminish. If the low points are beyond the limits established by the sunnah (for example, the person completely stops praying in congregation) then these low points will lead to destruction. According to this hadith, for a person to be rightly guided he must always stay within the limits established by the sunnah of the Prophet Muhammad (peace be upon him). Actually, even in periods of enthusiasm the person must be careful to stay within the limits set by the Prophet (peace be upon him), since his sunnah is the standard by which acts are judged. Thus, at either extreme, of activity or inactivity, the Muslim must stay within the sunnah. This is a clear warning for those who abandon the sunnah altogether and for those who introduce new concepts into the religion and try to add to the sunnah of the Prophet (peace be upon him).

In the following hadith the Messenger of Allah (peace be upon him) referred to his own judgment as "judging by the Book of Allah." Abu Hurairah and Zaid ibn Khaalid Juhani reported that two people quarreled and came to the Messenger of Allah (peace be upon him). One said, "O Messenger of Allah, decide between us in accordance with the Book of

---

[1] Recorded by Ahmad, ibn Hibbaan and others with a *sahib* chain. According to al-Albaani, it is *sahib*. See Muhammad Naasir al-Deen al-Albaani, *Saheeh al-Targheeb wa al-Tarheeb* (Riyadh: Maktabah al-Maarif, 1988), vol. 1, p. 98.

Allah." The other, who was more sensible, said, "Yes, Messenger of Allah, decide in accordance with the Book of Allah and permit me to speak." The Messenger of Allah (peace be upon him) allowed him to speak. He said, "My son was employed by this man and he [my son] committed adultery with his wife. The people said that my son deserves to be stoned. I gave the man one hundred sheep and a slave girl as a ransom on my son's behalf. I then asked the learned men and they said that my son should be whipped a hundred times and exiled for a year and that his wife is liable to be stoned to death as a punishment for her action." The Messenger of Allah (peace be upon him) said, "I will make a decision for you both in accordance with the Book of Allah. Your sheep and the slave girl are your property; take them back. The son shall be whipped a hundred times and exiled for a year." He then asked Unais Aslami to go to the other man's wife and see if she admitted to the crime, in which case he should have her stoned. She confessed and was stoned to death. (Recorded by al-Bukhari and Muslim.) This judgment, whipping a hundred times *with* an exile for a year, is not to be found in the Quran; yet the Prophet (peace be upon him) called it "deciding in accordance with the Book of Allah." This is because the commands of the Prophet (peace be upon him) are, in fact, on the same level in Islamic law as the Quran with respect to implementation (both of them being revelations from Allah). This is a result of the legislative authority of the Messenger (peace be upon him) that comes from Allah Himself in the Quran.

Al-Bukhari records the following moving hadith:

جَاءَتْ مَلاَئِكَةٌ إِلَى النَّبِيِّ صَلَّى اللَّهم عَلَيْهِ وَسَلَّمَ وَهُوَ نَائِمٌ فَقَالَ بَعْضُهُمْ إِنَّهُ نَائِمٌ وَقَالَ بَعْضُهُمْ إِنَّ الْعَيْنَ نَائِمَةٌ وَالْقَلْبَ يَقْظَانُ فَقَالُوا إِنَّ لِصَاحِبِكُمْ هَذَا مَثَلاً فَاضْرِبُوا لَهُ مَثَلاً فَقَالَ

بَعْضُهُمْ إِنَّهُ نَائِمٌ وَقَالَ بَعْضُهُمْ إِنَّ الْعَيْنَ نَائِمَةٌ وَالْقَلْبَ يَقْظَانُ
فَقَالُوا مَثَلُهُ كَمَثَلِ رَجُلٍ بَنَى دَارًا وَجَعَلَ فِيهَا مَأْدُبَةً وَبَعَثَ
دَاعِيًا فَمَنْ أَجَابَ الدَّاعِيَ دَخَلَ الدَّارَ وَأَكَلَ مِنَ الْمَأْدُبَةِ وَمَنْ
لَمْ يُجِبِ الدَّاعِيَ لَمْ يَدْخُلِ الدَّارَ وَلَمْ يَأْكُلْ مِنَ الْمَأْدُبَةِ فَقَالُوا
أَوِّلُوهَا لَهُ يَفْقَهْهَا فَقَالَ بَعْضُهُمْ إِنَّهُ نَائِمٌ وَقَالَ بَعْضُهُمْ إِنَّ
الْعَيْنَ نَائِمَةٌ وَالْقَلْبَ يَقْظَانُ فَقَالُوا فَالدَّارُ الْجَنَّةُ وَالدَّاعِي
مُحَمَّدٌ صَلَّى اللَّهم عَلَيْهِ وَسَلَّمَ فَمَنْ أَطَاعَ مُحَمَّدًا صَلَّى اللَّهم
عَلَيْهِ وَسَلَّمَ فَقَدْ أَطَاعَ اللَّهَ وَمَنْ عَصَى مُحَمَّدًا صَلَّى اللَّهم
عَلَيْهِ وَسَلَّمَ فَقَدْ عَصَى اللَّهَ وَمُحَمَّدٌ صَلَّى اللَّهم عَلَيْهِ وَسَلَّمَ
فَرْقٌ بَيْنَ النَّاسِ

Some angels came to the Messenger of Allah (peace be upon him) while he was sleeping. Some of the angels said, "He is sleeping [therefore leave him]." The others answered, "His eyes sleep but his heart is alert." They said, "Your companion is like this" and they propounded a similitude. They said, "His similitude is like a person who builds a house and provides a tablespread filled with provisions and calls the other people to it. Those who respond to his call enter the house and eat from the tablespread. Those who do not respond to his call do not enter the house nor do they eat from the tablespread." Some of the angels said, "Give him its interpretation." Others replied, "He is sleeping." They were answered by others who said, "His eyes sleep but his heart is alert." So they explained the parable to him, saying, "The house is Paradise and the one inviting is Muhammad (peace be upon him). Whoever obeys

Muhammad (peace be upon him) has verily obeyed Allah. Whoever disobeys Muhammad (peace be upon him) has verily disobeyed Allah. And Muhammad (peace be upon him) is a separator of humanity." In this hadith one can see the mistake committed by those who deny the sunnah or who give it little importance. The Prophet Muhammad (peace be upon him) with his perfect example, his orders and prohibitions, has made the way clear for Muslims and has called them to the path to Paradise in the same way that a person invites another to dinner. By ignoring this call a person would be ignoring, in fact, the path to Allah. The end result for those who do not bother to pattern their lives after the sunnah of the Prophet (peace be upon him) is that they will not be allowed to enjoy the fruits of Paradise. Lastly, the angels said that the Messenger of Allah (peace be upon him) separates mankind. That is to say that his message distinguishes the believers from the unbelievers and it distinguishes the people of Paradise from the people of Hell—that is, those who accept his invitation by following him and those who reject his invitation by rejecting his sunnah and way of life. This hadith, therefore, establishes the following of the sunnah as one of the vital signs of faith.

The Messenger of Allah (peace be upon him) said,

$$ كُلُّ أُمَّتِي يَدْخُلُونَ الْجَنَّةَ إِلاَّ مَنْ أَبَى $$

"All of my nation will enter Paradise except those who refuse." His companions asked, "Who would refuse?" He answered,

$$ مَنْ أَطَاعَنِي دَخَلَ الْجَنَّةَ وَمَنْ عَصَانِي فَقَدْ أَبَى $$

"Whoever obeys me will enter Paradise; whoever disobeys me has refused (to enter Paradise)." (Recorded by al-Bukhari and others.) Here again one can see the true and simple beauty of the Prophet's role. The Messenger of Allah (peace be upon him), by his sunnah or way of life, showed the path for Muslims that leads them directly to Paradise. If the Muslim accepts to follow him, he will not be refusing the invitation to Paradise. If the Muslim refuses to follow him, he is, in effect, refusing to enter Paradise. Note that the Prophet (peace be upon him) was referring to the people who believe in him ("his nation"), thus showing, as in other hadith, that Allah had informed the Prophet (peace be upon him) that there would exist people from his own nation who would refuse to follow his sunnah.

In another moving hadith, the Messenger of Allah (peace be upon him) said,

إِنَّمَا مَثَلِي وَمَثَلُ مَا بَعَثَنِي اللَّهُ بِهِ كَمَثَلِ رَجُلٍ أَتَى قَوْمًا فَقَالَ يَا قَوْمِ إِنِّي رَأَيْتُ الْجَيْشَ بِعَيْنَيَّ وَإِنِّي أَنَا النَّذِيرُ الْعُرْيَانُ فَالنَّجَاءَ فَأَطَاعَهُ طَائِفَةٌ مِنْ قَوْمِهِ فَأَدْلَجُوا فَانْطَلَقُوا عَلَى مَهَلِهِمْ فَنَجَوْا وَكَذَّبَتْ طَائِفَةٌ مِنْهُمْ فَأَصْبَحُوا مَكَانَهُمْ فَصَبَّحَهُمُ الْجَيْشُ فَأَهْلَكَهُمْ وَاجْتَاحَهُمْ فَذَلِكَ مَثَلُ مَنْ أَطَاعَنِي فَاتَّبَعَ مَا جِئْتُ بِهِ وَمَثَلُ مَنْ عَصَانِي وَكَذَّبَ بِمَا جِئْتُ بِهِ مِنَ الْحَقِّ

"My example and the example of that with which I have been sent by Allah is like a man whom came to a people and said, 'O people! I have seen an army with my own eyes. I am the naked warner,[1] so protect yourselves.' A group of his people

---

[1] The words, "naked warner," imply how serious the matter is, that the warned incident is very close and there is no reason to suspect the one who is giving the warning. The source for this expression comes from the concept of someone going out naked in order to get his people's immediate attention before the enemy is about to strike. Cf., al-Teebi, vol. 2, p. 612. Al-Teebi notes that there are three aspects of emphasis in the Prophet's statement: the mention of the naked

obeyed him and fled during the night, proceeding stealthily until they were saved. Another group did not believe him and stayed in their places until the morning, when the army came upon them. They destroyed and ruined them completely. That is the example of the one who obeys me and follows what I have brought and the example of the one who disobeys me and denies what I have brought of the truth." (Recorded by al-Bukhari and Muslim.) Note that after giving the parable, the Prophet (peace be upon him) said, "That is the example of the one who obeys me and therefore follows what I have brought," juxtaposed with, "one who disobeys me and denies what I have brought." This implies that the obedience is preceded by belief and affirmation in his message while denial and rejection is then followed by disobeying the Prophet (peace be upon him).[1] Indeed, the only reason imaginable why anyone would ever refuse[2] to follow what the Prophet (peace be upon him) brought is if he is somehow lacking in his faith. He is lacking when it comes to his complete belief in the Prophet (peace be upon him) and all what the Prophet (peace be upon him) taught. That is the real source of one's refusal to follow the sunnah of the Prophet (peace be upon him), as so subtly implied in this hadith.

Finally, in a hadith describing the comprehensiveness of the Prophet's guidance, thereby indicating the need to turn to his sunnah and the lack of need to turn to other supposed sources of guidance, the Prophet (peace be upon him) said,

---

warner, the mention of seeing with his own eyes and repeating the word, "I." This implies the closeness and seriousness of the matter that the Prophet (peace be upon him) is warning about.

[1] Al-Teebi, vol. 2, p. 613.

[2] Refuse as opposed to accepting and willing to submit but sometimes slipping and going against his commands.

ما بقي شيء يقرّب من الجنة ويباعد من النار إلا وقد بيّن لكم

"There is nothing left that takes one closer to Paradise or distances one from the Fire except that I have made it clear to you." In another narration, it states,

أيها الناس إنه ليس من شيء يقربكم من الجنة ويباعدكم من النار إلا وقد أمرتكم به وليس من شيء يقربكم من النار ويباعدكم من الجنة إلا وقد نهيتكم عنه

"O people, there is nothing that takes you closer to Paradise or that distances you from the Fire except that I have ordered it for you. And there is nothing that takes you closer to the Fire and distances you from Paradise except that I have prohibited it for you."[1]

Many more hadith can be added to the ones mentioned above but for the sake of brevity it will be best to stop here. The following are the conclusions that can be made from the hadith of the Prophet (peace be upon him):

(a) The Prophet (peace be upon him), in conveying the message as he was commissioned to by Allah, made it explicitly clear on many occasions that the Muslim must follow his sunnah in order to be rightly guided.

---

[1] The first narration is from al-Tabaraani in *al-Mujam al-Kabeer*. The second narration is from Hunaad ibn al-Sirri in *al-Zuhd*. Al-Albaani concludes that the first narration is *sahih*, but in his discussion he does not discuss the second narration. Muhammad al-Khairabaadi concludes that the second narration is *sahih* due to its corroborating evidence. See Muhammad Naasir al-Deen al-Albaani, *Silsilat al-Ahaadeeth al-Saheehah* (Kuwait: al-Daar al-Salafiyyah, 1983), vol. 4, pp. 416-417; Muhammad al-Khairabaadi, Footnotes to Hunaad ibn al-Sirri, *Al-Zuhd* (Published by the Ameer of Qatar, n.d.), vol. 1, pp. 584-585.

(b) Allah vouchsafed to the Prophet (peace be upon him) the knowledge that in later times there would come people who would reject his sunnah and refuse to follow his way of life. Therefore, the Prophet (peace be upon him) warned his followers about such people and about such concepts.

(c) From the hadith of the Prophet (peace be upon him) a Muslim can be certain that if he is following the Prophet's sunnah he is, in fact, on the straight path, the path leading directly to Allah's pleasure, forgiveness and Paradise.

The Prophet's Companions' View of the Sunnah

Next to the Messenger of Allah, it was his Companions who best understood the true meaning of the Quran and who best understood in what manner a believer should behave. The Messenger of Allah (peace be upon him) himself described his generation as the best of all generations:

$$ خَيْرُكُمْ قَرْنِي ثُمَّ الَّذِينَ يَلُونَهُمْ ثُمَّ الَّذِينَ يَلُونَهُم $$

"The best of you [my nation] is my generation, then the one that follows them, then the one that follows them." (Recorded by al-Bukhari.) Indeed, it was through the Companions (may Allah be pleased with all of them) that Allah safeguarded the Quran, and it was through them that the following generations learned vital and detailed aspects of Islam. Below are mentioned some of the most prominent and knowledgeable Companions and their positions toward the sunnah of the Prophet (peace be upon him).

Even before getting to some of the statements of the Companions about the sunnah, there is one thing that can be noticed about their behavior: The best generation immediately imitated and followed the Prophet (peace be upon him), without hesitation or questioning why the Prophet (peace be upon him) did a specific act.[1] For example, Al-Bukhari records on the authority of ibn Umar that the Prophet (peace be upon him) used to wear a gold ring, so the people also started wearing gold rings. Then the Prophet (peace be upon him) discarded it and said, "I will never wear it." So the people also immediately discarded their gold rings. On another occasion, the Prophet (peace be upon him) was praying and during his prayer, he removed his shoes. When the Companions saw him doing that, they all did the same. Afterwards, he asked them why they removed their shoes. They replied, "Because we saw you remove your shoes." He explained to them, "[The Angel] Gabriel had informed me that there was some filth on them."[2]

This behavior of the Companions and the fact that they were never reprimanded or corrected by either Allah or the Messenger (peace be upon him) is yet another evidence for the authority of the sunnah. This falls under a category known as the "tacit approval of Allah." It is inconceivable that Allah would allow them to continue to behave in this fashion without the slightest sign from Him indicating that what they were doing was wrong.

Besides their actions, the Companions stated their belief in the authority of the sunnah. Among the many quotes from them are the following:

Abu Bakr, the most virtuous of the Companions of the Prophet and therefore of this entire nation after the Prophet (peace be upon him) himself, stated, "I have not left anything that the Messenger of Allah (peace be upon him) used to do except that I also act upon it. I fear that if I were to leave any of his commands, I would become deviated."[3]

---

[1] Cf., al-Sibaa'ee, pp. 53-54; Abdul Khaaliq, pp. 283-291.

[2] Recorded by Ahmad and Abu Dawood. According to al-Albaani, it is *sahih*. See Muhammad Naasir al-Deen al-Albaani, *Saheeh Sunan Abi Dawood* (Riyadh: Maktab al-Tarbiyyah al-Arabi li-Duwal al-Khaleej, 1989), vol. 1, p. 128.

[3] Quoted in Ubaidullah ibn Battah al-Akbari, *al-Ibaanah an Shareeah al-Firq al-Naajiah* (Riyadh: Daar al-Raayah, 1988), vol. 1, p. 246. Commenting on Abu Bakr's statement, ibn Battah (Ibid., vol. 1, p. 246) stated, "This, my brothers, was

Al-Bukhari and Muslim record in their *Sahihs* that the companion Abdullah ibn Masood said, "Allah curses the one who tattoos, the one who asks to be tattooed, the one who plucks the eyebrows and the one who files her teeth in order to change the creation of Allah." This statement reached Umm Yaqoob, who came to him and said, "It has come to me that you said such and such." He answered her, "What is wrong with me if I curse what the Messenger of Allah has cursed and is to be found in the Book of Allah." She told him, "I have read [the Quran] from cover to cover yet I did not find [in there what you have stated]." Abdullah told her, "If you have read it you would have found it there. Did you not read, 'Verily, what the Messenger gives you, take; and what he forbids for you, abstain from' [*al-Hashr* 7]?" She said, "Yes." He replied, "He [the Messenger of Allah (peace be upon him)] forbade these things." In this incident there is a Companion mentioning a ruling of the Prophet (peace be upon him) as a ruling of Allah. The lady, Umm Yaqoob, misunderstood Abdullah and thought that he was referring to a specific verse wherein the actions he stated were specifically mentioned. In Abdullah's explanation he shows that what the Messenger of Allah (peace be upon him) prohibited has, in fact, the same status as something that Allah explicitly prohibited in the Quran. His proof was the seventh verse of *soorah al-Hashr*.

Abu Daawood recorded from Saeed ibn al-Musayyab that Umar said, "The widowed wife is not entitled to any inheritance out of the blood money [paid due to] her husband [having been killed]." Al-Dhuhaak ibn Sufyaan told Umar that the Messenger of Allah (peace be upon him) had once written to him that the wife of Ashyam al-Dhahabi was to be given an inheritance from the blood money of her husband. Umar then

the greatest truthful one fearing for himself that he would deviate if he contradicted anything that his Prophet (peace be upon him) ordered. And what could possibly be the case with an era whose people openly ridicule their Prophet (peace be upon him) and his commands and boast about going against him and ridicule his sunnah?"

reversed his decision and gave a portion of the blood money to the widow. This incident reveals the view of the sunnah held by Umar ibn al-Khattaab, the second caliph of Islam, who was known for his knowledge and insight into the religion. Unknowingly, he had taken a position that was contrary to the decision of the Messenger of Allah (peace be upon him). Upon finding out that his decision contradicted the sunnah, he immediately abandoned his opinion and completely submitted to the decision of the Prophet (peace be upon him).

In another situation involving Umar[1] a certain decision was made because one Companion reported a hadith of the Prophet (peace be upon him) concerning a similar incident. After this, Umar stated, "If we did not hear this [hadith] we would have given a different judgment. We would have judged according to our opinions." Here again, as al-Shaafi'ee commented, Umar's decision would not have been the same as the decision of the Prophet but since he was informed of the decision of the Prophet (peace be upon him), Umar knew that there was no say for him in the matter and, furthermore, he knew that the believer must accept the decision of the Prophet (peace be upon him) even if it goes against his own opinion.

In an incident recorded in the *Sahih*s of al-Bukhari and Muslim, it is reported that Umar had the intention to travel to al-Shaam ("Greater Syria"), where a plague had broken out. When he came upon the Companion Abdul Rahmaan ibn Auf, Abdul Rahmaan told him that the Prophet (peace be upon him) said, "If you hear that there is a plague in a certain land, do not set out for that land; and if you happen to be in that land, do not depart from that land." Upon hearing this Umar knew that it would not be right for him to proceed to al-Shaam; so he returned to Madinah. In another incident, also recorded by al-Bukhari, it is said that Umar abstained from taking the *jizyah* (the poll tax) from the Magians until Abdul Rahmaan

---

[1] Quoted in al-Suyooti, *Miftaab al-Jannab*, pp. 49-50.

ibn Auf bore testimony that the Prophet (peace be upon him) took it from them. This incident demonstrates that even the most important affairs of government are subservient to the commands and sunnah of the Prophet (peace be upon him). By hesitating in accepting the *jizyah* from the Magians (until he could confirm that the Prophet had actually done so), Umar was adversely affecting the budget of the expanding Islamic state.

Al-Baihaqi and al-Haakim record, with *sahih* chains, that Taawoos used to pray two units (Ar., *rakah*) after the obligatory afternoon prayer. Ibn Abbaas told him to refrain from doing so. He replied that he would not abandon them. Ibn Abbaas then said, "The Messenger of Allah (peace be upon him) forbade praying after the *Asr* (afternoon) prayer. Therefore I do not know if you will be punished or rewarded [for this prayer that you perform]. Verily Allah said, 'It is not becoming of a believing man or believing woman, after Allah and His Messenger have decided an affair, that they should have any choice in the matter' [*al-Ahzaab* 36]." From this incident one can see the importance of the commands of the Prophet (peace be upon him). Even in the virtuous acts of worship one must be aware of the regulations laid down by the Prophet (peace be upon him). Ibn Abbaas told Taawoos, "I do not know if you will be rewarded or punished" for the prayer Taawoos performed. How could it be that he might be punished for praying? It is because he was, in fact, violating the commands of the Prophet (peace be upon him). This shows that all deeds, no matter how virtuous they may seem, must be approved by the Quran or sunnah to be acceptable.

Abdullah ibn Umar narrated that the Messenger of Allah (peace be upon him) said, "Permit your women to go to the mosques at night." One of Abdullah's sons stated that he would not do so. Upon hearing this Abdullah condemned him in a very harsh manner, struck his chest and said, "I relate a

hadith of the Messenger of Allah to you and you say, 'No.'"1
In this incident Abdullah ibn Umar, the son of Umar ibn
al-Khattaab, who was also one of the most knowledgeable of
the Companions, struck his son's chest because his son showed
some inclination not to abide by a command from the Prophet
(peace be upon him). In Abdullah's statement it is clear that he
was implying, "I am telling you a statement of the Messenger
(peace be upon him) and you think you have some say in the
matter. Indeed, you do not."

The following incident was recorded by al-Bukhari
and Muslim (the wording of the report is Muslim's): Qataadah
narrated, "We were sitting in a group with Imraan ibn Husain
and Bushair ibn Kaab. Imraan narrated to us that on a certain
occasion the Messenger of Allah (peace be upon him) said,
'Modesty is a virtue through and through,' or said, 'Modesty is
completely good.' Upon hearing this Bushair ibn Kaab said,
'We find in certain books or books [of wisdom] that it is
God-inspired peace of mind or sobriety for the sake of Allah
and there is also some weakness in it.' Imraan was so much
enraged that his eyes became red and he said, 'I am narrating
to you a hadith of the Messenger of Allah (peace be upon him)
and you are contradicting it.'" Abdul Hamid Siddique
commented on this hadith, saying,

> This hadith explains the status of a Prophet. The
> source of prophetic knowledge is divine; it is,
> therefore, perfect and free from all kinds of error.
> Human wisdom is based on observation, experience
> and inference and can, therefore, be never infallible.
> This is the reason why humanity has always been
> exhorted to follow the commands of the Prophets and
> not those of the philosophers. This hadith also clearly
> brings into light the position of the Hadith. It is a part

---

1 This was recorded by Ahmad, Muslim and Abu Daawood.

of divine knowledge and, therefore, it should be accepted with religious devotion.[1]

In this hadith Bushair is referring to some of the old books of the Arabs which contained their "wisdom." But how can it be wisdom when it contradicts what the All-Wise has revealed? How could it be considered wisdom when the Messenger (peace be upon him) has stated the opposite to be true? How can one respect any contradictory statement after the Prophet (peace be upon him) has spoken?[2]

In fact, there are numerous examples of this nature of harsh treatment, such as people refusing to speak to others, because someone refused to accept a hadith of the Prophet (peace be upon him) or made some kind of negative comment. Such behavior in defense of the sunnah has been narrated from the Companions Abdullah ibn Mughafal, Ibaadah ibn al-Saamit, Abu al-Dardaa and Abu Saeed al-Khudri. Similar examples come from later scholars.[3] This harsh treatment can only be explained in one way: It is inconceivable for any Muslim to object to or reject any statement of the Prophet (peace be upon him). There is no room for such behavior and, therefore, the response to such an action must correspond to the gravity of the sin committed.

Al-Bukhari recorded that Ali and Uthmaan were on the road between Makkah and Madinah. At the time Uthmaan was preventing, for specific reasons, people from performing *muta*

---

[1] Abdul Hamid Siddiqui, trans. and commentator, *Sahih Muslim* (Lahore: Sh. Muhammad Ashraf, 1972), vol. 1, p. 28, fn. 87.

[2] Unfortunately, one can find Muslims who follow ideas that contradict what the Prophet (peace be upon him) has stated. For some, especially from lesser developed countries, anything that comes from the "scientific West" is considered superior to what they have of "traditional wisdom." This may be due to some kind of inferiority complex. However, a Muslim, one who worships and submits only to Allah, should never feel inferior to anyone or any civilization that is void of the great guidance from Allah.

[3] Cf., Abdul Qayyoom al-Sihaibaani, *Tadheem al-Sunnah wa Muwaqaf al-Salaf miman Aaridhuhaa au Istahza bi-Shain Minhaa* (Madinah: Maktabah ibn al-Qayyim, 1414 A.H.), pp. 35-41.

(that is, combining the *hajj* and *umrah* under one visit but with a break between them and with only one intention). Ali had made the intention: "We are coming for *hajj* and *umrah* together with a break in between them." Uthmaan said to him, "You see that I am preventing the people from doing so yet you do it?" Ali answered him, "I cannot leave the sunnah of the Messenger of Allah (peace be upon him) for the statement of anyone of mankind." In this incident one again sees that the Companions of the Prophet (peace be upon him) would accept no authority save that of Allah or His Messenger (peace be upon him). In this case Ali found Uthmaan's juristic reasoning to be wrong, as he noted that Uthmaan did not correctly understand the sunnah concerning *muta*. One point that should be noted is that this incident occurred while Uthmaan was the caliph of the Islamic state. This incident demonstrates that the Companions knew that even the highest authority in the land, as pious as he might be, cannot impose a law that goes against the sunnah of the Prophet (peace be upon him).

It is recorded concerning many Companions, through a number of authentic chains, that if any problem arose they would seek its solution, first, in the Book of Allah. If they did not find the solution there, they would search the sunnah of the Prophet (peace be upon him) for the answer.[1] Failing to find a solution, then, and only then, would they resort to personal reasoning. This was the way of Abu Bakr, the first caliph, and of Umar, Abu Bakr's successor, and, in fact, of all of the Companions of the Prophet (peace be upon him).[2]

From the above one may conclude the following:

---

[1] Whether the Quran should be looked to first and then the sunnah or if both of them should be taken together is a matter of dispute. A complete and detailed discussion of this question shall come later. However, it is clear that the above reports do not mean that the sunnah does not explain and further clarify the meaning of the Quran.

[2] One can find no report whatsoever of any Companion who did not behave in this manner.

(a) There was a consensus of opinion among the Companions (the best and most knowledgeable of all generations) that it was obligatory for them to follow the sunnah of the Prophet (peace be upon him), and none of them ever claimed to be free of this obligation.

(b) After the death of the Prophet (peace be upon him), Muslims still agreed that they must follow the sunnah of the Prophet (peace be upon him).

(c) The sunnah of the Prophet (peace be upon him) is to be applied to all aspects of life, from worship to government, and even the leader of the state does not have the right to rule in contradiction to the sunnah of the Prophet (peace be upon him).

Scholarly Opinion Regarding the Sunnah

In this section, commentary will be kept to minimum. After the preceding discussion, lengthy comments should not be necessary. Here will be recorded statements from some of the leading scholars throughout the ages to show that the great scholars of Islam have agreed that it is obligatory for all Muslims to follow the sunnah, or way, of the Prophet Muhammad (peace be upon him).[1]

Ibn Khuzaimah said, "No one can say anything if the Messenger of Allah (peace be upon him) has already spoken [on a topic] and it comes to us through a sound chain."

The famous scholar Mujaahid said, "We accept some sayings and reject others of everybody save the Messenger of Allah (peace be upon him)." In other words, all of the Messenger's statements are to be accepted.

Urwah said, "Following the sunnah is to establish the religion."

---

[1] Unless otherwise noted, the following statements can be found in al-Suyooti, *Miftah al-Jannah*, pp. 74f. The interested reader should also consult Abdul Khaaliq, pp. 345-382.

Abu Sulaimaan al-Daarimi said, "Perhaps there pricks my heart the problems and discussions of my day and I never accept anything except with the testimony of the two just witnesses: the Book and the sunnah."

Ahmad ibn Abu al-Huwari said, "Whoever does a deed that is not in accordance with the sunnah has, in fact, done a vain deed."

Abu Qilaabah said, "If you speak to a person with the sunnah and he says, 'Leave that from me and bring the Book of Allah,' then you should know that he is misguided."[1]

In fact, the authority of the sunnah is an issue that one can conclude that there is a unanimous opinion among the scholars. Shawaat noted,

> The authors writing on the topic of Islamic legal theory, like ibn Hazm, al-Baaji, al-Ghazaali, al-Amadi, al-Bazdawi and others, have discussed this issue [of the authority of the sunnah] and they have stated that there is a unanimity of the nation of Islam on this question. They do not mention in their books, either in a clear fashion or even by allusion, that there exists any difference of opinion concerning the authority of the sunnah. And these are the people who have scanned the books of their predecessors of their schools of fiqh and who followed up differences of opinion, whether reasonable or outlandish, and have taken the time to refute [rejected opinions]. How can anyone imagine that there could be a dispute among the Muslims on an issue that is from the fundamentals of the religion, which is known by necessity to be part of the religion of Islam and concerning which, if anyone disputes it, he is an apostate, outside the fold of the religion... Imam al-Shaafi'ee wrote in *Jimaa al-Ilm* in his book *al-Umm*,

---

[1] Quoted from *Tabaqaat ibn Saad* in al-Sihaibaani, p. 25.

"I have never heard of anyone who the people consider knowledgeable or who he considers himself knowledgeable differing about the fact that Allah has obligated the following of the orders of the Messenger of Allah (peace be upon him) and submitting to his rules and that Allah has not left open for anyone after him any other option except following him..." Even the sects who ascribed themselves to the Muslim community, although they have swerved from the truth and gone astray on this issue, none of them have been so bold as to reject the authority of the sunnah as a principle, for they knew that such would take them out of the religion.[1]

Note that although all of the above scholars (and thousands of other scholars) lived after the death of the Messenger of Allah (peace be upon him), none of them ever even remotely hinted at the possibility that the sunnah was only to be obeyed during the Prophet's lifetime and not for all time until the Day of Judgment. Indeed, such a thought is an innovation of recent times that has no foundation whatsoever, as can be seen from the preceding sections.

One important aspect that can be concluded from the statements of the Companions and other scholars: They all agreed that whatever comes from the Prophet (peace be upon him) must be accepted and whatever comes from anyone else can only be accepted if it is not in conflict with what is stated in the Quran or sunnah. Every other human is subject to err while the Prophet (peace be upon him) was guided by Allah and protected from committing error. In other words, if one is presented with an authentic hadith of the Messenger of Allah

---

[1] Shawaat, pp. 272-3. Abdul-Khaaliq, pp. 248-250 has a very similar passage with quotes from the leading legal theorists. Al-Shaafi'ee himself, in his works, debated with someone who seemed to reject the sunnah. However, as Abdul Khaaliq (pp. 260-266) has shown, he was questioning the attributing of the hadith to the Prophet (peace be upon him) and not objecting to the obligation of following the sunnah. Allah knows best.

(peace be upon him), he has no choice but to follow that hadith.[1] He must give up his own personal opinion in favor of what the Messenger of Allah (peace be upon him) said. He must give up the opinion of his school of fiqh, culture or traditions in favor of what has been authentically reported from the Prophet (peace be upon him). Issues are no longer open to debate, discussion or opinion once the Prophet (peace be upon him) has stated something unequivocally.

The Four Imams and Their View of the Sunnah

Over time, four schools of fiqh grew and flourished among the Muslims. To this day, those schools still hold a great deal of influence. These schools are[2]:

(1) The Hanafi school: This school developed in Kufah, where the Companions Abdullah ibn Masood and Ali ibn Abi Taalib lived. It is named after Abu Haneefah al-Numaan ibn Thaabit (80-150 A.H.). He has been recognized by all as one of the greatest juristic minds in the history of Islam. Along with Abu Haneefah himself, his students Abu Yoosuf, Muhammad ibn al-Hasan and Zafar, greatly contributed to the formation and development of this school. The Hanafi school is still dominant in modern-day Pakistan, India, Turkey, the ex-Soviet states and other parts of the Muslim world.

(2) The Maliki school: This school developed in Madinah, the adopted home of the Prophet (peace be upon him) and the residence of many of his Companions. The school is named after Maalik ibn Anas (95-179), a noted scholar of hadith and a jurist. This school spread quickly to North Africa,

---

[1] This is assuming, of course, that he has no other equally strong evidence to show that the particular hadith has been abrogated, particularized and so on.
[2] The historical discussion here is meant to be extremely brief. Those desiring to learn more about the history of the schools of fiqh may consult Bilal Philips, *The Evolution of Fiqh* (Riyadh: International Islamic Publishing House, 1995), pp. 52-90.

where it continues to hold sway, and was the dominant school in Muslim Spain.

(3) The Shaafi'ee school: This school is named after its founder, Muhammad ibn Idrees al-Shaafi'ee (150-204 A.H.). From a Makkan family, al-Shaafi'ee moved to Madinah and studied under Imam Maalik. He also went to Iraq and had a dialogue with Muhammad ibn al-Hasan, the student of Abu Haneefah. Al-Shaafi'ee was the first scholar to compile a work on Islamic legal theory or *usool al-fiqh* (أصول الفقه). This work was a great contribution and, among other things, clearly spelled out the authority and place of the sunnah in Islam. Today, the followers of the Shaafi'ee school can be found throughout Egypt, Syria, Malaysia, Indonesia and other places.

(4) The Hanbali school: This school is named after Ahmad ibn Hanbal (164-241). Imam Ahmad was a great scholar of hadith. He compiled one of the larger works of hadith, entitled *Musnad Ahmad*. With respect to his fiqh, he was greatly influenced by his teacher Imam al-Shaafi'ee. The Hanbali school is most dominant in modern-day Saudi Arabia.

It is important to understand these scholars' perception of the importance of the sunnah and hadith. This is because it is often their followers who have a strong resistance to following hadith when it seems that the hadith contradicts the tenets of their school. They assume that their scholars must have known the hadith and they must have a good reason for expressing an opinion that contradicts the hadith.

Among the statements concerning the sunnah and hadith quoted from these four Imams are the following:

Ibn al-Mubaarak reported that he heard Imam Abu Haneefah say, "If a report comes from the Messenger of Allah, then it is the head and eye [of the matter: there is no room for dispute in such a case]. If reports come from the Companions of the Prophet, we choose from among their statements."

Abu Haneefah said, "Beware of speaking about the religion of Allah based on personal opinion. You must adhere to the sunnah. Whoever goes away from it has strayed [from the straight path]." He also said, "If it were not for the sunnah, none of us would be able to understand the Quran." On another occasion, he said, "The people will continue to be in goodness as long as they continue to study and seek hadith. If they seek knowledge without the hadith, they will become rotten. No one should make any statement until he knows that the law of the Messenger (peace be upon him) accords with that statement."[1]

Abu Haneefah was asked, "If you made a statement that contradicts the Book of Allah [what should be done]?" He replied, "Leave my statement for the Book of Allah." It was then said, "[Suppose it contradicts a] report from the Messenger of Allah (peace be upon him)?" He replied, "Leave my statement for the report of the Messenger of Allah (peace be upon him)." The same has been narrated from Abu Haneefah's student Muhammad ibn al-Hasan. It is also narrated that he said, "If the hadith is authentic, it is my opinion (*madhhab*)."[2]

Uthmaan ibn Umar reported that a man came to Imam Maalik and asked him a question. Imam Maalik replied, "The Messenger of Allah (peace be upon him) said such and such." The man asked, "What is your opinion?" Maalik simply answered him with the following verse of the Quran which contains a stern warning,

فليحذر الذين يخالفون عن أمره أن تصيبهم فتنة أو يصيبهم

عذاب أليم

"Let those who contradict his orders beware lest a trial (Ar., *fitnah*) or a painful punishment befall them" (*al-Noor* 63).

Imam Maalik is also recorded to have said, "I am but a human being. I make mistakes and I am also correct [on other occasions]. Examine my opinions. Take whatever [of my opinions] which are in agreement with the Book and the

---

[1] The statements from Abu Haneefah were quoted in al-Salafi, pp. 77-78.
[2] Cf., Saalih al-Fulaani, *Eeqaadh Himam Ooli-l-Absaar* (Taif, Saudi Arabia: Maktabah al-Maarif, n.d.), p. 85.

sunnah. And leave whatever [of my opinions] which do not agree with the Book and the sunnah."[1]

Al-Rabeeah reported that Imam al-Shaafi'ee said, "If you find anything in my book that differs from the sunnah of the Messenger of Allah (peace be upon him), then speak according to the sunnah of the Messenger and leave what I have said."

Al-Shaafi'ee also said, "If the hadith is authentic, it is my opinion (*madhhab*)."[2]

Al-Humaidi stated that al-Shaafi'ee narrated a hadith one day and then al-Humaidi said to him, "Do you follow that?" He replied, "Do you see me leaving from a church or wearing a *zinaar* [a belt worn exclusively by non-Muslims] such that I would hear a hadith of the Messenger of Allah (peace be upon him) and not follow it?"[3] He was implying that only a non-Muslim, like a Christian who attends the church, would behave in such a fashion.

Ahmad was asked whether it was better to follow al-Auzaa'ee's opinions or Malik's, and he said, "In your religion, do not blindly follow any of those. Take what has come from the Prophet (peace be upon him) and his Companions..."[4]

In a lengthy passage describing the methodology of Imam Ahmad, ibn al-Qayyim begins by saying, "If Imam Ahmad found a text [meaning a Quranic verse or a hadith] on a matter, he would make a ruling according to what it implied and he would not look to anything which contradicted it or anyone who contradicted it, whoever he may be. For that

---

[1] Quoted, with its chain of transmitters, by al-Fulaani, p. 97.
[2] Al-Subki quoted this statement and then said, "This is a famous statement from him and no one differs about the fact that he said it. Its same meaning has been narrated from him in many different ways." Al-Subki goes on to give a large number of such narrations from al-Shaafi'ee. Ali al-Subki, *"Mana Qaul al-Imaam al-Mutalibi Idha Sah al-Hadeeth Fahuwa Madhhabi,"* in *Majmooah Rasaail al-Munairiyyah* (Riyadh: Maktabah Taibah, n.d.), vol. 3, p. 98.
[3] Quoted from *Hilyat al-Auliyaa* and *Seer Alaam al-Nubalaa* in al-Sihaibaani, p. 28; al-Fulaani, p. 135, also quotes this incident.
[4] Quoted in al-Fulaani, p. 145.

reason, he did not take into consideration Umar's opinion concerning the woman who had her final divorce as he would follow the hadith of Faatimah bint Qais..."[1]

As noted, the most stringent followers of these schools argue that their scholars would never intentionally go against a hadith of the Prophet (peace be upon him). On this point, there must be agreement. No one should accuse any of these noble and pious scholars of such a thing. It is recognized that they never, without reason, went against an authentic hadith. Given that point, the followers then argue that if one of their opinions contradicts a hadith, they must have had some overriding reason for ignoring that hadith. For example, that particular hadith may have been abrogated, is not actually authentic or does not truly refer to the particular issue at hand.[2]

There is no question that there may be some validity to such an argument. However, stronger arguments may demonstrate that the safer and more logical approach is quite the opposite.

It must be realized that the reasons they give for their scholar not following a particular hadith are not the only possible reasons why their scholar did not follow said hadith. Indeed, they may not even be the most plausible reasons. It is also possible, for example, that his scholar was unaware of the hadith. This is not an impossibility nor does it imply any blemish on his scholar's capability—none of the Companions themselves were aware of all of the hadith of the Prophet (peace be upon him). Furthermore, his scholar, who may not

---

[1] Ibn al-Qayyim, *Ilaam*, vol. 1, p. 29.

[2] Allah willing, no sincere and intelligent Muslim would ever willingly and knowingly go against a statement of the Prophet (peace be upon him). In most cases, unless the person has evil intentions or is a deviant, the reason why some people do go against the hadith is because they have trust in their scholars. It is reasonable for a Muslim to trust Abu Haneefah or Malik or any of the great scholars of Islam. This trust, though, causes them to ignore authentic hadith; this is, of course, a problem. The solution to this problem, Allah knows best, is to demonstrate to such people that the approach that they are taking to the authentic hadith is not the soundest or most logical approach.

be as specialized in hadith as the hadith specialists themselves, may consider the hadith to be weak, perhaps due to the way in which it reached him, while the hadith specialists have determined that the hadith is authentic. These are just as plausible assumptions as those given above for the person to follow his school instead of the hadith.

Suppose a person is presented with a hadith and he is told by trustworthy sources that the scholars of hadith have determined that hadith to be authentic. In fact, it is a hadith that the other schools of fiqh accept and apply. Suppose that the hadith contradicts the opinion of the school that he is following and he has no idea why his particular school is not applying that hadith.[1] The person has two choices: (a) Follow the hadith until he is shown that there is some reason not to follow it or (b) assume that there is some reason not to follow it and continue to follow the opinion of his school.

If he chooses (a), he will be following the better approach. It is the better approach for a number of reasons. First, on the Day of Judgment, he can stand in front of Allah and state that he followed what he was shown to be a true statement of the Prophet (peace be upon him). In the Quran, there are explicit verses obligating and commanding obedience to the Prophet (peace be upon him); however, there are such no commands to follow Abu Haneefah, Maalik, Ahmad, al-Shaafi'ee or any other specific individual. Therefore, even if it turns out that said hadith was abrogated, for example, his reasoning for following it would be sound and, Allah willing, he will be safe on the Day of Judgment. Secondly, he will be following the advice of his own Imam. As noted, all of the four Imams advised people to discard their teaching whenever their teaching contradicted anything that the Prophet (peace be upon him) said. Hence, he will be following the advice of the

---

[1] If he knows why his school is not applying that hadith, he may weigh their evidences and determine if their reasoning is strong or not. In general, it takes very strong evidence, such as other authentic hadith, to refuse to abide by the clear meaning of an authentic hadith of the Prophet (peace be upon him).

scholar he trusts, his own Imam, by excusing his Imam for his apparent mistake and following the sunnah of the Prophet (peace be upon him).

If the person chooses (b), then, in reality, he is following nothing more than an assumption and conjecture. In fact, he is following a three-prong assumption. First, he is assuming that his Imam or scholar was aware of the particular hadith in question. Second, he is assuming that his Imam or scholar knew the proper grading of the hadith (that it was acceptable) or that the hadith reached his Imam via its acceptable chains. Third, he is assuming that his Imam has strong enough reason not to abide by that particular hadith.[1] The law of probability shows that the more conditions or events that one must assume occurred, the less probable the incident.

Again, since he does not know why his school is not following that hadith, he must be assuming that they have a good reason for doing so. It is true that this is based on his trust in the excellence of his scholars, but that does not deny the fact that it is nothing more than an assumption on his part—an assumption with a seemingly small probability of being correct. A person's religion and actions should not be based on assumptions and mere conjecture. This is something that Allah has warned about in numerous places in the Quran. For example, Allah blames the idol worshippers for their following of conjecture in their religion and then Allah says,

---

[1] Some of the reasons that some of the schools of fiqh did not abide by apparently authentic hadith are the following: the hadith contradicted the practice of the people of Madinah, the hadith was contradicted by the same Companion who narrated the hadith, the hadith contradicts the result of analogy from other texts, the hadith contradicts a generally accepted principle. Upon close inspection, the arguments that they give to support these measures for rejecting hadith are, at best, frail.

وَمَا يَتَّبِعُ أَكْثَرُهُمْ إِلاَّ ظَنًّا إِنَّ الظَّنَّ لا يُغْنِي مِنَ الْحَقِّ شَيْئًا إِنَّ اللَّهَ عَلِيمٌ بِمَا يَفْعَلُونَ

"But most of them follow nothing but conjecture. Truly conjecture can be of no avail against truth. Verily Allah is well aware of all that they do" (*Yoonus* 36). Allah also says,

وَمَا لَهُمْ بِهِ مِنْ عِلْمٍ إِنْ يَتَّبِعُونَ إِلاَّ الظَّنَّ وَإِنَّ الظَّنَّ لا يُغْنِي مِنْ الْحَقِّ شَيْئًا

"But they have no knowledge therein. They follow nothing but conjecture; and conjecture avails nothing against truth" (*al-Najm* 28). If this is what the person is following, he may have no excuse or argument when he stands in front of Allah on the Day of Judgment. The words of the Prophet (peace be upon him) were presented to him, he had no reason to doubt that they were the words of the Prophet (peace be upon him) yet he did not follow those words because he assumed that his Imam must have had some reason for not following those words.

The correct approach, therefore, is that when one is presented with an authentic hadith of the Prophet (peace be upon him), he must believe in it wholeheartedly and he must have the intention to apply it to the best of his ability. When he does so, he will be following the most sound path in this life and the safest path for the Hereafter. One should abandon an authentic hadith of the Messenger of Allah (peace be upon him) if and only if he is presented with equally strong contrary evidence.[1]

---

[1] While discussing the hadith presented earlier, "Soon it will be that a man will recline on his couch and will be told a hadith of my hadith and will say, 'Between us and you is the Book of Allah. What we find allowed therein, we allow. What we find prohibited therein, we prohibit.' But truly, what the Messenger of Allah has forbidden is similar to what Allah has forbidden," al-Teebi notes that it is not acceptable for a person to refuse to follow a hadith in the name of following the Quran. He then says that if such is the case with respect to the Quran and hadith, what must be the case of the person who accepts personal opinion over the

Conclusions

This chapter could rightly be called the heart of this book. It has definitely proven the authority and importance of the sunnah of the Messenger of Allah (peace be upon him). If a person accepts the Quran, he must then accept the place of the sunnah—otherwise he is simply belying his belief in the Quran. If a person believes in the Messenger of Allah (peace be upon him) as a true messenger of God, then he must believe that the Prophet (peace be upon him) would not forge lies about his place and the importance of his own words. His own words once again demonstrate the importance and place of the sunnah. If a person believes in Allah's compassion and mercy, he would not believe that Allah would allow the Companions to emulate the Prophet (peace be upon him) in great detail without ever even hinting to them that what they were doing was not the proper mode of behavior. If a person believes in the Quran and the Prophet (peace be upon him) and what these two sources say about the Companions, he will realize that the Companions were blessed with guidance to the straight path. Yet, the Companions themselves put the Quran and the sunnah above anything else. They had an unwavering adherence to the sunnah of the Prophet (peace be upon him). If one puts any trust in any of the later scholars, including the four famous Imams, one will accept their conclusion that the sunnah is an authority. None of them ever put their opinions and thoughts above what had authentically come from the Prophet (peace be upon him). Indeed, the Muslim community as a whole, from the time of the Companions to their Followers, unanimously agreed about the authority and place of the sunnah. Allah would not allow this Islamic community to all err. This is yet another sign of the definitive place of the sunnah.

---

hadith? These people, when presented with an authentic hadith, will then say, "I need not act by it for I have a school of fiqh that I follow." Cf., al-Teebi, vol. 2, p. 631.

The conclusion is that the sunnah is definitively an authority in Islamic law. This means that it is an indication of the law and rule of Allah, the One whom all must worship and to whom all must submit. Therefore, a believer with true faith has no other option except to submit and accept whatever decision, command, statement or ruling the Prophet Muhammad (peace be upon him) made.

Chapter Three:
The Roles of the Messenger
(peace be upon him)

Upon further study, one can see that the importance of the Messenger of Allah (peace be upon him) lies in certain roles that he fulfills for the Muslim nation. These roles further establish the indispensability of following the sunnah and hadith. Many scholars have enumerated these roles. Although many roles of the Prophet (peace be upon him) could be discussed, the discussion here will be limited to the following four roles: explainer of the Quran, independent legislator, perfect example, and object of obedience.[1]

The Prophet Muhammad (peace be upon him) as the Explainer of the Quran

Those who oppose Islam try to separate the Quran and Islam from the sunnah of the Prophet (peace be upon him). It has already been demonstrated that such a view is unacceptable. The sunnah is, as some have described it, the living Quran. As Aishah said, "The character of the Messenger of Allah was the Quran." (Recorded by al-Bukhari and others.) Umar ibn al-Khattaab warned the Muslims about those who would try to interpret the Quran without reference to the

---

[1] Cf., Mustafa Azami, *Studies in Hadith Methodology*, pp. 5-7; Habib-ur-Rahman Azami, *The Sunnah in Islam: The Eternal Relevance of the Teaching and Example of the Prophet Muhammad* (Leicester, United Kingdom: UK Islamic Academy, 1989), pp. 34-38.

sunnah, "A people will come who will argue with you based on the ambiguous verses of the Quran. Restrict them by the sunnah for the people of the sunnah are the most knowledgeable of the Book of Allah."[1]

Undoubtedly, one of the most important roles of the Prophet Muhammad (peace be upon him) was to convey the wording of the Quran to mankind and to teach, explain and implement its meaning.[2] The following verse is one of a number of verses referred to earlier in which this role of the Prophet (peace be upon him) is alluded to:

لَقَدْ مَنَّ اللَّهُ عَلَى الْمُؤْمِنِينَ إِذْ بَعَثَ فِيهِمْ رَسُولاً مِنْ أَنْفُسِهِمْ يَتْلُوا عَلَيْهِمْ آيَاتِهِ وَيُزَكِّيهِمْ وَيُعَلِّمُهُمُ الْكِتَابَ وَالْحِكْمَةَ وَإِنْ كَانُوا مِنْ قَبْلُ لَفِي ضَلالٍ مُبِينٍ

"Allah has clearly shown grace to the believers by sending unto them a Messenger of their own who recites unto them His revelations, and causes them to grow and teaches them the Book and the *Hikmah*, although before they were in flagrant error" (*ali-Imraan* 164). The Prophet (peace be upon him) is specifically referred to as "reciting unto them the revelation" and also "teaching them the Book." This implies two separate roles that the Prophet (peace be upon him) fulfilled—otherwise

---

[1] Quoted in Salafi p. 71. Ibn al-Qayyim (*Ilaam*, vol. 1, pp. 54-55) says that this report reaches the highest levels of authenticity.

[2] There is a difference of opinion concerning how much of the Quran did the Prophet (peace be upon him) actually explain. The different opinions, their evidences and this author's conclusion may be found in Jamaal al-Din M. Zarabozo, *The Methodology of the Quranic Commentators* (Falls Church, VA: American Open University, 1997), pp. 40-47. For a collection of authentic hadith in which the Prophet (peace be upon him) directly commented upon verses of the Quran, by mentioning the verse before or after his speech, see Al-Sayyid Ibraaheem ibn Abu Amuh, *Al-Saheeh al-Musnad min al-Tafseer al-Nabawi li-l-Quran al-Kareem* (Tanta, Egypt: Daar al-Sahaabah lil-Turaath, 1990), *passim*, or Saalih Al-Buqaawi, *al-Talaazim Bain al-Kitaab wa al-Sunnah min Khilaal al-Kutub al-Sittah* (Riyadh: Daar al-Maarij al-Dauliyyah lil-Nashr, 1416 A.H.), *passim*.

the passage would be redundant. The Prophet (peace be upon him) received the revelation from the Angel Gabriel and recited it to the Muslims. At the same time, though, he also taught them the meaning of the revelation. Habib-ur-Rahman Azami writes,

> In all three verses above[1], two things are distinctively and separately mentioned. Firstly recitation of the revelations, and secondly the teaching of the Book.
>
> The meaning of the first, 'recitation' of the Book, is clear. But the second, the 'teaching' of the Book, requires some elucidation. If the expression denoted the reading (aloud) of the Quran in a systematic manner, making people commit it to memory, there was no need to specify it as something different from 'recitation'. It evidently, therefore, signifies the explanation and interpretation of the Quranic verses and the exposition of their meaning, wisdom and commands.
>
> It is thus apparent from the Quran itself that just as direct recitation and preaching of the Divine revelations are part of the Prophetic duties of the Prophet, so too are their exposition and interpretation. It follows logically that the text of the Quran is binding and absolute. As is its interpretation, as provided by the Prophet. Otherwise it would have been meaningless to charge him with the teaching of the Book and make it part of his Prophetic mission. In sum, on the basis of these Quranic statements, the Prophet is not only the

---

[1]That is, *al-Baqara* 151, *ali-Imraan* 164 and *al-Jumuah* 2.

Messenger of Allah but also the teacher and interpreter of the Divine message.[1]

Allah also says in the Quran,

وَأَنزَلْنَا إِلَيْكَ الذِّكْرَ لِتُبَيِّنَ لِلنَّاسِ مَا نُزِّلَ إِلَيْهِمْ وَلَعَلَّهُمْ يَتَفَكَّرُونَ

"And We have revealed unto you (Muhammad) the reminder so you may expound unto all of mankind that which has been revealed for them. So perchance they may ponder" (*al-Nahl* 44). Al-Albaani writes that this verse has two meanings. First, the Messenger of Allah (peace be upon him) is not to conceal anything of the revelation that he has received but he must convey all of it to mankind. Second, it means that the Messenger of Allah (peace be upon him) has the duty of explaining the finer details of the Quran and of demonstrating how the Quran is to be applied.[2]

Obviously, Allah would not burden the Messenger (peace be upon him) with that second duty of explaining the meaning of the Quran unless He also gave the Prophet (peace be upon him) the necessary knowledge to explain the Quran. Otherwise, "expounding unto mankind what has been revealed" would be an impossible task and Allah does not burden any soul beyond what it can bear. Thus the Prophet (peace be upon him), when he spoke or acted, was implementing and explaining the Quran according to the knowledge that Allah had bestowed upon him for this purpose. This was in order for him to fulfill the role of "the explainer of the revelation." Hence, whenever the Messenger of Allah (peace be upon him) explained or applied any verse, this explanation or application was based on Allah's intention or purpose behind the verse, the knowledge of which Allah had vouchsafed unto the Prophet (peace be upon him). This is also the implication of the following verses from *soorah al-Qiyaamah*,

---

[1] Habib-ur-Rahman Azami, p. 9.
[2] See al-Albaani, *Manzalat al-Sunnah*, p. 6.

لاَ تُحَرِّكْ بِهِ لِسَانَكَ لِتَعْجَلَ بِهِ إِنَّ عَلَيْنَا جَمْعَهُ وَقُرْآنَهُ فَإِذَا قَرَأْنَاهُ
فَاتَّبِعْ قُرْآنَهُ ثُمَّ إِنَّ عَلَيْنَا بَيَانَهُ

"Move not your tongue [O Muhammad] concerning [the Quran] to make haste therewith. It is for Us to collect it and to promulgate it. But when We have promulgated it, follow its recital (as promulgated). Nay more, it is upon Us to explain it (and make it clear)" (*al-Qiyaamah* 16-19). The Prophet (peace be upon him) was instructed to receive the Quran in the proper way and then Allah would make its meaning clear—first to him and then, through him, to the rest of mankind.

The verse also states that if anyone truly seeks Allah's explanation and application of the Quran, then, as Allah states, he must look to the sunnah of the Messenger of Allah (peace be upon him). In the above verse it is clearly stated that this is one of the roles of the Prophet (peace be upon him); he is to explain the Quran to mankind. If such a role was not necessary, the Quran could have been revealed unto a mountain with no need for a Messenger to accompany it. But Allah, in His infinite wisdom, did not do that and He left it to mankind to ponder over the reason for this action.

The Ways in Which the Prophet (peace be upon him) Explained the Meaning of the Quran

In general, one will see that it could have only been the Prophet (peace be upon him) who could have explained numerous aspects of the Quran because they require certain knowledge that rests only with the One who revealed the Quran, Allah. These aspects include those described below in the following subsections:

The Prophet (peace be upon him) Explained the Meanings of Words Whose Meanings Were Vague For Different Reasons

Sometimes the wording of the Quran could be slightly difficult for a person to understand. This could be the case for various reasons. For example, a word used in the Quran could have more than one meaning or different shades of meanings and the reader cannot be certain which is meant. The only way to know for certain which is meant is to turn to the one to whom the book was revealed and to whom was given the knowledge of the book—and whose role it was to explain the Quran—the Prophet Muhammad (peace be upon him).

Al-Albaani gives many examples wherein the Companions themselves did not understand the intent of the Quran correctly and it was necessary for the Prophet (peace be upon him) to explain the Quran to them.[1] This demonstrates that possessing knowledge of the Arabic language, which the Companions did possess, is not always sufficient for the correct understanding of the Quran. One must turn to the sunnah to understand the Quran correctly.

For example, Allah says in the Quran,

الَّذِينَ آمَنُوا وَلَمْ يَلْبِسُوا إِيمَانَهُمْ بِظُلْمٍ أُولَٰئِكَ لَهُمُ الْأَمْنُ وَهُمْ مُهْتَدُونَ

"Those who believe and obscure not their belief by *dhulm*, theirs is safety; they are rightly guided" (*al-Anaam* 82). The Companions understood the word *dhulm* (translated by Pickthall as "wrongdoing") in a wide sense covering all types of wrongdoing. Hence they questioned who it was who was not guilty of such an act. They asked the Messenger of Allah (peace be upon him) about it and he told them that this verse did not have the meaning that they suspected. He told them

---

[1] Al-Albaani, *Manzalah*, pp. 7-10.

108

that the word *dhulm* in this case referred specifically to associating partners with Allah and he quoted the Quranic verse, *Luqmaan* 13,

إنَّ الشِّرْكَ لَظُلْمٌ عَظِيمٌ

"Verily associating partners with Allah is a great *dhulm*."[1] In this example, the Messenger of Allah (peace be upon him) had to save the Companions from their distress due to their misunderstanding of the verse.

In another verse, Allah says,

وَإِذَا ضَرَبْتُمْ فِي الأَرْضِ فَلَيْسَ عَلَيْكُمْ جُنَاحٌ أَنْ تَقْصُرُوا مِنْ الصَّلاة إنْ خِفْتُمْ أَنْ يَفْتِنَكُمْ الَّذِينَ كَفَرُوا

"And when you go forth in the land, it is no sin upon you if you curtail (your) worship if you fear that those who disbelieve may attack you" (*al-Nisaa* 101). The apparent meaning of this verse is that one may shorten one's prayers while traveling only during occasions in which one fears an attack from the enemies of Islam. This was the meaning that some of the Companions derived from this verse and therefore they went to the Messenger of Allah (peace be upon him) and asked him how they could possibly continue to shorten their prayers while they were no longer in fear of any enemy. The Messenger of Allah (peace be upon him) cleared up their misunderstanding and explained to them that the shortening of the prayers while travelling, even if there was no fear, is a charity from Allah and the Muslims should accept His charity.[2] This means that the words of the verse did not imply

---

[1]Recorded by al-Bukhari, Muslim and others. This implies that Pickthall's translation of *dhulm* as "wrongdoing" is not proper. Incidentally, according to Abdul Raheem, this example shows that the Prophet (peace be upon him) approved of the use of the Quran as a source of *tafseer*. Abdul Jaleel Abdul Raheem, *Lughat al-Quran al-Kareem* (Amman, Jordan: Maktabah al-Risaalah al-Hadeethah, 1981), p. 419.

[2]Recorded by Muslim.

a condition action but they were simply alluding to a common occurrence at the time of the revelation of the verse.

In another example, Allah says in the Quran,

وَكُلُوا وَاشْرَبُوا حَتَّى يَتَبَيَّنَ لَكُمُ الْخَيْطُ الْأَبْيَضُ مِنَ الْخَيْطِ الْأَسْوَدِ مِنَ الْفَجْرِ

"And eat and drink until the white thread becomes distinct from the black thread of the dawn" (*al-Baqarah* 187).[1] After this verse was revealed, a Companion used to keep two threads, one black and one white, under his pillow and checked to see if he could distinguish between the two at the appropriate time of dawn. The Messenger of Allah (peace be upon him) heard about this and he remarked that this Companion must have a very large pillow as the verse is referring to the differentiation between the white streak of the dawn and the blackness of the night.[2]

The above examples should be sufficient to render the point clear. They demonstrate that knowledge of the Arabic language is not sufficient to completely or correctly understand the Quran. Indeed, even knowledge of the other verses of the Quran is not sufficient to interpret all of the Quran. One must also look to the deeds and statements of the Messenger of Allah (peace be upon him) and how he applied the Quran to correctly understand the Quran. One cannot possibly do without his sunnah. The Companions of the Messenger were all fluent in Arabic yet they, at times, misunderstood the real meaning of certain verses. In the above examples there was no possible way for the Companions to know the exact nature of the verses, how general or how specific they are and what exactly they were referring to, without the aid of the Prophet (peace be upon him).

---

[1] When this verse was first revealed, the words, "of the dawn" were not present as part of the verse.
[2] Recorded by Muslim.

The Prophet (peace be upon him) Corrected the Misunderstandings of His Companions or of Others

Muslim records that al-Mugheerah ibn Shubah was asked by the Christians of Najraan about the verse that says about Mary,

يَاأُخْتَ هَارُونَ مَا كَانَ أَبُوكِ امْرَأَ سَوْءٍ وَمَا كَانَتْ أُمُّكِ بَغِيًّا

"O sister of Aaron, your father was not a man who used to commit adultery, nor was your mother an unchaste woman" (*Maryam* 28). The Christians argued that Mary was definitely not Aaron's sister. Hence, the verse must contain an anachronism. When al-Mugheerah returned to Madinah, he asked the Prophet (peace be upon him) about that issue. The Prophet (peace be upon him) told him,

إِنَّهُمْ كَانُوا يُسَمُّونَ بِأَنْبِيَائِهِمْ وَالصَّالِحِينَ قَبْلَهُمْ

"They used to call themselves by the names of their prophets and pious people before them."[1]

Al-Bukhari and Muslim recorded the following in their *Sahih*s from ibn Abu Mulaikah:

أَنَّ عَائِشَةَ زَوْجَ النَّبِيِّ صَلَّى اللَّهم عَلَيْهِ وَسَلَّمَ كَانَتْ لَا تَسْمَعُ شَيْئًا لَا تَعْرِفُهُ إِلَّا رَاجَعَتْ فِيهِ حَتَّى تَعْرِفَهُ وَأَنَّ النَّبِيَّ صَلَّى اللَّهم عَلَيْهِ وَسَلَّمَ قَالَ مَنْ حُوسِبَ عُذِّبَ قَالَتْ عَائِشَةُ فَقُلْتُ

---

[1] This clear and authentic hadith is a refutation of many Christian writers. In particular, Rodwell, in his translation of the Quran, puts a footnote to the above verse and notes how such misinformation, as he claims it to be, should be used against the Muslims.

111

أُوَلَيْسَ يَقُولُ اللَّهُ تَعَالَى (فَسَوْفَ يُحَاسَبُ حِسَابًا يَسِيرًا)
قَالَتْ فَقَالَ إِنَّمَا ذَلِكِ الْعَرْضُ وَلَكِنْ مَنْ نُوقِشَ الْحِسَابَ
يَهْلِكْ

"If Aisha, the wife of the Prophet (peace be upon him), would ever hear anything that she did not understand, she would research it until she understood it. The Prophet (peace be upon him) once said, 'Whoever will [have his deeds] reckoned will be punished.' Aisha said, 'But didn't Allah say, "They shall certainly face a light reckoning"?' He said, 'That is the presentation of their deeds. However, whoever has his deeds reckoned in detail shall be destroyed.'"

The Prophet (peace be upon him) Qualified the Unrestricted and Particularized the General

A very important aspect of the Prophet's explaining and applying of the Quran is wherein he (peace be upon him) showed the extent to which the verses are to be applied. A general term, for instance, seems to apply to all of the members of a category or set. However, the Messenger of Allah (peace be upon him) showed that sometimes a general term did not necessarily refer to all of its members; that is, there are sometimes exceptions that fall outside of the scope of the general term.

For example, Allah says in the Quran,

وَالسَّارِقُ وَالسَّارِقَةُ فَاقْطَعُوا أَيْدِيَهُمَا

"For the male and female thief, cut off their hands" (al-Maaidah 38). The only way to know how exactly this verse is to be applied is by reference to the sunnah of the Messenger of Allah (peace be upon him). This is because both "thief" and "hand" are general, unrestricted terms. This would imply, for example, that every "thief" must have his hand cut off. However, as is known from the Prophet (peace be upon him), their general, unrestricted meanings are not what are implied here.

The word commonly translated as hand in the above verse, *yad*, in Arabic can imply anything from the hand itself all the way up to the armpit. The Prophet (peace be upon him) has explained, though, that the commandment means that the hand to the wrist is all that is to be cut off.[1] He also showed that not every thief will have his hand cut off. For example, the Messenger of Allah (peace be upon him) said,

$$تُقْطَعُ الْيَدُ فِي رُبُعِ دِينَارٍ فَصَاعِدًا$$

"The hand is to be cut [only when something is stolen whose value is] a quarter of a *deenaar* or more." (Recorded by al-Bukhari and Muslim.)

There are many other verses in the Quran whose true import could not possibly be known without looking to what the Prophet (peace be upon him) said about such verses. In the following verse, "blood" is used in a general connotation but the Prophet (peace be upon him) explained that there are some exceptions to that general statement:

$$حُرِّمَتْ عَلَيْكُمُ الْمَيْتَةُ وَالدَّمُ وَلَحْمُ الْخِنْزِيرِ$$

---

[1] For a discussion of the different hadith stating that the Prophet (peace be upon him) would cut the hand of the thief from the wrist, see Muhammad Naasir al-Deen al-Albaani, *Irwaa al-Ghaleel fi Takhreej Ahaadeeth Manaar al-Sabeel* (Beirut: al-Maktab al-Islaami, 1979), vol. 8, pp. 91-83. The Khawaarij were an early, extremist group who did not accept narrations from people outside of their sect. Hence, they would cut the arm all the way to the shoulder. For more about the conditions and rulings of cutting the hand of the thief, see Muhammad Ali al-Saayis, *Tafseer Ayaat al-Ahkaam* (Kulliyat al-Shareeah, Azhar), vol 2, pp 188-193. It is amazing how many among those groups today who claim the sunnah need not be followed will automatically state that the hand of the thief is to be cut from the wrist. They do not realize that this is not what the Quran states but it is how the Messenger of Allah (peace be upon him) explained the verse.

"Forbidden unto you are carrion [non-slaughtered, dead animals] and blood and swine flesh" (*al-Maaidah* 3). The Messenger of Allah (peace be upon him) explained to the Muslim nation that two types of blood are allowable as well as two types of carrion. He said,

$$\text{أُحِلَّتْ لَكُمْ مَيْتَتَانِ وَدَمَانِ فَأَمَّا الْمَيْتَتَانِ فَالْحُوتُ وَالْجَرَادُ}$$
$$\text{وَأَمَّا الدَّمَانِ فَالْكَبِدُ وَالطِّحَالُ}$$

"Permissible for you are two types of carrion [dead, non-slaughtered animals] and two [sources of] blood. As for the two carrion, they are fish and locusts. As for the two bloods, they are the liver and the spleen."[1] Without the Messenger of Allah (peace be upon him) expounding upon this verse, the Muslims would deny themselves some of the good things that Allah has, in fact, made lawful for them.

Similarly, Allah says,

$$\text{قُلْ لا أَجِدُ فِي مَا أُوحِيَ إِلَيَّ مُحَرَّمًا عَلَى طَاعِمٍ يَطْعَمُهُ إِلاَّ أَنْ}$$
$$\text{يَكُونَ مَيْتَةً أَوْ دَمًا مَسْفُوحًا أَوْ لَحْمَ خِنزِيرٍ}$$

"Say: I find not in that which is revealed to me anything prohibited to an eater that he may eat except if it be carrion or blood poured forth or swine flesh" (*Al-Anaam* 145). In addition to these, the Messenger of Allah (peace be upon him) has prohibited other types of food. For example, he prohibited the flesh of donkeys, which was not mentioned by Allah in this verse.

---

[1] With this wording it was recorded by ibn Maajah. According to al-Albaani, it is *sahih*. See al-Albaani, *Saheeh al-Jaami*, vol. 1, p. 102.

The Prophet (peace be upon him) Clarified Which Verses of the Quran Are Abrogated

Al-Shafi'ee wrote, "[M]ost of the abrogating (communications) of the Book can be known only by [indications provided in] the sunnah of the Apostle."[1] Indeed, such knowledge had to be known through the Prophet (peace be upon him), the one who was receiving the revelation and its explanation, as otherwise no one during his lifetime could truly claim that one verse abrogated another.

Allah says in the Quran,

وَاللَّاتِي يَأْتِينَ الْفَاحِشَةَ مِنْ نِسَائِكُمْ فَاسْتَشْهِدُوا عَلَيْهِنَّ أَرْبَعَةً مِنْكُمْ

فَإِنْ شَهِدُوا فَأَمْسِكُوهُنَّ فِي الْبُيُوتِ حَتَّى يَتَوَفَّاهُنَّ الْمَوْتُ أَوْ يَجْعَلَ

اللَّهُ لَهُنَّ سَبِيلاً

"And those of your women who commit illegal sexual intercourse, take the evidence of four witnesses from among you against them; and if they testify, confine them [the women] to houses until death comes to them or Allah ordains for them some way" (*al-Nisaa* 15). This verse was abrogated by *Surah al-Noor*, verse 2. The Prophet (peace be upon him) explained this when he came saying,

خُذُوا عَنِّي فَقَدْ جَعَلَ اللَّهُ لَهُنَّ سَبِيلاً الثَّيِّبُ بِالثَّيِّبِ وَالْبِكْرُ

بِالْبِكْرِ الثَّيِّبُ جَلْدُ مِائَةٍ ثُمَّ رَجْمٌ بِالْحِجَارَةِ وَالْبِكْرُ جَلْدُ مِائَةٍ

ثُمَّ نَفْيُ سَنَةٍ

"Take it from me. Allah has made for them a way. If it is a married person and a married person or a virgin and a virgin: the married one will be flogged one hundred times and then

---

[1] Al-Shafi'ee, p. 184.

115

stoned. The virgin will be flogged one hundred times and then banished for one year." (Recorded by Muslim.)

The Prophet (peace be upon him) Implemented the Non-Detailed Commands of the Quran, Giving Them Their Needed Details

The Prophet (peace be upon him) explained the details of the Quranic ordinances. For example, Allah orders the Muslims to pray but Allah never explains exactly how this prayer is to be performed. The answer to the question of how to pray is not explicitly found in the Quran but the Messenger of Allah (peace be upon him) answered it by saying,

صَلُّوا كَمَا رَأَيْتُمُونِي أُصَلِّي

"Pray as you have seen me praying."[1]

The Prophet (peace be upon him) also explained the details of the laws of zakaat, fasting, pilgrimage, marriage, divorce, jihad and so on. One can find numerous Quranic verses exhorting people concerning these topics. However, the vast majority of the details of these essential portions of Islam are not to be found in the Quran. It was the Prophet's role to explain and demonstrate by his speech and practice the laws and details concerning these maters.

Concerning on this aspect of the Prophet's (peace be upon him) role vis-a-vis the Quran, Maudoodi wrote,

> The Quran, to put it succinctly, is a Book of broad general principles rather than of legal minutiae.[2] The Book's aim is to expound, clearly and adequately, the

---

[1] Recorded by al-Bukhari.

[2] This statement by Maudoodi can be considered correct in a general sense; obviously, there are numerous exceptions to that general description of the Quran.

intellectual and moral foundations of the Islamic programme for life. It seeks to consolidate these by appealing both to man's mind and to his heart. Its method of guidance for practical Islamic life does not consist of laying down minutely detailed laws and regulations. It prefers to outline the basic framework for each aspect of human activity, and to lay down certain guidelines within which man can order his life in keeping with the Will of God. The mission of the Prophet was to give practical shape to the Islamic vision of the good life, by offering the world a model of an individual character and of a human state and society, as living embodiments of the principles of the Quran.[1]

The importance of this facet of the Prophet's clarification and implementation of the Quran is great. The majority of the laws of the Quran are stated without their required details. Those details are only known—and can only be known—by returning to the sunnah of the Prophet (peace be upon him).

The Prophet (peace be upon him) Made Statements Whose Meanings Were Similar to Verses in the Quran, Which Emphasized and Further Clarified the Point of the Quran

The Messenger of Allah (peace be upon him) stressed and emphasized the meanings of many of the verses of the Quran with his own statements; that is, many of his statements have the same meaning as some verses of the Quran and they simply emphasize or further elucidate the meaning of the verse. This is also a type of commentary or explanation as

---

[1]Abul Ala Maudoodi, *An Introduction to Understanding the Quran* (Riyadh: WAMY, 1990), p. 44.

elaboration or emphasis strengthens the truth and, when stated in different words, makes its meaning even clearer.

For example, Allah says in the Quran,

$$\text{فَمَا مَتَاعُ الْحَيَاة الدُّنْيَا فِي الآخِرَة إلاَّ قَلِيلٌ}$$

"Little is the comfort of this life as compared to the Hereafter" (*al-Taubah* 38). The purport of this verse was emphatically underscored by the Prophet (peace be upon him) when he said,

$$\text{وَاللَّهِ مَا الدُّنْيَا فِي الآخِرَة إلاَّ مِثْلُ مَا يَجْعَلُ أَحَدُكُمْ إِصْبَعَهُ}$$

$$\text{هَذِهِ وَأَشَارَ يَحْيَى بِالسَّبَّابَةِ فِي الْيَمِّ فَلْيَنْظُرْ بِمَ تَرْجِعُ}$$

"By Allah, this world with respect to the Hereafter is not but like one of you taking this finger—and Yahya [the narrator] pointed to his index finger— and putting it into the ocean and seeing what comes out with it [as compared to what remains in the ocean]." (Recorded by Muslim.)

In another verse, Allah says,

$$\text{حَتَّى إِذَا مَا جَاؤُوهَا شَهِدَ عَلَيْهِمْ سَمْعُهُمْ وَأَبْصَارُهُمْ وَجُلُودُهُمْ بِمَا}$$

$$\text{كَانُوا يَعْمَلُونَ}$$

"At length, when they reach the (Fire), their hearing, their sight, and their skins will bear witness against them, as to (all) their deeds" (*Fussilat* 20). Exactly what will occur is made clear in the following hadith from *Sahih Muslim*:

$$\text{عَنْ أَنَسِ بْنِ مَالِكٍ قَالَ كُنَّا عِنْدَ رَسُولِ اللَّهِ صَلَّى اللَّهم عَلَيْهِ}$$

$$\text{وَسَلَّمَ فَضَحِكَ فَقَالَ هَلْ تَدْرُونَ مِمَّ أَضْحَكُ قَالَ قُلْنَا اللَّهُ}$$

$$\text{وَرَسُولُهُ أَعْلَمُ قَالَ مِنْ مُخَاطَبَةِ الْعَبْدِ رَبَّهُ يَقُولُ يَا رَبِّ أَلَمْ}$$

$$\text{تُجِرْنِي مِنَ الظُّلْمِ قَالَ يَقُولُ بَلَى قَالَ فَيَقُولُ فَإِنِّي لا أُجِيزُ}$$

عَلَى نَفْسِي إِلاَّ شَاهِدًا مِنِّي قَالَ فَيَقُولُ كَفَى بِنَفْسِكَ الْيَوْمَ
عَلَيْكَ شَهِيدًا وَبِالْكِرَامِ الْكَاتِبِينَ شُهُودًا قَالَ فَيُخْتَمُ عَلَى فِيهِ
فَيُقَالُ لِأَرْكَانِهِ انْطِقِي قَالَ فَتَنْطِقُ بِأَعْمَالِهِ قَالَ ثُمَّ يُخَلَّى بَيْنَهُ
وَبَيْنَ الْكَلَامِ قَالَ فَيَقُولُ بُعْدًا لَكُنَّ وَسُحْقًا فَعَنْكُنَّ كُنْتُ
أُنَاضِلُ

On the authority of Anas ibn Maalik who said: We were with
the Messenger of Allah (peace be upon him) and he laughed.
He said, "Do you know what made me laugh?" We said,
"Allah and His Messenger know best." He replied, "[I
laughed] due to what the human will say to his Lord. He says,
'O my Lord, did You not make a pact not to commit
injustice?' He [the Lord] says, 'Certainly.' He [the human]
then says, 'I would not be pleased with any witness against me
except one who is from me.' He [the Lord] then says, 'Today,
your soul will be sufficient as a witness against you, as will the
noble recording witnesses.' Then He says, 'Seal his mouth.'
Then it will be said to his body parts, 'Speak.' Then they shall
speak about his deeds. Then the person is allowed to speak
again and he will say [to his limbs], 'Get away, Allah's curse
may be upon you. It was on your behalf that I was pleading.'"
(Recorded by Muslim.)

The Prophet (peace be upon him) Supplied Details of Incidents That the Quran Did Not Mention

Actually, in many cases the Prophet (peace be on him)
supplied more information that what was stated in the Quran.
For example, the Prophet (peace be upon him) gave more
details about what happens on the Day of Judgement, the Hell-
fire and so on. But two glaring examples stand out:

In *Soorah al-Kahf*, verses 60-82, Allah recounts the story of Khidr and Moses. The Prophet (peace be upon him) also discussed the same incident. However, there are a number of details in the Prophet's narrative that are not to be found in the Quran. For example, the beginning of the Prophet's narrative is as follows,

> Moses got up to deliver a speech before the Tribe of Israel and he was asked, "Who is the most learned person among the people?" Moses replied, "I am." Allah admonished him for he did not ascribe the knowledge to Allah alone. So Allah revealed to him: "At the junction of the two seas there is a servant of Ours who is more learned than you." Moses said, "O my Lord, how can I meet him?" Allah said, "Take a fish and put it in a basket and then proceed..."

Here the Messenger of Allah (peace be upon him) explained why Moses set out to find Khidhr as well as the significance of the fish that is mentioned in the *soorah* of the Quran. Like this beginning, the Prophet (peace be upon him) has added a number of important and beneficial points to the incident as narrated in the Quran. Commenting on this story, al-Sid wrote,

> Now this hadith combined with another hadith in which the Prophet says, "I have been given the Book and what is like it," point to Muhammad's possession of substantial knowledge pertinent to the Quran. This gives to him alone authority to elaborate on the Quran by adding factual details not mentioned in the text. His exegesis is authoritative and Muslims do not take it for granted.[1]

Another excellent example of this nature concerns *Surah al-Burooj* and the Prophet's lengthy explanation,

---

[1] Muhammad Al-Sid, "The Hermeneutical Problem of the Quran in Islamic History," (Ph.D. Dissertation, Temple University, 1975), p. 208.

recorded in *Sahih Muslim*, as to the exact details surrounding those people who were burnt alive in the pit due to their belief in Allah.

The Messenger of Allah (peace be upon him) also explained the meaning of the terms that do not have a clear and specific reference in the Quran. For example, with respect to *soorah al-Faatiha*, the Messenger of Allah (peace be upon him) explained that those whose portion is wrath refers to the Jews while those who have gone astray refers to the Christians.[1] This particular reference cannot be known by a look at the verse itself but since the Prophet (peace be upon him) explained it, it is clear that it is they who the verse is referring to.

Reference to the Prophet's Life in Understanding the Quran

There is yet another aspect that demonstrates that one must return to the life and sunnah of the Prophet (peace be upon him) in order to understand the Quran properly. To put it another way, Allah has made it a necessity for the one who wants to understand the Quran that he must have a good understanding of the sunnah and life of the Prophet (peace be upon him) as otherwise the meanings of many verses of the Quran would simply be unreachable. Habib-ur-Rahman Azami has explained this concept well when he wrote,

> If there is no authentic source of knowledge than the Quran, and if the reports of the Prophet (peace be upon him) are rejected as untrustworthy, then the meaning and significance of many of the verses of the Quran itself will remain unclear and incomplete. For instance, it is declared in the Quran:

---

[1] Recorded by al-Tirmidhi. According to al-Albaani, it is *sahih*. See al-Albaani, *Saheeh Sunan al-Tirmidhi*, vol. 3, p. 20.

"So when Zaid had performed the necessary formality (of divorce) from her, We gave her unto thee in marriage" (*al-Ahzab* 33-37). Can the full significance of this verse be appreciated without recourse to the Traditions[1] and a placing of reliance upon them? Or is it possible to know solely from the Quran who Zaid was, who his wife was, and what actually happened?...

Likewise, if the whole store of Traditions is discarded as useless and unreliable, what way will remain open to us to find out details of the events mentioned in the Quran concerning the battles of Ahzab, Hunain, etc. Once again we read in the Quran: "And when Allah promised you one of the two bands that it should be yours" (*al-Anfal* 7). Can anyone tell simply from the Quran what were the two bands referred to? Where in the Quran is the promise that is here recalled? If it is not contained in the Quran, must there also be some other kind of revelations come to the Prophet from Allah?...

[After presenting a number of examples, Azami concludes:] These are only a few examples, and many more instances could be given. Our aim, however, is only to show that it is almost impossible to understand or explain the meaning of a large

---

[1] In the translation of Azami's work, the word "Traditions" is used for the Arabic word *hadith*. This author prefers not to refer to hadith as "traditions." Indeed, it is this author's belief that the word "tradition" was intentionally chosen by Western authorities as a translation for the word hadith in order to downplay the legitimacy and reliability of hadith. The word "tradition" gives the impression of something passed down, perhaps in a haphazard fashion, or something that is simply legend and not verified. None of these impressions hold true for hadith and, therefore, this author prefers not to refer to hadith as "traditions." Allah knows best.

number of Quranic verses if the Traditions are rejected as useless and inauthentic.[1]

Conclusions Concerning the Prophet (peace be upon him) As Explainer of the Quran

The functions of the Prophet (peace be upon him) with respect to the Quran may, therefore, be summarized as follows:

(1) Explaining the general and specific ordinances, specifying or restricting many of the general and unrestricted commands, of the Quran.[2]

(2) Explaining the details and applications of the Quranic commandments or prohibitions.

(3) Giving the exact meaning of some phrases whose meanings were ambiguous or had many possible meanings.[3] In addition, correcting misconceptions that existed concerning the meanings of verses of the Quran.

(4) Giving additional ordinances and regulations that are not to be found in the Quran but which make up part of the religion of Islam.

(5) Clarifying which verses are abrogated and which are not.

(6) Emphasizing and stressing, by his own speech, the meanings of numerous Quranic verses.

(7) Prividing further details for incidents mentioned in the Quran.

In addition, one must have a knowledge of the Prophet's life and sunnah in order to have any real

---

[1] Habib-ur-Rahman Azami, pp. 29-31.

[2] For more examples of this nature, see Abdul Raheem, p. 409.

[3] Al-Suyooti has a long section containing the Prophet's *tafseer* of specific words and phrases in the Quran. See Jalaal al-Deen al-Suyooti, *al-Itqaan fi Uloom al-Quran* (Beirut: Daar al-Marifah, 1978), vol. 2, pp. 244-263. Also see Abdul Raheem, pp. 411-414.

understanding of the many references made in the Quran to incidents and aspects of the Prophet's biography.

There is yet other evidence from the Quran that proves that the Muslim must look to the Messenger of Allah's (peace be upon him) sunnah to truly see how to live according to the Quran. There is no question that the way of life expounded by Allah in the Quran is the straight path, the way of life that is pleasing to Allah. At the same time, Allah states,

لَقَدْ كَانَ لَكُمْ فِي رَسُولِ اللَّهِ أُسْوَةٌ حَسَنَةٌ لِمَنْ كَانَ يَرْجُو اللَّهَ
وَالْيَوْمَ الآخِرَ وَذَكَرَ اللَّهَ كَثِيرًا

"Verily in the Messenger of Allah you have an excellent example for him who looks unto Allah and the Last Day and remembers Allah much" (*al-Ahzaab* 21). When Allah declares that the Messenger of Allah (peace be upon him) is the best example for Muslims to follow, this is a declaration from Allah that the Messenger of Allah (peace be upon him) is following the straight path, the path that is pleasing to Allah. Or, in other words, it means that the way of life or sunnah of the Messenger of Allah (peace be upon him) is the same way of life that is in accord with the teachings of the Quran. In essence, Allah is telling the believers, "If you wish to see how to properly and best apply the Quran, look to the example of the Messenger of Allah." This thought was echoed by the Prophet's wife Aishah who, as noted earlier, when asked about the Prophet's character, replied, "His character was the Quran."[1] In essence, the Prophet (peace be upon him) was the practical application of the Quran, "a walking Quran" as some people have called him.

Allah also states,

---

[1] Recorded by Muslim.

وَإِنَّكَ لَتَهْدِي إِلَى صِرَاطٍ مُسْتَقِيمٍ صِرَاطِ اللَّهِ الَّذِي لَهُ مَا فِي

السَّمَاوَاتِ وَمَا فِي الْأَرْضِ أَلاَ إِلَى اللَّهِ تَصِيرُ الْأُمُورُ

"And verily you (O Muhammad) do guide (men) to the straight way— the Way of Allah to whom belongs whatever is in the heavens and whatever is on earth. Behold how all affairs tend towards Allah" (*al-Shoora* 52-53); and Allah states,

كَمَا أَرْسَلْنَا فِيكُمْ رَسُولاً مِنْكُمْ يَتْلُو عَلَيْكُمْ آيَاتِنَا وَيُزَكِّيكُمْ

وَيُعَلِّمُكُمُ الْكِتَابَ وَالْحِكْمَةَ وَيُعَلِّمُكُمْ مَا لَمْ تَكُونُوا تَعْلَمُونَ

"A similar (favor have you already received) in that We have sent among you a messenger of your own, rehearsing to you Our signs, and purifying you and instructing you in Scripture and Wisdom, and that which you knew not" (*al-Baqarah* 151).[1]

In *al-Shoora* 52-53 quoted above, Allah pronounces that the Messenger of Allah (peace be upon him) guides to the straight path. In the Quran, it states that the straight path is the path expounded by the Quran itself. Hence, both the Messenger of Allah (peace be upon him) and the Quran are showing and guiding Muslims to one and the same straight path that leads to Allah's pleasure. Hence, they must both be consistent with one another and both of them must be taken together as guides.

From all of the above it should become clear that the correct understanding of the Quran cannot be achieved without reference to the Prophet (peace be upon him) and the manner in which he applied the Quran. This is why all of the scholars of Quranic exegesis are in agreement that the first source of attaining the meaning of the verses of the Quran is other relevant verses of the Quran itself. The second source is, undoubtedly, the sayings and actions of the Messenger of

---

[1]Verses similar to this last verse may be found in *ali-Imraan* 164 and *al-Jumuah* 2.

Allah (peace be upon him) as, indeed, it was one of his roles that he should explain the Quran and put it into practice in the exact manner in which it was meant to be put into practice. Saeed ibn Jubair was absolutely correct when, after he related some hadith of the Prophet (peace be upon him), a man came to him and said, "In the Book of Allah is something that differs from what you have said." Saeed replied, "The Messenger of Allah knows the Book of Allah much better than you do."[1] Indeed, the Messenger of Allah (peace be upon him) knows the Book of Allah better than anyone of this creation and anyone who claims to know it or understand it better than the Prophet (peace be upon him) is, in fact, an apostate.

Two very important sources of *tafseer* have been established in the discussion here: the Quran and the sunnah of the Prophet (peace be upon him). It is not allowed for any explanation of a verse to contradict either of these two sources. This is true because both of these sources come directly from Allah and no one knows the Book of Allah better than the one who revealed it. These are the two definitive sources of *tafseer* that may not be contradicted by personal reasoning or *ijtihaad*. Abdul Raheem has succinctly concluded,

> It is established that whatever the Prophet (peace be upon him) stated in interpreting the Quran and explaining what Allah's words mean was based on revelation and what Allah had imprinted on his heart of understanding and what he was exclusively given of knowledge and erudition. In fact, Allah obliged him to explain the Quran and expound the meanings of His words... Therefore it is absolutely necessary for anyone who interprets the Quran to base his interpretation upon what has been narrated of its interpretation by the Messenger (peace be upon him) and not to deviate from it and [instead] turn to

---

[1] Quoted in al-Suyooti, *Miftaah*, p. 108.

ijtihaad and personal judgment by looking at the Arabic wording to determine its meaning.[1]

The Messenger of Allah (peace be upon him) as an "Independent Source of Law "

One of the roles of the Messenger of Allah (peace be upon him) was to be a "source of law" and what he decreed must be accepted as part of the Islamic law or *Shareeah*. In other words, some of the commands and directives from Allah are known only through the mouth of the Prophet (peace be upon him), independent of what was revealed in the Quran.

The Prophet (peace be upon him) himself made it clear that stating new laws and rules was one of his responsibilities and Muslims must look towards him as having that right and duty. In a hadith mentioned earlier, the Messenger of Allah (peace be upon him) is reported to have prohibited the flesh of domestic donkeys and then he emphatically stated,

يُوشِكُ الرَّجُلُ مُتَّكِئًا عَلَى أَرِيكَتِهِ يُحَدَّثُ بِحَدِيثٍ مِنْ حَدِيثِي فَيَقُولُ بَيْنَنَا وَبَيْنَكُمْ كِتَابُ اللَّهِ عَزَّ وَجَلَّ مَا وَجَدْنَا فِيهِ مِنْ حَلَالٍ اسْتَحْلَلْنَاهُ وَمَا وَجَدْنَا فِيهِ مِنْ حَرَامٍ حَرَّمْنَاهُ أَلَا وَإِنَّ مَا حَرَّمَ رَسُولُ اللَّهِ صَلَّى اللَّهِ عَلَيْهِ اللَّهم وَسَلَّمَ مِثْلُ مَا حَرَّمَ اللَّهُ

"Soon it will be that a man will recline on his couch and will be told a hadith of my hadith and will say, 'Between us and you is the Book of Allah. What we find allowed therein, we allow. What we find prohibited therein, we prohibit.' But truly,

---

[1]Abdul Raheem, p. 415.

127

what the Messenger of Allah has forbidden is like what Allah has forbidden."[1]

In the previous pages, there are other examples in which the Prophet (peace be upon him) stated legislation that was not found in the Quran. Allah, the Most High and the All-Knowing, did not include all of the laws of Islam in the Quran. Some of the Islamic laws Allah instituted only through the sayings and deeds of His Messenger (peace be upon him).

Allah says in the Quran,

يَأْمُرُهُمْ بِالْمَعْرُوفِ وَيَنْهَاهُمْ عَنِ الْمُنكَرِ وَيُحِلُّ لَهُمُ الطَّيِّبَاتِ وَيُحَرِّمُ عَلَيْهِمُ الْخَبَائِثَ وَيَضَعُ عَنْهُمْ إِصْرَهُمْ وَالأَغْلاَلَ الَّتِي كَانَتْ عَلَيْهِمْ فَالَّذِينَ آمَنُوا بِهِ وَعَزَّرُوهُ وَنَصَرُوهُ وَاتَّبَعُوا النُّورَ الَّذِي أُنزِلَ مَعَهُ أُوْلَئِكَ هُمُ الْمُفْلِحُونَ

"For he [the Prophet (peace be upon him)] commands them what is just and forbids them what is evil; He allows them as lawful what is good and pure and prohibits them from what is bad and impure. He releases them from their heavy burdens and from the yokes that are upon them. So it is those who believe in him, honor him, help him, and follow the Light which is sent down with him, it is they who will prosper" (*al-Araaf* 157). This verse is a description of the Messenger of Allah (peace be upon him). In this verse Allah describes the Messenger of Allah as being the one who "allows them as lawful..." This is because the Messenger of Allah (peace be upon him) himself has been commissioned by Allah to give commandments and issue regulations, under inspiration from Allah. In this manner, what the Messenger of Allah (peace be upon him) ordered is similar to what Allah has ordered. Usmani also notes that at the end of the verse, Allah refers to following the light which is sent with the Prophet (peace be

---

[1] Recorded by al-Baihaqi, Ahmad, al-Tirmidhi and ibn Maajah. According to al-Albaani, it is authentic. See al-Albaani, *Saheeh al-Jaami*, vol. 2, p. 1360.

upon him). Allah did not specifically mention the Book but instead mentioned "the Light," which is inclusive of all of the guidance—both the Book and the *Hikmah*—that the Prophet (peace be upon him) received.[1]

Al-Baihaqi recorded that Imraan ibn Husain mentioned the intercession of the Prophet (peace be upon him). A person said to him, "O Abu Najeed, you relate hadith [concerning topics] not found in the Quran." Imraan became angered and told that person, "Have you read the Quran?" The man answered, "Yes." Imraan told him, "Did you find therein that the night prayer is four units, and the sunset prayer is three and the morning prayer is two and the noon prayer is four and the afternoon prayer is four?" Imraan told him further, "From whom do you take these ordinances? Do you not take them from the Messenger of Allah?"[2] No Muslim claims that the morning prayer's being only two units is not part of the Islamic law because it is not explicitly mentioned in the Quran. Hence, one is forced to admit that this ordinance came not from the Quran but from the Messenger of Allah (peace be upon him) who is, therefore, an independent source of law.

Allah's Sanctioning of the Prophet's Legislation

Allah's sanctioning of this role and place of the Prophet (peace be upon him) is further substantiated by practices that definitely form a part of Islam that were initiated by the Prophet (peace be upon him) and supported by Allah in the Quran. (Of course, the inspiration for the Prophet's acts was Allah.)

For example, there is the funeral prayer which is referred to in *soorah al-Taubah*:

ولا تصل على أحد منهم مات أبدا ولا تقم على قبره

---

[1] Usmani, p. 47.
[2] For the rest of the incident see al-Suyooti, *Miftaah al-Jannah*, p. 21.

"Never [O Muhammad] pray for any of them [that is, the hypocrites] who dies, nor stand at his grave" (*al-Taubah* 84). This verse is generally understood to be a reference to the funeral prayer. Commenting on this verse, H. Azami writes,

> The verse implies that such funeral services had begun to be performed and that the Prophet used to offer prayers at the burial of the dead before this particular verse was revealed; yet no verse revealed earlier than this one can be cited as enjoining such services or prayers upon the Prophet and the Muslims. It must, therefore, be conceded that the command for the burial service was given through the Sunnah.[1]

Another example that H. Azami gives is the call to prayer (*adhaan*). He states,

> No one claiming to be a Muslim could deny that the *Adhan* or call to prayer given before *Salah* is a religious act, continuously observed among the Muslims since the time of the Prophet. In the Quran, the *Adhan* is mentioned once in *Surah al-Ma'idah* as part of the statement of fact that the foolish disbelievers made fun of it by imitating it derisively, and with mocking gestures ("And when ye call to prayer they take it for a jest and sport") (*al-Ma'idah* 5:58) and on another occasion, in *Surah al-Jumu'ah* in connection with another command... But though it is known from these verses that the *Adhan* was current religious practice among the Muslims, not a single verse can be found in the Quran through which the *Adhan* may be said to have been prescribed to the believers. It naturally follows that the command for

---

[1] H. Azami, p. 32.

the *Adhan* was not given through the Quran but the Sunnah.[1]

The purport of the above discussion is to demonstrate that what the Prophet (peace be upon him) established as part of the religion is approved by Allah. In the two examples given above, there is a somewhat explicit approval of some practices that the Prophet (peace be upon him) established. One cannot find anywhere in the Quran any type of censure of the Prophet (peace be upon him) for establishing acts that are not found in the Quran. Furthermore, if the final Prophet (peace be upon him), whose message and teachings are for everyone until the Day of Judgment, made any statement or established any practice that should not form part of the religion, one would expect that Allah would have clearly and unequivocally demonstrated that such practices do not form part of the religion or that the Prophet (peace be upon him) does not have

---

[1] H. Azami, p. 33. Azami also gives another example of the *khutbah* or address of the Friday Prayer. He writes, "Similarly, a passing reference to the Friday sermon, in the course of a parable or complaint, is made in the following verse of *Surah al-Jumu'ah*: 'But when they spy some merchandise or pastime they break away to it and leave you standing' (*al-Jumu'ah* 62:11). Surely not even the Traditions' rejectors [*sic*] would deny that the Friday sermon is a religious observance ordained by the *Shari'ah* and that the Prophet himself used to deliver a Friday sermon and that his practice has been kept on in the *Ummah* without break or interruption ever since. Yet no Quranic verse can be quoted in which the Friday sermon is enjoined as such." However, this particular example may not be proper. This is because in the books explaining the occasions behind revelations of the Quran (*asbaab al-nuzool*), mention is made of *al-Jumuah* 11, which Azami referred to, as being revealed after a number of Muslims left the Prophet (peace be upon him) standing delivering the *khutbah*. However, it seems—and Allah knows best—that the verse previous to that was already a portion of the Quran: "O believers, when the call is proclaimed for the prayer on Friday, come to the remembrance of Allah and leave off business" (*al-Jumuah* 9). In this verse, the meaning of the "remembrance of Allah" as given by the early commentators is the *khutbah* itself. In fact, Al-Tabari records no other opinion; no one stated that it is in reference to the Prayer. Hence, this is a command from Allah to "go and attend the *khutbah*." Cf., Jamaal al-Din Zarabozo, *The Friday Prayer: Part I: The Fiqh* (Ann Arbor, MI: Islamic Assembly of North America, 1998), p. 107.

the right to establish any practice in the religion. One does not find anything of that nature. Indeed, one finds only the opposite: approval or acceptance of what the Messenger of Allah (peace be upon him) established, in addition to the numerous verses quoted earlier ordering Muslims to accept and follow whatever the Prophet (peace be upon him) instructs them to do.

A Sunnah with No Basis in the Quran

With respect to its relationship to the Quran, the scholars have divided the sunnah into three categories: (1) The sunnah that emphasizes or reaffirms what is already found in the Quran. (2) The sunnah that explains or gives the details of the injunctions found in the Quran. (3) The sunnah that has no direct basis in the Quran itself. Al-Shaafi'ee wrote,

> I know of no scholar who does not agree that the sunna of the Prophet falls in three categories, two of which were agreed upon unanimously... First, for whatever acts there is textual [legislation] provided by God in the Book, the Apostle [merely] specified clearly what is in the text of the Book. Second, as to any [ambiguous] communication in the Book laid down by God, [the Prophet] specified the meaning implied by Him. These are the two categories on which the scholars do not disagree. The third category consists of what the Apostle has laid down in the sunna and concerning which there is no text in the Book.[1]

The scholars all agree upon the first two categories. About the third category there is some difference of opinion. The majority of the scholars believe in the existence of the third category. They cite the following rulings that are derived

---

[1] Al-Shaafi'ee, p. 120.

from the hadith with no apparent source in the Quran: the obligation of banishing the unmarried fornicator for one year, the penalty for having sexual intercourse during the daytime of the month of Ramadhaan, the prohibition of men wearing either gold or silk and so on. Actually, all of the scholars agree that these types of sunnah exist. Some, though, claim the even these sunnah can somehow be traced back to the Quran.

Among those who believe that even the third category can be traced back to the Quran is al-Shaatibi. He wrote,

> The sunnah, in its meaning, always returns to the Book—for it is the details of what [the Quran] has left undetailed, clarification of its difficult matters and explanation of what it touched upon briefly. That is because it is [only] the explanation for it [the Book]. And this is what is indicated by Allah's words, "We have revealed to you the *Dhikr* ('reminder') that you may explain unto mankind what has been revealed to them" [*al-Nahl* 44]. There is not found in the sunnah any command except that the Quran points to its meaning, by either a general or specific indication.[1]

Muhammad Abu Zahrah, a specialist in Islamic legal theory of this century, wrote, "One can hardly find any example of a ruling from the sunnah except that we find for it a Quranic source, either direct or indirect."[2]

Again, these scholars will admit the fact that one can find a sunnah for which there is no direct source in the Quran. What they are claiming is that for every sunnah, if one searches and contemplates well, one can find a Quranic verse that somehow alludes to that sunnah of the Prophet (peace be upon him)—even though that allusion may be very obscure.

---

[1] Ibraaheem al-Shaatibi, *Al-Muwaafaqaat* (Al-Khobar, Saudi Arabia: Daar ibn Affaan, 1997), vol. 4, p. 314-316.
[2] Muhammad Abu Zahrah, *Usool al-Fiqh* (Cairo: Daar al-Fikr al-Arabi, n.d.), p. 88.

There is no question that al-Shaatibi's and Abu Zahrah's opinion is the weaker opinion. Even al-Shaatibi is forced to admit that sometimes they have to go to extremes to make their theory seem feasible.[1] More importantly, the command in the Quran to obey the Prophet (peace be upon him) is an unrestricted command, meaning obedience to him is required in whatever he promulgates, regardless of whether he is explaining the Quran or laying down new legislation.[2]

In reality, this difference of opinion boils down to one of semantics only, as al-Sibaa'ee, al-Turki and others have concluded.[3] In other words, both groups of scholars accept everything that comes in the sunnah. None of them ever claimed that one only follows a sunnah if he is able to research and discover some source for it in the Quran.

This last point, though, is why it is important to realize the weakness of the opinion that every sunnah has to have a basis in the Quran. That opinion leaves the door open for

---

[1] Al-Shaatibi's theory falls apart when he tries to force everything under the Quran. Obviously, if one makes broad enough statements, everything will fit under the Quran. Al-Shaatibi offers five possible explanations for those sunnah that have no apparent relation to a verse in the Quran: (1) The Quran says one must follow the sunnah. Therefore, following the sunnah is actually applying the Quran. (2) The Quran is *mujmal* (un-detailed) and the sunnah is simply the details. (3) Taking into consideration the general purposes of the Quranic commands, one finds that they are to meet three types of needs: necessities, needs and amenities. Every command in the sunnah fits into one of these three goals of the Quran. (4) These sunnah are simply a matter of applying different types of analogy to the Quran. For example, Allah allows the *tayyibaat* (the pure things) and forbids the *khabaaith* (impure and evil things). The sunnah rules showing permissibility or impermissibility fall under one of these two general categories. (5) Simply from the wording of the Quran, one can derive the laws of the sunnah. (Cf., al-Shaatibi, *Al-Muwaafaqaat*, vol. 4, pp. 340-402.) Al-Shaatibi's goal is a noble goal: the word of Allah is the fountainhead for Islam and everything must return to it. But there is no need to resort to this type of explanation and theory since both the Quran and sunnah are equally revelations from Allah.

[2] For a detailed refutation of al-Shaatibi's opinion, see Abdul Khaaliq, pp. 504-537.

[3] Al-Sibaa'ee, p. 385; Abdullah al-Turki, *Usool al-Imaam Ahmad* (Riyadh: Maktabah al-Riyaadh al-Hadeethah, 1977), p. 220.

people to make the claim that one does not have to follow a particular sunnah if there is no relevant source for it in the Quran. In other words, they may refuse to follow a hadith based on their claim that what is found in that hadith has no basis in the Quran and every sunnah must have a basis in the Quran, arguing that the Quran is the basis for Islam and every ruling must have some source for it in the Quran.[1]

This argument, although sometimes resorted to, is a fallacious argument. The Prophet (peace be upon him) himself has warned against it in the hadith quoted earlier,

يُوشِكُ الرَّجُلُ مُتَّكِئًا عَلَى أَرِيكَتِهِ يُحَدَّثُ بِحَدِيثٍ مِنْ حَدِيثِي فَيَقُولُ بَيْنَنَا وَبَيْنَكُمْ كِتَابُ اللهِ عَزَّ وَجَلَّ مَا وَجَدْنَا فِيهِ مِنْ حَلَالٍ اسْتَحْلَلْنَاهُ وَمَا وَجَدْنَا فِيهِ مِنْ حَرَامٍ حَرَّمْنَاهُ أَلَا وَإِنَّ مَا حَرَّمَ رَسُولُ اللهِ صَلَّى اللهم عَلَيْهِ وَسَلَّمَ مِثْلُ مَا حَرَّمَ اللهُ

"Soon it will be that a man will recline on his couch and will be told a hadith of my hadith and will say, 'Between us and you is the Book of Allah. What we find allowed therein, we allow. What we find prohibited therein, we prohibit.' But truly, what the Messenger of Allah (peace be upon him) has forbidden is similar to what Allah has forbidden."[2]

Therefore, tt is because the Messenger of Allah (peace be upon him) is an independent source of Islamic law that one can find certain sunnah actions that seem to have no source or

---

[1] This author has personally received many questions in which the questioner states, "What is the proof for such and such an act, and I want a verse in the Quran only and not a hadith..." Although not uncommon, this type of question definitely reflects some kind of misunderstanding with respect to the status of the sunnah in Islam.

[2] Recorded by al-Baihaqi, Ahmad, al-Tirmidhi and ibn Maajah. According to al-Albaani, it is authentic. See al-Albaani, *Saheeh al-Jaami*, vol. 2, p. 1360.

related text in the Quran. On this point Imam al-Shaafi'ee has written,

> For the Apostle has laid down a sunnah [on matters]
> for which there is a text in the Book of God as well
> as for others concerning which there is no [specific]
> text. But whatever he laid down in the sunnah God
> has ordered us to obey, and He regards [our]
> obedience to him as obedience to Him, and [our]
> refusal to obey him as disobedience to Him for which
> no man will be forgiven.[1]

Finally, al-Ameen points out that if there were no such sunnah that are not somehow derived from the verses of the Quran, the idea of obeying the Prophet (peace be upon him) would be moot. In other words, in reality, one would actually be obeying the Quran only and not the Prophet (peace be upon him) because everything he orders must somehow be traced back to a relevant verse in the Quran. This would make the numerous verses ordering obedience to the Prophet (peace be upon him) superfluous and meaningless.[2]

The Prophet Muhammad (peace be upon him) as a Model of Behavior

Allah says in the Quran,

لَقَدْ كَانَ لَكُمْ فِي رَسُولِ اللَّهِ أُسْوَةٌ حَسَنَةٌ لِمَنْ كَانَ يَرْجُو اللَّهَ وَالْيَوْمَ الآخِرَ وَذَكَرَ اللَّهَ كَثِيرًا

"An excellent model you have in Allah's Messenger, for all whose hope is in Allah, and in the Final Day and who often

---

[1] Al-Shaafi'ee, *Risala*, p. 119.

[2] Cf., Al-Ameen al-Saadiq al-Ameen, *Mauqaf al-Madrasah al-Aqliyyah min al-Sunnah al-Nabawiyyah* (Riyadh: Maktabah al-Rushd, 1998), vol. 1, p. 51.

remember Allah" (*al-Ahzaab* 21). This verse brings to light another role of the Messenger of Allah (peace be upon him). Instead of sending an angel or something similar to an angel with the message of Islam, Allah always sent human beings as messengers and prophets. Allah even states in the Quran that these humans married and had children and lived among the people. In fact, Allah sometimes sent messengers without them having a specific book to read to the people. But it has never been the case that Allah simply revealed a book—to a mountainside, for example—without it being accompanied with a messenger.

Allah alone knows the complete wisdom behind this course of action. Some scholars point to the fact that Allah sent such humans in order to give the believers a perfect example of how the message is to be applied in everyday human affairs. Believers have an actual human example before them. The example has shown the believers their capabilities as human beings (as well as their limitations) and proves to them that they are, in fact, capable of fulfilling the requirements and commands of the religion in a manner comparable to the manner in which the prophets (peace be upon all of them) themselves had performed them. Furthermore, these prophets taught the people and instructed them in how to understand and apply the teachings from Allah.

Imagine the problem the believers would have faced if they had not been given such a perfect example. One can look to the example of the ascetics of Christianity (who no longer possessed the perfect example of their messenger because of the loss of historic material) to see to what extremes many may go to "please their Lord." Allah praises fasting, but how often should one fast? Possibly every day? What about continuous fasting? In Islam, the answers to all of these types of questions are found in the example of the Prophet (peace be upon him). His exact mode of behavior is known and captured in the hadith literature. Therefore, a Muslim knows "how far" he needs to go to please His Lord. He can also understand at what point he is going "too far," to an extreme that is not in accord with what Allah wants from His creatures.

One is reminded by *al-Ahzaab*, verse 21, of the story of the three who, upon asking about the Messenger of Allah's sunnah, said that they could do more than what the Prophet (peace be upon him) was doing. One said that he would fast every day, another would spend the whole night in prayer, while the other would never marry. Upon hearing this the Messenger of Allah (peace be upon him) became angry and stated that sometimes he would fast and sometimes he would not, he would sleep part of the night and pray part of the night, and he would wed. After stating this the Prophet (peace be upon him) clearly warned,

$$\text{فَمَنْ رَغِبَ عَنْ سُنَّتِي فَلَيْسَ مِنِّي}$$

"One who turns away from my sunnah is not of me."[1] In other words, one who rejects the Prophet's sunnah is, in fact, rejecting his role as Messenger and Example for the believers and is in effect rejecting him as the Prophet of Allah (peace be upon him). On another occasion a Companion asked about kissing while fasting. A wife of the Prophet (peace be upon him) informed him that she and the Prophet (peace be upon him) would kiss while he was fasting. The Companion replied that he was not of the same nature as the Messenger of Allah (peace be upon him) and therefore he would refrain from kissing while fasting although he knew that the Prophet (peace be upon him) considered it lawful. The Prophet (peace be upon him) replied to this man's misconception by stating that he was the most aware of Allah and the most knowledgeable regarding Allah and what He likes and dislikes. He clearly stated,

---

[1] Recorded by al-Bukhari and Muslim.

مَا بَالُ أَقْوَامٍ يَتَنَزَّهُونَ عَنِ الشَّيْءِ أَصْنَعُهُ فَوَاللَّهِ إِنِّي أَعْلَمُهُمْ
بِاللَّهِ وَأَشَدُّهُمْ لَهُ خَشْيَةً

"What is wrong with a people that they refrain from doing something that I do. By Allah, I am certainly the most knowledgeable of Allah and the most fearful of Him." (Recorded by al-Bukhari.) Hence, he is the example that the believer must follow.

A Muslim, by the grace of Allah, can read the hadith of the Messenger of Allah (peace be upon him) and practically visualize the actions of this perfect model. This is a special blessing that has been vouchsafed to the nation of Muhammad (peace be upon him) only. The previous communities never established the system of reports from their prophets that allowed them to preserve the details of their prophets' lives. That valuable information was lost for them but it was saved in the case of the final Prophet (peace be upon him), so that all of mankind may learn this information and follow that excellent example.

Many authors have noted the importance of this role of the Prophet (peace be upon him). Many times, those who insist on ignoring the sunnah are, in reality, trying to escape the concrete practices of the noble teachings of Islam. They make claims to have piety and to believe in the moral tenets of Islam. Their claims, though, are not backed up by any practices of the Prophet (peace be upon him) except for those practices that they find acceptable and easy. They have taken their own standards as the standard for piety instead of the example set by the Prophet (peace be upon him). However, Allah has stated that the Prophet (peace be upon him) is the perfect example along the straight path. If a person refuses to emulate the Prophet's example, no matter how pious he may claim to be or how much he may claim to believe in the moral teachings of Islam, he has actually missed the point of what it means to act and behave in the proper moral fashion.

Furthermore, it is easy to talk about virtues and good practices in the abstract, but for humans to have a real conception of how to behave and act, something more is needed. S. M. Yusuf refers to this example of the Messenger of Allah (peace be upon him) as "the concrete form" and he noted,

> The simple natural wisdom of man would also regard the concrete form as crucial in the matter of heavenly guidance. So far as the values are concerned, they belong to the realm of *maruf*, i.e., intuitive knowledge of good and evil. It is only in determining the particular form of virtue in specified circumstances that man by himself would feel somewhat perplexed and helpless. And it is just at the point where man's natural wisdom wavers and feels at a loss to make a definite choice—it is just there that the choice of Allah is made known to him in the form of actual practice fostered under the aegis of a prophet in intimate communion with Himself. Now the actual practice of virtue with all the details of form and manner represents the real outside help to man in his predicament, which is to devise form and shape for the practice of intuitively known values in actual life. It is but due that the faithful should treasure and stick unflinchingly to the formalities of the Sunnah because it is the forms of virtue that constitute the real art of religion...
>
> But as soon as it comes to actual practice calling for a definite choice of form, the imprudence of both the intuition and the rational thought is fully exposed. Then there appear only two alternatives: either to acknowledge in all humbleness that the choice of

form is to be determined by the Sunnah, i.e. the example of a Divinely-guided person, or to resort to bullying and assert that the forms are just inconsequential. The former is the way of religion, the latter the way of no-religion. Naturalism, humanism and liberalism are essentially non-religious attitudes, not because they deny any moral values of life but just because they discount the specific forms of virtue as enjoined by religion...

So far as the value is concerned, it is ingrained in human nature; there is no grace of God in revealing the same through a prophet. It is only the prescription through Sunnah of the dimensions and particulars of the acts containing, embodying as well as preserving and promoting the value, which constitutes the real "grace". And it is the height of folly on the part of man to belittle or cast away this very distinctive element of grace from the solid structure of practical religion.[1]

Allah also says about the Prophet (peace be upon him),

وَكَذَلِكَ أَوْحَيْنَا إِلَيْكَ رُوحًا مِنْ أَمْرِنَا مَا كُنْتَ تَدْرِي مَا الْكِتَابُ وَلَا الْإِيمَانُ وَلَكِنْ جَعَلْنَاهُ نُورًا نَهْدِي بِهِ مَنْ نَشَاءُ مِنْ عِبَادِنَا وَإِنَّكَ لَتَهْدِي إِلَى صِرَاطٍ مُسْتَقِيمٍ

"And thus have We inspired in you [Muhammad] a spirit of Our command, you knew not what the scripture was, nor what the faith was. But We have made it a light whereby We guide whom We will of Our bondmen. And lo! You verily do guide unto a right path" (*al-Shooraa* 52). In the Quran, Allah describes two very general types of guidance: the type of guidance that only Allah gives, which is actually an opening of

---

[1] Yusuf, pp. 3-6.

the heart to the truth, as in the verse, "Allah guides whomsoever He wills"; and a second type of guidance in the form of showing what is the correct path to follow, as in the verses,

$$ذَلِكَ الْكِتَابُ لا رَيْبَ فِيهِ هُدًى لِلْمُتَّقِينَ$$

"This is the book in which there is no doubt. Guidance for those who are aware of Allah..." (*al-Baqarah* 2). From the verse of *soorah al-Shooraa*, quoted above, one can conclude that the Prophet (peace be upon him), by his behavior, speech and example, is establishing for believers a "guide to the straight path," as in the second type of guidance mentioned above. All Muslims supplicate to Allah in their prayers, "Guide us to the straight path..." Allah has clearly answered this prayer with the Quran[1] and with the sunnah of the Messenger (as is clear from *al-Shooraa* 52). In fact, Allah declares that the Prophet (peace be upon him) himself is upon a straight path:

$$إِنَّكَ لَمِنَ الْمُرْسَلِينَ عَلَى صِرَاطٍ مُسْتَقِيمٍ$$

"Verily, you are from among the messengers upon a straight path" (*Ya Seen* 3-4). He is also upon the true path:

$$فَتَوَكَّلْ عَلَى اللَّهِ إِنَّكَ عَلَى الْحَقِّ الْمُبِينِ$$

"So put your trust and reliance in Allah. You are upon the clear truth" (*al-Naml* 79).

Sometimes, those who neglect to follow the example of the Prophet (peace be upon him) are also those who claim that they have the most hope in Allah and claim some kind of spiritual awareness for themselves. However, as Al-Shaukaani noted, the verse from *al-Ahzaab* noting that the Prophet (peace be upon him) is the perfect example states that he is the example for "the one who hopes for Allah." This is the person

---

[1] As is clear from *al-Baqarah* 2, "This is the book in which there is no doubt, a guidance for the pious..."

who believes in Allah and is seeking His pleasure and reward. Hence the verse implies that if one truly believes in Allah and the Last Day, puts his hope in Allah and remembers Allah often, he should pattern his life after the one whom Allah Himself called "the excellent example."[1]

Hence, the Muslim has the Book and the sunnah; these are the two guides that Allah has revealed to guide mankind to the straight path and the clear truth. One must realize this fact and set his life according to the pattern and example set by the example *par excellence*, the Prophet Muhammad (peace be upon him).

The Prophet Muhammad (peace be upon him) as a Recipient of Obedience

The last role of the Messenger of Allah (peace be upon him) to be discussed here is related to the Prophet (peace be upon him) having been sent by Allah as someone who is to be obeyed. Allah says in the Quran,

وَمَا أَرْسَلْنَا مِنْ رَسُولٍ إِلاَّ لِيُطَاعَ بِإِذْنِ اللَّهِ

"We never sent any messenger except for him to be obeyed, by Allah's leave" (*al-Nisaa* 64).[2] Allah has sent the message of Islam in a clear and beautiful manner in order for all of mankind to respond to the call of Allah and His guidance.

---

[1] Al-Shaukaani, *Fath*, vol. 4. p. 270.

[2] After quoting this verse, al-Salafi (p. 33) makes a noteworthy point: "It cannot be said that it is obligatory to obey the Messenger (peace be upon him) only with respect to what he conveyed of the Noble Quran. Allah has said, 'We never sent any messenger except for him to be obeyed, by Allah's leave,' and how many were the messengers who were sent without any recited book. If the obedience is only in accepting what is in the Book, concerning what were [these messengers'] peoples supposed to obey them, if it were not their statements [alone that must be obeyed]?"

Allah has left man free to choose between truth and falsehood. Allah says in the Quran,

تَبَارَكَ الَّذِي بِيَدِهِ الْمُلْكُ وَهُوَ عَلَى كُلِّ شَيْءٍ قَدِيرٌ الَّذِي خَلَقَ الْمَوْتَ وَالْحَيَاةَ لِيَبْلُوَكُمْ أَيُّكُمْ أَحْسَنُ عَمَلاً وَهُوَ الْعَزِيزُ الْغَفُورُ

"Blessed is He in whose hand is the Sovereignty, and He is able to do all things— Who has created life and death that He may try you [and see] which of you is best in conduct; and He is the Mighty, the Forgiving" (*al-Mulk* 1-2).

In the same way that Allah created mankind and is testing them to see if they follow His Book, He is also testing them to see if they will follow and obey the sunnah of the Prophet (peace be upon him). It is not enough for them to claim by their tongues that they are believers, but they must also demonstrate their truthfulness by willingly submitting to the complete truth of the Quran and the sunnah. Allah says,

أَحَسِبَ النَّاسُ أَنْ يُتْرَكُوا أَنْ يَقُولُوا آمَنَّا وَهُمْ لا يُفْتَنُونَ وَلَقَدْ فَتَنَّا الَّذِينَ مِنْ قَبْلِهِمْ فَلَيَعْلَمَنَّ اللَّهُ الَّذِينَ صَدَقُوا وَلَيَعْلَمَنَّ الْكَاذِبِينَ

"Do the people think that they will be left alone on saying, 'We believe,' and that they will not be tested? We did test those before them, and Allah will certainly know those who are true from those who are false" (*al-Ankaboot* 2-3).

Until recent times, very few Muslims who passed the first test of following the Quran failed to pass the second test of following the sunnah. Only recently have many people claimed that they are following the Quran and they need not follow the sunnah. It is a prerequisite of belief for a person to follow both the Quran and the sunnah. This fact can be proven by many verses of the Quran, some of which have already been discussed.

In the Quran one may find the following:

قُلْ أَطِيعُوا اللَّهَ وَالرَّسُولَ فَإِنْ تَوَلَّوْا فَإِنَّ اللَّهَ لا يُحِبُّ الْكَافِرِينَ

"Say: Obey Allah and the Messenger. And if you turn away [know that] verily Allah does not love the unbelievers" (*ali-Imraan* 32). In this verse those who turn away from Allah and the Messenger are implicitly referred to as unbelievers. Ibn Katheer points out that this verse proves that whoever differs from the Messenger (peace be upon him) and refuses to follow his sunnah becomes an unbeliever.[1] There is, in fact, no way to get close to Allah and to receive His love save by following the Messenger (peace be upon him), as is stated in the verse,

قُلْ إِنْ كُنْتُمْ تُحِبُّونَ اللَّهَ فَاتَّبِعُونِي يُحْبِبْكُمُ اللَّهُ وَيَغْفِرْ لَكُمْ ذُنُوبَكُمْ

"Say [O Muhammad]: If you truly love Allah, then follow me and Allah will love you and forgive your sins" (*ali-Imraan* 31).

Allah says in the Quran,

مَنْ يُطِعِ الرَّسُولَ فَقَدْ أَطَاعَ اللَّهَ

"Whoever obeys the Messenger verily obeys Allah" (*al-Nisaa* 80). The Messenger of Allah (peace be upon him) added that whoever disobeys the Messenger has disobeyed Allah. This verse needs no further amplification.

Imam al-Shaafi'ee perceptibly noted,

In whatever form it may take, God made it clear that He imposed the duty of obedience to His Apostle, and has given none of mankind an excuse to reject any order he knows to be the order of the Apostle of God. God has rather made men have a need for him in [all matters of] religion and He has given the proof for it by providing that the sunnah of the Apostle make clear the meanings of the duties laid down in His Book, so that it might be known that the sunnah—whether in the form specifying the meaning of God's commands as provided in the text of the Book which they can read or in the form of legislation in the absence of such a text—in either

---

[1] Ibn Katheer, p.236.

145

form represents God's command and is in [full] agreement with that of His Apostle; both are [equally] binding in all circumstances.[1]

Conclusion: The Roles of the Prophet (peace be upon him) Indicate the Indispensability of Following the Sunnah

In the previous chapter, verses of the Quran and hadith were presented that definitively establish the authority and importance of the sunnah of the Prophet (peace be upon him). In this chapter, once again, further evidence was presented to demonstrate the place of the sunnah. In discussing the roles of the Prophet (peace be upon him), one is, in reality, proving that the sunnah is indispensable to Islam and an authority in Islamic law. Indeed, there is no real Islam without the sunnah.

The Prophet (peace be upon him) explained the Quran. Without his explanation and implementation of the Quran, there would be no way for anyone to know exactly and correctly how the Quran is to be applied. In other words, Allah revealed the Quran but He revealed it in such a way that it cannot be divorced from the sunnah of the Prophet (peace be upon him). Any claims or attempts to do so are nothing but folly.

It was also proven through the Quran and hadith that the Prophet (peace be upon him) was an "independent source of law." Muslims are obliged to obey him (peace be upon him) in the same manner that they are obliged to obey the Quran—because both his words and the Quran have their source with Allah and it is actually Allah that one is worshipping. Hence, if one is truly seeking to worship Allah properly, he must follow

---

[1] Al-Shaafi'ee, pp. 121-2.

and obey whatever comes from the Prophet (peace be upon him), regardless of that law or aspect having any source in the Quran or not.

The Prophet (peace be upon him) was also the perfect example. He was following the straight path and it is incumbent upon all who wish to know and follow that path to look to his example. There is no way of life better than his. If a Muslim emulates the Prophet (peace be upon him) in the proper manner, he can be certain that he is behaving in a way that is pleasing to Allah.

Finally, obedience to the Prophet (peace be upon him) is a type of trial for mankind. One may read the Quran and find it beautiful and wonderful but the question is if he is really willing to put it into concrete form in the proper way, in the way demonstrated by the Prophet (peace be upon him). Similarly, one may study the Prophet's life and be fully impressed by his character and struggle but, again, is he willing to submit to what the Prophet (peace be upon him) has commanded. Without a willingness to submit, the other aspects are worthless. If one is not willing to submit, he is demonstrating to Allah that he is failing when it comes to this trial that Allah has, in His wisdom and knowledge, laid down for mankind.

Chapter Four:
The Authority of the Sunnah vis-a-vis the Quran

Now that the authority of the sunnah has been established without any doubt, via numerous verses of the Quran and hadith, the next question is what place or rank does that sunnah have. In particular, what place has it with respect to the Quran? Does it come second to the Quran with respect to authority or it is equivalent to the Quran in authority? Finally, the significance and ramifications of this question need to be addressed.

On this question, there are three opinions among the scholar. Each opinion shall be discussed separately with a conclusion afterwards.

The First Opinion: The Quran Takes Precedence Over the Sunnah

A well-known opinion is that the Quran takes precedence to the sunnah or, in other words, the sunnah is relegated to a secondary position vis-a-vis the Quran. One of the leading proponents of this opinion was the famous legal theorist al-Shaatibi.[1] Al-Salafi also favors this position as he states clearly,

---

[1] He presents his case in al-Shaatibi, *Al-Muwaafaqaat*, vol. 4, pp. 294-313. Al-Tartoori also ascribes this opinion to al-Shaafi'ee. However, he ascribes this opinion to al-Shafi'ee due to the fact that al-Shaafi'ee says it is not permissible for the sunnah to abrogate the Quran. [See Husain al-Tartoori, *"Mabaahith al-Sunnah ind al-Usooliyeen,"* *Majallat al-Buhooth al-Islaamiyyah* (No. 20, Dhul-Qaadah/Dhul-Hijjah 1407 A.H./Muharram/Safar 1408 A.H.), p. 241.] However, in

149

There is no doubt that the sunnah is in second ranking to the Quran from the point of view of using it as an authority and returning to it to derive shareeah rulings. The *mujtahid*[1] does not turn to the sunnah to research an issue unless he does not find in the Quran a ruling for that case...[2]

The most important proofs for this position are the following:

(1) The Quran is a miracle, a challenge to all of mankind to produce anything similar to it. Such is not the case with the sunnah. This, in itself, demonstrates the superiority of the Quran, which implies that it is to be given a position above and beyond that of the sunnah.

(2) All of the Quran is *mutawaatir* (متواتر) or *qati'ee al-thaboot* (قطعــــــي الثبـــــوت) definitively confirmed or authenticated).[3] *Mutawaatir*, again, means that the Quran has been transmitted in such a way and by so many people that there is no possibility of them all having made the same mistakes or agreed upon some fabrications. *Qati'ee al-thaboot* means that it is definitively confirmed as authentic. This flows from the fact that it is *mutawaatir*. On the other hand, only a

---

doing so, he has misunderstood al-Shaafi'ee's reasoning. This is demonstrated by the fact that al-Shafi'ee also does not allow the Quran to abrogate the sunnah. Based on al-Tartoori's conclusion, this would mean that al-Shafi'ee also says that the sunnah takes precedence over the Quran. In reality, in al-Shaafi'ee's thought, the non-permissibility of one abrogating the other has nothing to do with the question of which source takes precedence. As shall be noted, it seems that al-Shaafi'ee's actual position is that the Quran and sunnah are equal in status; in fact, they are inseparable from one another.

[1] A *mujtahid* is the one who makes *ijtihaad*, meaning that he uses his efforts and ability to determine a new ruling.

[2] Al-Salafi, p. 93.

[3] The opposite of *qati'ee al-thaboot* is *dhanni al-thaboot* (ظني الثبوت), meaning that something is confirmed in a conjectural or less than definitive manner.

small portion of hadith are considered *mutawaatir*. Hence, the Quran must be given preference based on this fact.[1]

(3) The recitation of the Quran is, in itself, considered an act of worship that entails a special reward. This fact is based on the Prophet's statement,

مَنْ قَرَأَ حَرْفًا مِنْ كِتَابِ اللَّهِ فَلَهُ بِهِ حَسَنَةٌ وَالْحَسَنَةُ بِعَشْرِ أَمْثَالِهَا لا أَقُولُ الم حَرْفٌ وَلَكِنْ أَلِفٌ حَرْفٌ وَلامٌ حَرْفٌ وَمِيمٌ حَرْفٌ

"Whoever reads a *harf* [word or letter] of the Book of Allah shall have a good deed [recorded for him] and every good deed receives a tenfold [reward]. I do not say that *Alif Laam Meem* is a *harf* but *alif* is a *harf*, *laam* is a *harf* and *meem* is a *harf*."[2]

(4) The following hadith is very important evidence from the sunnah itself that the Quran takes precedence over the sunnah:

عَنْ أُنَاسٍ مِنْ أَهْلِ حِمْصَ مِنْ أَصْحَابِ مُعَاذِ بْنِ جَبَلٍ أَنَّ رَسُولَ اللَّهِ صَلَّى اللَّهم عَلَيْهِ وَسَلَّمَ لَمَّا أَرَادَ أَنْ يَبْعَثَ مُعَاذًا إِلَى الْيَمَنِ قَالَ كَيْفَ تَقْضِي إِذَا عَرَضَ لَكَ قَضَاءٌ قَالَ أَقْضِي بِكِتَابِ اللَّهِ قَالَ فَإِنْ لَمْ تَجِدْ فِي كِتَابِ اللَّهِ قَالَ فَبِسُنَّةِ رَسُولِ اللَّهِ صَلَّى اللَّهم عَلَيْهِ وَسَلَّمَ قَالَ فَإِنْ لَمْ تَجِدْ فِي سُنَّةِ رَسُولِ

---

[1] This is not the proper place to enter into a detailed discussion of this point. For the sake of argument, what is stated above will be considered true and acceptable.

[2] Recorded by al-Tirmidhi and others. According to al-Albaani, it is *sahih*. See al-Albaani, *Saheeh al-Jaami*, vol. 2, pp. 1103-1104.

اللَّهِ صَلَّى اللَّهم عَلَيْهِ وَسَلَّمَ وَلَا فِي كِتَابِ اللَّهِ قَالَ أَجْتَهِدُ

رَأْيِي وَلَا آلُو فَضَرَبَ رَسُولُ اللَّهِ صَلَّى اللَّهم عَلَيْهِ وَسَلَّمَ

صَدْرَهُ وَقَالَ الْحَمْدُ لِلَّهِ الَّذِي وَفَّقَ رَسُولَ رَسُولِ اللَّهِ لِمَا

يُرْضِي رَسُولَ اللَّهِ

On the authority of persons from Hims from among the Companions of Muaadh ibn Jabal: When the Messenger of Allah (peace be upon him) wanted to send Muaadh to Yemen, he said, "How will judge when you are presented with a matter to judge?" He replied, "I will judge by the Book of Allah." He [the Prophet (peace be upon him)] then said, "And if you do not find [it] in the Book of Allah?" He replied, "Then [I will judge] by the sunnah of the Messenger of Allah (peace be upon him)." He then said, "And if you do not find it in the sunnah of the Messenger of Allah (peace be upon him) or in the Book of Allah?" He replied, "I shall exert myself [to come up with] my opinion and I will not spare any means." The Messenger of Allah (peace be upon him) then struck his chest and said, "Praise be to Allah [for the fact that the] messenger of the Messenger of Allah is in accord with what pleases the Messenger of Allah."

(5) In addition to that hadith, there also the established practice of Abu Bakr, Umar and others showing that they would resort first to the Quran and then, only after not finding something relevant in the Quran, would turn to the sunnah of the Prophet (peace be upon him). In his famous letter to the judge Shuraih, Umar ibn al-Khattaab wrote, "If a matter comes to you that is in the Book of Allah, judge in accordance with what is in the Book of Allah. If something that is not in the Book of Allah comes to you, judge in accordance with what the Messenger of Allah (peace be upon

him) established..." Similar statements have been recorded on the authority of ibn Masood and ibn Abbaas.[1]

(6) The Quran is the thing that establishes the authority of the sunnah; therefore, the sunnah is its *far'* (فرع branch) and the *asal* (أصل root) takes precedence over the *far'*.

(7) What came from the Prophet (peace be upon him) may have been the result of his *ijtihaad* and may be subject to mistakes.[2] Hence, one cannot hold that to be equivalent to the Quran.

(8) The sunnah is either an explanation of the Quran or an addition to its ruling. If it is an explanation, it comes second to the thing that it is explaining. If the thing being explained is discarded, then the explanation is also discarded. But if the explanation is discarded, the thing being explained is not necessarily discarded. If the sunnah is an addition to what is found in the Quran, it is only turned to after a search of the Quran turns up nothing on that topic. Once again, this demonstrates that the Quran takes precedence to the sunnah.

Comments on the Proofs for the First Opinion

The above proofs can be criticized with the following points:

(1) The fact that the Quran is a miracle in and of itself is actually irrelevant to the present discussion. It being a miracle does not give it any more status in Islamic law. This is proven by the fact that if the Prophet (peace be upon him) were given a book which were not a miracle, it would have the same legal status as the Quran. Furthermore, there are many facets to the miraculous nature of the Quran. One of those aspects is the

---

[1] Quoted in al-Salafi, p. 94.

[2] There is a disagreement among the legal theorists as to whether or not the Prophet (peace be upon him) himself ever made *ijtihaad*. Without entering into detail on that question here and for the sake of argument, it will be accepted that the Prophet (peace be upon him) did in fact make *ijtihaad* and, since he was a human, he may have made mistakes in his *ijtihaad*.

law and teachings that it offers for all mankind until the Day of Judgment. But in that particular facet, it encompasses the sunnah and the sunnah, therefore, also has a miraculous aspect to it.

(2) Even if just for the sake of argument one wants to accept the premise of this proof (that the Quran is *mutawaatir* and definitively confirmed while the sunnah is not), it still is not sufficient to prove that the Quran takes precedence over the sunnah. This is because its historical confirmation or authenticity is only one aspect in its strength as a proof. Another aspect is how definitive the text is with respect to its indication or meaning. If a text is definitive and conclusive with respect to its legal indication, it is termed *qati'ee dalaalah* (قطعي الدلالة).[1]

The following example should make this point clearer: After mentioning the categories of women that a man is not allowed to marry, Allah then says,

$$\text{وَأُحِلَّ لَكُمْ مَا وَرَاءَ ذَلِكُمْ أَنْ تَبْتَغُوا بِأَمْوَالِكُمْ مُحْصِنِينَ غَيْرَ}$$
$$\text{مُسَافِحِينَ}$$

"Except for these, all others are lawful, provided you seek (them in marriage) with gifts from your property, desiring chastity, not lust" (*al-Nisaa* 24). Verse 23, just preceding this statement, specifically prohibits marriage to two sisters at one and the same time. However, the question of being married to a woman and her aunt is not specifically addressed. Indeed, it is covered in a general sense by the words, "Except for these, all others are lawful..." Hence it touches upon them in a *dhanni* or less than conclusive manner. These words, "Except for these, all others are lawful," are general and they are open to particularization. However, the Prophet (peace be upon him) said,

---

[1] The opposite of *qati'ee al-dalaalah* is *dhanni al-dalaalah* (ظني الدلالة), where something is indicated by the text but in less than a definitive manner.

لَا يُجْمَعُ بَيْنَ الْمَرْأَةِ وَعَمَّتِهَا وَلَا بَيْنَ الْمَرْأَةِ وَخَالَتِهَا

"A woman and her paternal aunt are not to be combined [in marriage], nor is a woman with her maternal aunt." (Recorded by al-Bukhari and Muslim.) This hadith, it could be argued, is not as definitive with respect to its authenticity as the verse in the Quran. However, with respect to the question of marrying both a woman and her aunt, it is conclusive with respect to its indication. Therefore, it takes precedence over the verse above, which is not conclusive with respect to this particular case. Hence, the claim that the Quran takes precedence in Islamic law over the sunnah because it is all *mutawaatir* and *qati'ee al-thaboot* is truly a bogus argument because it may have the advantage of being *qati'ee al-thaboot* but a hadith may take precedence over it because it is *qati'ee al-dalaalah* with respect to a particular issue.[1]

Furthermore, if one is talking about the essential nature of the Quran and sunnah, this argument is moot. If a Companion hears either a verse of the Quran or a hadith of the Prophet (peace be upon him) directly from the Prophet (peace be upon him) himself, then it would be definitively confirmed in his eyes. This implies that they must be equal in rank to that Companion. Certainly, al-Shaatibi, and those who also use this point as an argument, could not mean to imply that the Quran and sunnah were of equal status to the Companions but for later generations the Quran comes first and then the sunnah. Al-Shaatibi never makes this argument and, therefore, his claim that the Quran is superior because—that is, for one reason—all of it is *mutawaatir* falls apart.

---

[1] This line of reasoning would hold true for most scholars, except for those, like the Hanafis, who say that general statements (like the verse stated above) are also definitive with respect to their indicativeness. However, even they would accept the conclusion given above because they would say that the hadith quoted is a *nass* (a clear, definitive statement whose purport is to explain that particular issue) while the verse in question is not. Hence, once again, the hadith would take precedence even though it is not *mutawaatir*.

(3) The fact that the recitation of the Quran is an act of worship in itself has no bearing on this particular question of which takes precedence, the Quran or sunnah. Again, even if such reading were not an act of worship, one would still have to accept the Quran as an authority in Islamic law. Furthermore, seeking knowledge can also be an act of worship. Seeking knowledge would include studying hadith. Thus, it is acceptable for studying hadith to also be considered an act of worship. Hence, there is some equality between the two in this case.

(4) The hadith of Muaadh is a well-known and famous hadith. It was recorded by Abu Dawood al-Tayaalisi in his *Musnad*, Ahmad, Abu Dawood al-Sijistaani, al-Tirmidhi and others. One can find it quoted in a number of classic works on fiqh and Islamic legal theory. There have been some scholars of note who have accepted this hadith as *hasan* or *sahih*. Most notable among them are ibn Katheer and ibn al-Qayyim.

A detailed discussion of this hadith has been presented by the late scholar of hadith Muhammad Naasir al-Deen al-Albaani and by Mashhoor Hasan Salmaan.[1] They both consider this a weak hadith. The hadith has three defects. First, according to its strongest narratives, it is narrated by the companions of Muaadh ibn Jabal without them mentioning if that they heard it directly from Muaadh. Hence, the link between them and the Prophet (peace be upon him) is broken. Second, it is not specified in any of the narrations of this hadith who the companions of Muaadh are.[2] These are

---

[1] Muhammad Naasir al-Deen al-Albaani, *Silsilat al-Ahadeeth al-Dhaeefah wa al-Maudhooah* (Beirut: al-Maktab al-Islaami, 1399 A.H.), vol. 2, pp. 273-286; Mashoor Hasan Salmaan, footnotes to Ibraaheem al-Shaatibi, *Al-Muwaafaqaat* (Al-Khobar, Saudi Arabia: Daar ibn Affaan, 1997), vol. 4, pp. 298-306.

[2] Ibn al-Qayyim (*Ilaam*, vol. 1, p. 234, also quoted in al-Albaani, Ibid., vol. 2, p. 276; Salmaan, vol. 4, p. 303) has answered this criticism by saying that this is not a damaging defect. He says that the way it is narrated indicates how well-known the hadith was. He further argues that the companions of Muaadh were known for their knowledge, piety and honesty. Therefore, this is not a defect at all. Al-Albaani (Ibid., vol. 2, p. 276) and Salmaan (vol. 4, p. 303) are impressed by that

unknown narrators and unknown narrators are not acceptable. Third, one of the narrators who appears in the chain, al-Haarith ibn Amr, is also unknown. After discussing the hadith for many pages, both al-Albaani and Salmaan conclude that all of the different chains do not overcome these weaknesses. Hence, the hadith is considered weak. Al-Albaani further notes that all of the following scholars also considered this hadith weak: al-Bukhari, al-Tirmidhi, al-Uqaili, al-Daaraqutni, ibn Hazm, ibn Taahir, ibn al-Jauzi, al-Dhahabi, al-Subki and ibn Hajr. The arguments that al-Albaani and Salmaan present are strong and it must be concluded that this hadith is weak. Therefore, it cannot be used as evidence that the Quran takes precedence over the sunnah of the Prophet (peace be upon him) as an authority in Islamic law or beliefs.

(5) The established practice and statements of Abu Bakr, Umar and others give the impression that they first turned to the Quran and then, only after not finding something relevant in the Quran, would turn to the sunnah of the Prophet (peace be upon him). This proof is a stronger proof than the previous one. However, it must be admitted that there are numerous reports from these same noted personalities demonstrating that as soon as they would hear something from the sunnah, they would follow it. It is not recorded from any of them, for example, that they were of the opinion that it is allowed to be married to a woman and her aunt at the same time simply because the Quran does not prohibited that. In

---

response. Al-Albaani, for example, wrote, "That response is sound if the defect were limited only to that defect." Personally, this author does not find ibn al-Qayyim's argument very convincing. In particular, if that argument is taken to its logical conclusion, one could say that the Followers, for example, were known for their piety and knowledge and, therefore, if the name of the Follower is missing from a chain, it is not a damaging defect. In other words, just because the companions of Muaadh as a whole were known for their piety and knowledge, it does not mean that all of them were pious and knowledgeable; it also does not mean that they were all proficient and acceptable as narrators. Until the actual narrator is identified, one cannot make the assumption that he is an acceptable narrator.

fact, the Quran states, "Except for these, all else are permissible for you" (*al-Nisaa* 24), as noted above. None of the Companions applied the apparent conclusion from that verse. Of even greater importance is the fact that they would apply the sunnah in cases where the sunnah abrogates or restricts the application of the Quran. If they were not applying the two together, as one integrated unit, they would have stopped at the verse of the Quran and ignored the abrogating or restricting sunnah—which is the impression that these reports give. For example[1], Allah says in the Quran,

كُتِبَ عَلَيْكُمْ إِذَا حَضَرَ أَحَدَكُمُ الْمَوْتُ إِنْ تَرَكَ خَيْرًا الْوَصِيَّةُ
لِلْوَالِدَيْنِ وَالأَقْرَبِينَ بِالْمَعْرُوف حَقًّا عَلَى الْمُتَّقِينَ

"It is prescribed, when death approaches any of you, if he leave any goods, that he make a bequest to parents and next of kin, according to reasonable usage; this is due from the God-fearing" (*al-Baqarah* 180). This verse is considered abrogated by the statement of the Prophet (peace be upon him),

فَلا وَصِيَّةَ لِوَارِثٍ

---

[1] Earlier the example of the punishment for the fornicator was given, wherein the Prophet's statement abrogated or explained the abrogation of the relevant verse of the Quran. A second, admittedly more controversial, example is given in this section. In fact, the question of whether a sunnah can abrogate the Quran is a debated question among the scholars. The Shafi'ees and Hanbalis do not allow the sunnah to abrogate the Quran. They interpret all of the examples of the proponents of such abrogation to be, in reality, cases of particularization or restriction of an unrestricted rule rather than abrogation. The Hanafis consider particularization, adding of new rules to what is stated in the Quran and other topics to be types of abrogation. Hence, they allow only certain hadith (*mutawaatir* and *mustafeedh*) to abrogate the Quran. The Shafi'ees, as a whole, say that these are not types of abrogation but they are simply further explanations or clarifications as to the original intent of the verses. A number of cases of the sunnah possibly abrogating the Quran and replies to such possibilities are given in al-Tartoori, pp. 241-245.

"There is no bequeathing to a rightful heir."[1] After this statement of the Prophet (peace be upon him), it was no longer permissible to make a bequest for one's parents, which is the command that is mentioned in the verse above. The Companions understood this concept and did not stop at the verse, as some of their statements would lead one to believe, but they applied the hadith of the Prophet (peace be upon him) even though the Quran had touched upon that subject.

Hence, it seems that the overall situation has to be taken into consideration when evaluating their statements. It was known and already established at that time that the Quran is explained by the sunnah. As Kamali writes, "Furthermore, according to the majority opinion, before implementing a Quranic rule one must resort to the sunnah and ascertain that the ruling in question has not been qualified in any way or given an interpretation on which the text of the Quran is not self-evident."[2] What Kamali described was the way of the Companions themselves. Hence, quoting particular statements of the Companions to show that the Quran took precedence to the sunnah in their eyes is, in reality, simply distorting what they meant by such statements.

(6) The sixth proof mentioned above is that the Quran is the thing that establishes the authority of the sunnah; therefore, the sunnah is its *far'* (فرع branch) and the *asal* (أصل root) takes precedence over the *far'*. This logical argument is very faulty on a number of counts. First, one knows what is or is not part of the Quran by the testimony of the Prophet (peace be upon him). In other words, it was only the Prophet's statements, "This is part of the Quran and forms part of such and such *soorah*," that establishes the Quran in the first place. Hence, it is the sunnah (the Prophet's words) that states what is the Quran. Therefore, if one wants to make such an argument,

---

[1] Recorded by al-Tirmidhi and others. According to al-Albaani, it is *sahih*. See al-Albaani, *Saheeh al-Jaami*, vol. 2, p. 1256.
[2] Mohammad Hashim Kamali, *Principles of Islamic Jurisprudence* (Selangor, Malaysia: Pelanduk Publications, 1989), p. 76.

one should say that the sunnah should be considered the root and not the branch. Second, there is nothing in the Quranic verses that imply that the sunnah comes second in authority to the Quran. As noted earlier, one does not find a verse ordering obedience to Allah except that it will order obedience to the Prophet (peace be upon him) while, on the other hand, one can find a verse ordering obedience to the Prophet (peace be upon him) without any mention of obedience to Allah. Third, as Abdul Khaaliq points out, pointing this argument on its head, the sunnah also points to the necessity of following the Quran. This does not mean that the sunnah is the root and that the Quran, again, must be considered the branch.[1] In conclusion, this argument is irrelevant or meaningless.

(7) The seventh proof was that what came from the Prophet's (peace be upon him) sunnah may have been the result of his *ijtihaad* and may be subject to mistakes. This is a straw hat argument. If the Prophet (peace be upon him) ever made a mistake, Allah would not allow him to continue in that mistake and propagate it to others; instead, the Prophet (peace be upon him) would be immediately corrected by Allah. Hence, his sunnah would not be his mistaken *ijtihaad* but the act corrected made by Allah. That is defined as his sunnah and, therefore, there is no fear of any mistake occurring therein.

(8) The eighth argument is related to the fact that the sunnah is the explanation of the Quran. This may very well be an argument against the superiority of the Quran. In general, an explanation and clarification of something is in less need of the original, explained text than vice-versa.

---

[1] Cf., Abdul Khaaliq, pp. 486-487.

The Second Opinion: The Quran and Sunnah Are Equal in Authority

The second opinion is that the Quran and sunnah are equal in authority and are to be taken together as the sources of the Shareeah. This was the clear opinion of ibn Hazm.[1] It is the view that Abdul Ghaani Abdul Khaaliq solidly supports in his dissertation *Hujjiyah al-Sunnah*. He begins by noting,

> There is no dispute that the book is distinguished from the sunnah and superior to it because its wording is a revelation from Allah, its recitation is a type of worship and mankind is not able to produce anything like it. In these aspects, the sunnah is inferior to it. But those aspects do not require superiority between them from the point of view of *hujjah* [authority, proof], such that one only acts by the Quran in the face of any apparent contradiction between the two. That is so because the authority of the Quran is actually due to it being a revelation from Allah and not due to any of the aforementioned aspects. If the Book were not a miracle nor were its recitation a type of worship and the Messengership was confirmed by other miracles, it would still be necessary to say that the Quran is a *hujjah*, as was the same case with the earlier books. But the sunnah is equivalent to the Quran in this respect, as it is also a type of revelation. Therefore, one must say that the sunnah does not come after the Quran in authority.[2]

Yusuf argues that this is definitely the view of al-Shafi'ee,

---

[1] Al-Tartoori (p. 240) also attributes this opinion to the Hanafis and Malikis. However, the reason that he makes that attribution is because they allow the abrogation of the Quran by certain hadith (*mutawaatir* hadith). Allah knows best if this implies that they consider the two to be of equal strength.

[2] Abdul Khaaliq, p. 485.

Al-Shafi'ee insisted on taking the Quran and the Sunnah together and at par so as to eliminate the very prospect of having the one set against the other. Most significant is his denial that the Quran constitutes the test of the veracity of the Sunnah. If it were so, then it would be quite easy to brush aside a good deal of the Sunnah. Al-Shafi'ee countered by asserting and working out the unquestionable basic theory that there could not possibly be any inherent contradiction or discrepancy between the Quran and the Sunnah, both owing their origin to the same divine source. This theory was best formulated by him in the famous dictum: The Quran can be repealed only by the Quran and the Sunnah can be repealed only by another Sunnah. The net result is the integration of "the Kitab and the Sunnah"...[1]

The proofs for this position are the following:

(1) The obligation to obey a messenger is independent of whether he has received a book or not. Allah says,

$$وَمَا أَرْسَلْنَا مِنْ رَسُولٍ إِلاَّ لِيُطَاعَ بِإِذْنِ اللَّهِ$$

"We never sent any messenger except for him to be obeyed, by Allah's leave" (al-Nisaa 64). If this is the case, then whatever the Prophet (peace be upon him) said must be followed and obeyed, regardless of whether it be from a book or not. The basis of his authority is that he is a messenger of Allah and not that he has a book.[2]

(2) The real basis for the authority of the Quran is the fact that it is a revelation from Allah. All of the other points mentioned (such as the fact that it is all *mutawaatir*, it is a miracle, reading it is an act of worship) are, as noted earlier, completely irrelevant to the question of authority. Furthermore, it has been proven through verses of the Quran

---

[1] Yusuf, p. 19.
[2] Abdul Khaaliq, pp. 486-487.

itself that the sunnah is also a revelation from Allah. Hence, those who say that the Quran takes precedence over the sunnah are really saying, "This revelation [the Quran] from Allah to the Prophet Muhammad (peace be upon him) takes precedence over that revelation [the sunnah] from Allah to the Prophet Muhammad (peace be upon him)." Since they are both revelations from Allah, this claim is unfounded.

(3) The verses of the Quran command an unrestricted obedience to the Prophet (peace be upon him). Furthermore, in reference to obedience to Allah and the Prophet (peace be upon him), the conjunction و ("and") is always used while the conjunction ثم ("then") is never used. This notable aspect of all of these verses implies that the obedience to the Book of Allah and obedience to the sunnah of the Prophet (peace be upon him) must have the same authority in Islamic law.

The very purpose for life is to worship and obey Allah. But Allah says,

$$ \text{مَنْ يُطِعْ الرَّسُولَ فَقَدْ أَطَا عَ اللَّه} $$

"Whoever obeys the Messenger verily obeys Allah." (*al-Nisaa* 80). The book of Allah is followed as an act of worship of Allah. The Messenger (peace be upon him) is followed as an act of worship of Allah. Whatever comes from the Prophet (peace be upon him) is followed and obeyed because such obedience constitutes an act of worship—not of the Prophet (peace be upon him) but of Allah Himself. Hence, what the Prophet (peace be upon him) conveys of revelation from Allah—be it in the form of the Book or in the form of the sunnah—is to be obeyed unquestionably as a worship of Allah. There is no room for distinguishing between the two types of revelation that have come via the Prophet (peace be upon him).

The Third Opinion: The Sunnah Takes Precedence to the Quran

The third opinion on this issue is that the sunnah takes precedence over the Quran. The basis for this opinion is that the Quran is in need of the sunnah to explain it and demonstrate how it is to be applied. However, without the Quran, one could still apply the sunnah which encompasses the teachings of the Quran. Al-Auzaa'ee is quoted to have said, "The Book [the Quran] is in more need of the sunnah than the sunnah is of the Book."[1] The same statement has been narrated from Makhool. Yahya ibn Katheer even said, "The sunnah judges the Quran but the Quran does not judge the sunnah."[2] In other words, the sunnah shows how the Quran is to be applied. If the sunnah shows that a certain verse does not apply to a particular issue, even though its apparent meaning would imply that it does, then the ruling of the sunnah takes precedence over the apparent meaning of the verse. This is, in essence, showing that the sunnah takes precedence over the Quran.

Another argument used to support this opinion is that one only knows what the Quran is based on a statement of the Prophet (peace be upon him). If the Prophet (peace be upon him) said, "This is from the Quran," it is considered from the Quran. If the Prophet (peace be upon him) said, "Allah has said...," like what is found in *hadith qudsi*, yet he never said that it is from the Quran, then it is not considered part of the Quran. When viewed in this manner, it is clear that the sunnah—the Prophet's statement—is the entire basis for knowing what is the Quran. Hence, it takes precedence.

---

[1] This statement is recorded by ibn Abdul Barr in *Jaami Bayaan al-Ilm*. According to Abu al-Ashbaal al-Zuhairi, it is authentic. See Abu al-Ashbaal al-Zuhairi, footnotes to Yoosuf ibn Abdul Barr, *Jaami Bayaan al-Ilm wa Fadhlihi* (Al-Damaam, Saudi Arabia: Daar ibn al-Jauzi, 1996), vol. 2, pp. 1193-1194.

[2] The quotes from Makhool and Yahya ibn Katheer may be found in ibn Abdul Barr, *Jaami*, vol. 2, p. 1194. Al-Zuhairi did not comment on their authenticity.

Probably this opinion has more evidence for it than the first opinion. However, most scholars would hesitate to go this far. For example, Ahmad ibn Hanbal said about the statement that the sunnah is a judge over the Quran, "I would not be so bold as to venture that far. But I would say that the sunnah explains and clarifies [the Quran]."[1]

Conclusions on The Authority of the Sunnah vis-a-vis the Quran

After reviewing the three opinions concerning the authority of the sunnah vis-a-vis the Quran, the following conclusions seem apparent:

(1) The proponents of the view that the Quran takes precedence over the sunnah seemed to have built a strong case for their opinion. However, upon closer inspection, none of their "proofs" withstand the objections to them. In the end, it seems that they have no real evidence for their opinion.

(2) The proponents of the view that the Quran and sunnah are to be taken as one united, equal partnership definitely have the strongest of all the arguments. Indeed, the main point is that both the Quran and the sunnah are revelations from Allah and they are submitted to and followed for that reason. The burden of proof falls upon the one who claims that one of these two types of revelations takes precedence over the other. Although some have tried to prove that, their proofs, as noted above, are faulty.

(3) The third view is that the sunnah takes precedence over the Quran. Again, the same major criticism can be directed at this argument: One must have strong proof to say that one of these two types of revelation takes precedence over the other. No such proof seems to be available. Instead, this

---

[1] Quoted in ibn Abdul Barr, *Jaami*, vol. 2, p. 1194. Al-Zuhairi did not comment on its authenticity.

third view simply emphasizes, once again, to take the Quran and sunnah as two entities which are indispensably linked to one another; a person cannot follow one of them correctly without following the other.

The clear conclusion from the above is that the Quran and sunnah are equal in status when it comes to being authorities in Islamic law. Fortunately, this difference of opinion among the scholars did not have much effect in their fiqh opinions. In other words, once again, among the scholars the difference is mostly one of semantics only—with the possible exception of allowing the sunnah to abrogate the Quran, a question which al-Shafi'ee views from a completely different perspective.

This conclusion is in no way meant to downplay the importance of the Quran but it is a matter of understanding and applying the Quran correctly. Someone once said to al-Mutraf ibn Abdullah ibn al-Sukhair, "Do not talk to us except with the Quran." He replied, "By Allah, we do not want any substitute for the Quran but we want the one [meaning the Messenger of Allah (peace be upon him)] who is more knowledgeable of the Quran than us."[1]

The Importance of This Realization

Allah repeatedly says in the Quran that one must obey Allah and obey the Messenger. The two go hand in hand. The obedience to the Messenger (peace be upon him), as Allah states in another verse, is indeed obedience to Allah. Hence, there is no room for a person to think about the Quran and sunnah as, "the Quran first and then the sunnah."

In reality, there is no contradiction between the Quran and sunnah since they are both revelations from Allah. The

---

[1] Quoted in ibn Abdul Barr, *Jaami*. According to al-Zuhairi, its chain is *sahib*. See al-Zuhairi, vol. 2, p. 1193.

two go together. Both are indispensable. The *shareeah* is made up of two sources, as the Prophet (peace be upon him) himself reminded all Muslims:

$$تَرَكْتُ فِيكُمْ أَمْرَيْنِ لَنْ تَضِلُّوا مَا تَمَسَّكْتُمْ بِهِمَا كِتَابَ اللَّهِ وَسُنَّةَ نَبِيِّهِ$$

"I have left among you two matters that if you adhere to them you will never be misguided: the Book of Allah and the sunnah of His prophet."[1]

Again, it is true that this issue of which takes precedence, the Quran or the sunnah, may be one of semantics only, as al-Salafi has concluded, since all the scholars involved agreed that the sunnah may particularize a verse in the Quran, restrict its application and so forth.[2] Therefore, the dispute definitely has no real effect when it comes to how the scholars deal with both the Quran and sunnah. However, it may have some influence on others who have this perception that first comes the Quran and then the sunnah. This may lead them to emphasize the study of the Quran while not giving the sunnah its appropriate amount of study and devotion. This may cause them, even if very subtly, to downplay the role of the sunnah and to downplay the importance of the hadith they hear. Hence, this misunderstanding must be removed. When it is realized that the two are of equal status because they are both revelations from Allah, it should then be realized that they are both deserving of intense and regular study.

Furthermore, the idea that the Quran comes first and then the sunnah has been used by some writers in ways that are very misleading. Abdul Khaaliq notes that some authors state their agreement with al-Shaatibi's view, that the sunnah comes second to the Quran in authority, but their goal or conclusion

---

[1] Recorded by Maalik, al-Haakim and al-Baihaqi. It is *sahih*.

[2] Al-Salafi, p. 95.

from that stance is unacceptable. They use this argument as a smokescreen to conclude that those sunnah that are explaining the Quran are, in reality, contradicting the apparent meaning of the Quran. Since the sunnah is second to the Quran, such sunnah are then to be rejected and one only follows the apparent meaning of the Quran.[1] Once it is established that the sunnah is on an equal footing with the Quran, the door to such fallacious arguments should be closed forever.

Another important conclusion that is established upon concluding that the sunnah is of equal authority to the Quran is that it is not necessary for a belief or act to be specifically mentioned in the Quran for it to have validity. This conclusion was mentioned earlier while discussing the Prophet (peace be upon him) as an "independent source of legislation." However, it is good to spell it out again because it can be a sticky point concerning which some are confused and others are misled.

Conclusions

There is no question that both the Quran and the sunnah have as their source Allah. They are both inspirations from Allah and, therefore, they both must be submitted to on an equal basis. In legal authority and purpose, there is no difference between the one revelation that is recited as part of the Book and that revelation which is not recited as part of the Book: Together they constitute the guidance for mankind.

---

[1] Abdul Khaaliq refers to Abdul Azeez al-Khauli in a work entitled *Miftaah al-Sunnah* and the authors of a work entitled *Mudhakirah Tareekh al-Tashree al-Islaami*. Abdul Khaaliq, p. 489, fn. 4.

Chapter Five:
Allah's Preservation of the Sunnah

Proofs that Allah preserved the sunnah are both textual (Ar., *naqli*) and logical (Ar., *aqli*). The textual argument is based on the verse,

$$\text{إِنَّا نَحْنُ نَزَّلْنَا الذِّكْرَ وَإِنَّا لَهُ لَحَافِظُونَ}$$

"We reveal the reminder (Ar., *al-dhikr*) and We, verily, are its guardians" (*al-Hijr* 9).[1] The word *al-dhikr* and its derivatives have numerous meanings in the Quran.[2] It is sometimes used for the Quran, as in,

$$\text{وَهَذَا ذِكْرٌ مُبَارَكٌ أَنزَلْنَاهُ}$$

"This is a blessed Reminder that We have revealed" (*al-Anbiyaa* 50); and it is sometimes used for the sunnah, as in,

$$\text{وَأَنزَلْنَا إِلَيْكَ الذِّكْرَ لِتُبَيِّنَ لِلنَّاسِ مَا نُزِّلَ إِلَيْهِمْ وَلَعَلَّهُمْ يَتَفَكَّرُونَ}$$

---

[1] Perhaps no translation can even come close to doing justice to this verse. This verse is filled with literary tools of stress and emphasis. The first word is a word implying emphasis. The second word of the verse, نحن, also implies emphasis as a repetition of the connected pronoun. The verb نزّلنا also implies emphasis because the verb form فعّل implies stress. The repeating of the word إنّا is also done for emphasis. Putting the word له before the verb is also done as a form or mode of emphasis. Finally, the letter ل in the word لحافظون is a letter inserted for the purpose of emphasis. It could be translated something like, "Of a surety, We certainly reveal the *dhikr*, and We certainly are its definite guardians." When one finishes reading the verse, he is absolutely certain that Allah has revealed the *dhikr*, Allah has the ability to preserve the *dhikr* and that Allah is definitely going to preserve the *dhikr*. Cf., Ahmad Uqailaan, *Min Lataaif al-Tafseer* (Al-Mansoorah, Egypt: Daar al-Yaqeen, 1998), vol. 1, p. 7.

[2] See Majud al-Deen al-Fairoozabaadi, *Basaair Dhuwi al-Tamyeez* (Beirut: al-Maktabah al-Ilmiyyah, n.d.), vol. 3, pp. 9-17.

"We have revealed to you the Reminder that you may explain to mankind that which has been revealed for them" (*al-Nahl* 44). In addition, the word *dhikr* may be used to be in reference to Allah's religion (*deen*) and law as a whole. This is its purport in the verse,

$$\text{فَاسْأَلُوا أَهْلَ الذِّكْرِ إِنْ كُنْتُمْ لَا تَعْلَمُونَ}$$

"So ask of those who know the revelation (*al-dhikr*), if you know not" (*al-Nahl* 43). The word *dhikr* here means Allah's religion, or everything that Allah has revealed as guidance for mankind.

Therefore, *a priori*, it cannot be stated that *al-dhikr* in,

$$\text{إِنَّا نَحْنُ نَزَّلْنَا الذِّكْرَ وَإِنَّا لَهُ لَحَافِظُونَ}$$

"We reveal the Reminder and We, verily are its Guardian," is referring only to the Quran. In fact, it will be argued, in this verse *al-dhikr* is either referring to both the Quran and the sunnah or only the sunnah; it is not possible that it is referring to the Quran only. This is true because it is inconceivable that only the wording of the Quran would be preserved. Preserving the Quran must imply preserving both its wording and meaning. But, as was shown earlier, the meaning of the Quran is captured in the sunnah of the Prophet (peace be upon him); that is, its meaning cannot be had without the sunnah. Therefore, in this verse wherein Allah promises to preserve the *dhikr*, it is possible that He is speaking about both the Quran and the sunnah or just the sunnah by itself.[1] The important point for the discussion here is that the sunnah is definitively included in what Allah has promised to preserve.

In fact, the strongest view is that *dhikr* in, "We reveal the reminder (Ar., *al-dhikr*) and We, verily, are its guardians" (*al-Hijr* 9), is referring to Allah's promise to preserve both the Quran and sunnah. On this point, ibn Hazm noted,

---

[1] There are many other verses that state that the Quran cannot be tampered with. Therefore, there is no compelling argument for this verse (*al-Hijr* 15) to be applied to the Quran.

170

There is no difference of opinion from anyone among the specialists in language or of the *shareeah* that all of what Allah revealed is [referred to as] the sent-down *dhikr*. And all of the inspiration is preserved with certainty by its preservation by Allah. Anything that Allah preserves with His preservation will not have anything lost from it. Nor will anything ever be distorted of it except that there will appear clear proof showing the falsehood [of that distortion].[1]

Furthermore, if someone claims that the word *dhikr* in *al-Hijr* 9 is referring to only the Quran, then the burden of proof is upon him to support that claim. This is because such an interpretation restricts the general purport of the word *dhikr*. However, one cannot restrict the meaning of the word without any sound proof. In this case, there is no sound proof presented to restrict the term but, on the contrary, as shown above, the word *dhikr* must be understood to be inclusive of both the Quran and the sunnah, the two forms of revelation or *dhikr* that the Prophet Muhammad (peace be upon him) received.[2]

The logical argument runs as follows: According to Islamic belief, the Quran is Allah's final revelation and the Prophet Muhammad (peace be upon him) is Allah's final messenger. Allah orders Muslims to follow the sunnah of the Prophet (peace be upon him). If Allah did not preserve the sunnah, the true sunnah would have been lost and Allah would be ordering Muslims to follow something that they could not possibly follow. This would not be consistent with what is known of the mercy, wisdom and justice of Allah. Therefore, logically speaking, Allah must have preserved the sunnah.

These arguments do not mean that Allah did not use some earthly means to preserve the Quran and the sunnah. The manner in which Allah, through the Companions, preserved

---

[1] Ibn Hazm, vol. 1, p. 109.
[2] Cf., ibn Hazm, vol. 1, pp. 109-110.

the Quran is well-known and fairly clear.[1] However, the ways and means by which the sunnah was preserved are not that well-known. Hence, some of the means by which the sunnah was preserved will be discussed here.

Some of the Means by Which Allah Preserved the Sunnah

Allah, through humans, used many means by which He preserved the sunnah. Some of these aspects are unique to the Muslim nation. This is a great blessing and bounty from Allah for which every Muslim should be sincerely grateful— grateful to Allah and grateful to those individuals who sacrificed their time and wealth in order to preserve the teachings of the final Prophet (peace be upon him).

A detailed discussion of the different means used to preserve the hadith is beyond the scope of this work, as this chapter is not meant to be the main focus of this book.[2] However, a brief sketch of a number of those different means is indeed called for as one of the problems encountered while discussing the sunnah is that many people have a false conception of how the hadith were preserved.

Obviously, the means of preservation had to be followed from the earliest times in order to truly preserve the hadith of the Prophet (peace be upon him). Therefore, following aspects will be discussed briefly by tracing them back to the earliest years of the preservation of hadith:

---

[1] Cf., Ahmad von Denffer, *Ulum al-Quran: An Introduction to the Sciences of the Quran* (Leicester, England: The Islamic Foundation, 1983), pp. 31-56.

[2] Much of this chapter is excerpted from the author's three part series, "Recording, Traveling and *Isnad* of Hadith: From the Early Years (I-III)," *Al-Basheer* (Vol. 8, No. 3, Sept.-Oct. 1994; vol. 8, no. 4, Nov.-Dec. 1994; vol. 8, no. 5, Jan.-Feb. 1995). Many topics found in those articles have not been touched upon here, such as the Prophet's prohibition and subsequent permission for recording hadith and a detailed discussion of some of the early written works.

(1) First, there was the understanding of the Companions of their responsibility for conveying the hadith of the Prophet (peace be upon him). In addition, they must have understood that they must convey the words of the Prophet (peace be upon him) with the utmost accuracy.

(2) In the early years, there began the work of hadith criticism and criticism of the narrators. This developed into a science known as *al-jarh wa al-tadeel* (الجرح والتعديل).

(3) There was also the recording or writing down of the hadith of the Prophet (peace be upon him). Obviously, in general, one of the ways of preserving something is to record it. There have been many claims and misconceptions surrounding the recording of hadith. Hence, this topic deserves some attention here.

(4) A very important and unique aspect that worked to preserve the sunnah was the use of the *isnaad* (إسناد) or chain of narrators, tracing one's source all the way back to the Prophet (peace be upon him).

(5) Another unique phenomena the appeared and assisted in the preservation of the sunnah was the traveling in search of hadith, in order to check the sources and gather more hadith together.

Finally, another topic that shall be discussed briefly is the first occurrence of the fabrication of hadith.

There are yet other aspects in the preservation of hadith that "do not appear in the statistics," as they say in the world of sports. For example, one cannot look at the chains of hadith and see the great desire that the early Muslims had in learning, memorizing and gathering the hadith of the Prophet (peace be upon him). This great desire to learn the hadith of the Prophet (peace be upon him) has been demonstrated in many different ways. As noted, here there shall be a discussion of one of these channels: the journeying (and sacrificing of time and wealth) to learn and record the hadith of the Prophet (peace be upon him).

The Companions' Understanding of Their Heavy Responsibilities

The Prophet (peace be upon him) made the Companions understand that it was their responsibility to take what he said and to convey it to others. This instruction from the Prophet (peace be upon him) can be seen in a number of his statements, some of which have been narrated from numerous Companions. For example, the Prophet (peace be upon him) said,

نَضَّرَ اللَّهُ امْرَأً سَمِعَ مِنَّا حَدِيثًا فَحَفِظَهُ حَتَّى يُبَلِّغَهُ غَيْرَهُ فَرُبَّ حَامِلِ فِقْهٍ إِلَى مَنْ هُوَ أَفْقَهُ مِنْهُ

"May Allah make radiant the man who has heard what I said and has preserved it in his memory until he conveys it to another. Perhaps the one he conveyed it to has a better understanding than him."[1] This hadith has been narrated from numerous Companions. From this hadith, the Companions could understand that it was their responsibility to convey the sunnah—and to convey it exactly in the way that they heard it from the Prophet (peace be upon him).

Another hadith states,

---

[1] The particular wording quoted above is from al-Tirmidhi. Abdul Muhsin al-Abbaad has written a 263-page book entirely about this hadith. This hadith is, without question, a *mutawaatir* hadith. He concludes that twenty-four Companions narrated this hadith from the Prophet (peace be upon him). In addition, it has been recorded in more than forty-five books of hadith. One hundred and seventy-five different chains can be traced for this hadith. See Abdul Muhsin al-Abbaad, *Diraasat Hadeeth Nadhara Allahu imraan Sama Muqaalati...: Riwaayah wa Diraayah* (no publication information given), *passim*.

بَلِّغُوا عَنِّي وَلَوْ آيَةً وَحَدِّثُوا عَنْ بَنِي إِسْرَائِيلَ وَلَا حَرَجَ وَمَنْ
كَذَبَ عَلَيَّ مُتَعَمِّدًا فَلْيَتَبَوَّأْ مَقْعَدَهُ مِنَ النَّارِ

"Convey from me, even if it is just a verse. And narrate
[stories] from the Tribes of Israel and there is no harm. And
whoever falsely attributes something to my authority shall take
his own seat in the Hell-fire." (Recorded by al-Bukhari.) Here
again is the instruction from the Prophet (peace be upon him)
to convey his words. Along with that instruction is the stern
warning at the end of the hadith: "And whoever falsely
attributes something to my authority shall take his own seat in
the Hell-fire." It seems that the Prophet (peace be upon him)
stated that warning on a number of occasions, as those words
have been recorded from the Prophet (peace be upon him)
through over fifty Companions.[1]

The Companions understood from the Quran that they
had the obligation to convey the message. For example, during
Abu Hurairah's lifetime, he was known for transmitting more
hadith than others. Some even questioned why he was
transmitting more than some of the other Companions who
were closer to the Prophet (peace be upon him). Abu Hurairah
replied to these queries by saying, "The people are saying,
'Abu Hurairah narrates too much.' If it were not for two verses
in the Book of Allah, I would not have narrated a single
hadith." He then recited the following two verses,

إِنَّ الَّذِينَ يَكْتُمُونَ مَا أَنزَلَ اللَّهُ مِنْ الْكِتَابِ وَيَشْتَرُونَ بِهِ ثَمَنًا قَلِيلاً
أُوْلَئِكَ مَا يَأْكُلُونَ فِي بُطُونِهِمْ إِلاَّ النَّارَ وَلَا يُكَلِّمُهُمْ اللَّهُ يَوْمَ الْقِيَامَةِ
وَلَا يُزَكِّيهِمْ وَلَهُمْ عَذَابٌ أَلِيمٌ

---

[1] Cf., Sulaimaan al-Tabaraani, *Turuq Hadeeth Man Kadhaba Alayya Mutamadan* (Beirut: al-Maktab al-Islaami, 1990), *passim.*

"Those who conceal Allah's revelations of the Book, and purchase for them a miserable profit, they swallow into themselves naught but Fire; Allah will not address them on the Day of Resurrection, nor purify them. Grievous will be their penalty" (*al-Baqarah* 174).

إِنَّ الَّذِينَ يَكْتُمُونَ مَا أَنزَلْنَا مِنَ الْبَيِّنَاتِ وَالْهُدَى مِنْ بَعْدِ مَا بَيَّنَّاهُ

لِلنَّاسِ فِي الْكِتَابِ أُوْلَئِكَ يَلْعَنُهُمُ اللَّهُ وَيَلْعَنُهُمُ اللَّاعِنُونَ

"Those who conceal the clear (Signs) We have sent down, and the Guidance, after we have made it clear for the people in the Book, on them shall be Allah's curse, and the curse of those entitled to curse" (*al-Baqarah* 159). Abu Hurairah then continued by saying that the other Muslims were busy with their trading or their wealth while he spent his whole time with the Prophet (peace be upon him), being present while they were not present. (Recorded by al-Bukhari and Muslim.)

The Companions also realized that they had to be very careful in their narratives. They understood the warning stated above concerning one who falsely attributes something to the Prophet (peace be upon him) as applying to one who does so intentionally as well as unintentionally.[1] In a report recorded in *Sahih al-Bukhari*, the Companion al-Zubair was asked why he did not narrate as many hadith as some of the others did. He replied, "As for me, I never parted from him [that is, the Prophet (peace be upon him)]. However, I heard him say, 'Whoever falsely attributes something to my authority shall take his own seat in the Hell-fire.'" Commenting on this statement, ibn Hajr noted that al-Zubair is obviously not speaking about himself forging something in the Prophet's name. Instead, he feared that if he narrated a lot, he would make mistakes. And those mistakes would put him under the warning mentioned in that hadith.[2]

---

[1] The word *kadhaba* in the language of the people of Hijaz meant to say something which is false; it did not necessarily mean to lie.

[2] Ibn Hajr, *Fath*, vol. 1, p. 201.

Anas ibn Maalik also said, "If I did not fear that I may make a mistake, I would narrate to you some of the things that I heard from the Messenger of Allah (peace be upon him). However, I heard him say, 'Whoever falsely attributes something to my authority shall take his own seat in the Hell-fire.'"[1] This, once again, implies that Anas, a Companion, understood that the threat stated in that hadith also applies to the one who makes unintentional mistakes while narrating hadith.

In reality, some of the Companions, like Abu Hurairah, continued to study and memorize the hadith they learned from the Prophet (peace be upon him). Therefore, they did not have as much to fear with respect to making mistakes. On the other hand, those who were not dedicated to such study had more to fear because their memories may fail them when they narrated from the Messenger of Allah (peace be upon him).

The Recording or Writing Down of the Hadith

Before discussing this topic, it should be noted that, in order for something to be preserved, it is not a necessary condition that it be recorded or written down. That is, simply because something was not written down, it does not mean that it was not accurately and correctly preserved. Furthermore, the writing of something down itself is not sufficient for the preservation of something. It is possible that something is recorded incorrectly. Both of these points were duly noted by the scholars of hadith. They did not require hadith to be written down for them to be accepted although they did recognize the importance of such a physical recording and many times,

---

[1] This narration was recorded by al-Daarimi. According to Abdul Rahmaan al-Birr, its chain is *sahih*. Cf., Abdul Rahmaan al-Birr, *Manaahij wa Adaab al-Sahaabah fi al-Taallum wa al-Taleem* (Al-Mansoorah, Egypt: Daar al-Yaqeen, 1999), p. 183.

depending on the personality involved, preferred the written record over the verbal record. These scholars also realized that the mere recording of something is not sufficient. It must also be ascertained that it was recorded properly. Hence, scholars of hadith would accept or prefer written reports of scholars over memorized reports only if it was known that those scholars were proficient and correct in their writing.

It has been one of the favorite practices of many of the Orientalists to constantly state the "fact" that hadith were not recorded at first but were, instead, passed on only orally for the first two centuries after the Hijrah. Therefore, hadith are not much more than folklore and legend that was passed on orally and in a haphazard fashion for many years. Unfortunately, this is a misconception that is also held by a number of Muslims today. A recently converted Muslim may get the impression that the hadith are "no more reliable than the Gospels."[1]

There are, in many hadith, references to the secretaries of the Prophet (peace be upon him) who would record the Quran and any letters he may have dictated. Al-Kattaani concluded that the Prophet (peace be upon him) must have had at least fifty secretaries. Al-Azami has also done research in this area and has published his findings in a work entitled *Kutaab al-Nabi*, in which he traces over sixty scribes. In addition, ibn Hajr and ibn Saad recorded that Companions such as Abdullah ibn Saeed ibn al-As, Saad ibn al-Rabee, Basheer ibn Saad ibn Thalaba, Abaan ibn Saeed ibn al-As and others used to teach reading and writing inside the very mosque of the Prophet (peace be upon him). And, of course,

---

[1] This is a rather clever phrase used by some people who wish to attack hadith. Many converts have studied the Gospels and know how unreliable they are. Therefore, such a statement will quickly shake their faith in hadith. The recording of hadith is one topic that has been discussed in the English literature on hadith in great detail. The interested reader should consult Azami, *Studies in Early Hadith Literature, passim.*

this could not have been done without the Prophet's explicit approval or encouragement.[1]

The recording of the hadith of the Prophet (peace be upon him) began during the time of the Prophet (peace be upon him) himself. Al-Baghdaadi records a number of hadith that show that the Prophet (peace be upon him) explicitly allowed the recording of his hadith. Here are some examples:

1. Al-Daarimi and Abu Dawood in their *Sunan*s recorded that Abdullah ibn Amr ibn al-As stated that they used to record everything they heard from the Prophet (peace be upon him). They were warned against doing so as, it was argued, the Prophet (peace be upon him) was a human being who may be angry at times and pleased at times. Abdullah stopped writing his hadith until they could ask the Prophet (peace be upon him) about this issue. The Messenger of Allah (peace be upon him) told him,

اكْتُبْ فَوَالَّذِي نَفْسِي بِيَدِهِ مَا يَخْرُجُ مِنْهُ إلاَّ حَقٌّ

"Write [my hadith], by the One in whose hand is my soul, nothing leaves it [the Prophet's mouth] save the truth."[2] That is, whether he was angry or pleased what he spoke was always the truth.

2. Al-Bukhari, in his *Sahih*, recorded that Abu Hurairah said, "One can find none of the Companions of the Messenger of Allah relating more hadith than I, except Abdullah ibn Amr because he used to record the hadith while I did not do so."[3]

---

[1] Ibn Hajr, *Fath*, vol. 3, p. 531.
[2] According to al-Albaani, this hadith is *sahih*. See Muhammad Naasir al-Deen al-Albaani, *Saheeh Sunan Abi Dawood* (Riyadh: Maktah al-Tarbiyyah al-Arabi li-Duwal al-Khaleej, 1989), vol. 2, p. 695.
[3] Ibn Hajr, commenting on this hadith, explained how Abu Huraira could have narrated so many more hadith than Abdullah ibn Amr. See Ahmad ibn Hajr, *Fath al-Baari* (Riyadh: Riaasah Idaarah al-Buhooth al-Ilmiyyah wa al-Ifta, no date),

3. Al-Bukhari recorded that a person from Yemen came to the Prophet (peace be upon him) on the day of the Conquest of Makkah and asked him if he could get the Prophet's speech recorded and the Prophet approved and told someone, "Write it for the father of so and so."

4. Anas narrated the statement, "Secure knowledge by writing it." This hadith has been related by a number of authorities but mostly with weak chains. There is a dispute concerning whether or not it is actually a statement of the Prophet (peace be upon him) or of some Companion. However, according to al-Albani, the hadith, as recorded by al-Haakim and others, is authentic.[1]

Al-Azami writes, "The Prophet himself sent hundreds of letters. Many of these were very lengthy, containing formulas for prayers and worship."[2] These are, in reality, nothing more than hadith of the Prophet (peace be upon him).

There is no question, therefore, that the recording of hadith began during the lifetime of the Messenger of Allah (peace be upon him) himself. This practice of writing hadith continued after the death of the Messenger of Allah (peace be upon him). Al-Azami, in his work *Studies in Early Hadith Literature*, has listed and discussed some fifty Companions of the Prophet who had recorded hadith.[3] Note the following:

> Abd Allah B. Abbas (3 B.H.-68 A.H.)... He was so eager for knowledge that he would ask as many as 30 Companions about a single incident... It seems he wrote what he heard and sometimes even employed his slaves for this purpose... The following derived

---

vol. 1, pp. 206-8. One aspect that he neglected to mention is Abu Hurairah's dying some sixteen years after Abdullah ibn Amr.

[1] Al-Albani, *Saheeh al-Jaami al-Sagheer*, vol. 2, p. 816.

[2] Al-Azami, *Early Hadith*, p. 23. Muhammad ibn Tooloon al-Dimishqi (880-953 A.H.) compiled a number of such letters in a book: Muhammad ibn Tooloon al-Dimishqi, *Ilaam al-Saaileen an Kutub Sayyid al-Mursaleen* (Beirut: Muassasah al-Risaalah, 1987), *passim*.

[3] Al-Azami, *Early Hadith*, pp. 34-60.

hadith from him in written form: Ali b. Abdullah ibn Abbas, Amr b. Dinar, Al-Hakam b. Miqsam, Ibn Abu Mulaikah, Ikrimah... Kuraib, Mujahid, Najdah... Said b. Jubair.[1]

Abd Allah B. Umar B. al-Khattab (10 B.H.-74 A.H.). He transmitted a large number of *ahadith*, and was so strict in relating them that he did not allow the order of a word to be changed even though it would not have altered the meaning... He had books. One *Kitab* [book] which belonged to Umar, and was in his possession, was read to him by Nafi several times... The following derived hadith from him in written form: Jamil b. Zaid al-Tai... Nafi client of ibn Umar, Said b. Jubair, Abd al-Aziz b. Marwan, Abd al-Malik b. Marwan, Ubaid Allah b. Umar, Umar b. Ubaid Allah...[2]

Anas B. Malik (10 B.H.-93 A.H.)... He advised his sons to write *ahadith* of the Prophet and to learn them. He used to say, "We do not value the knowledge of those who have not written it down." Here knowledge means *ahadith* of the Prophet. His Books: Hubairah b. Abd al-Rahman says, "When Anas b. Malik imparted the *ahadith* many people gathered and he brought books and gave them to the people saying, 'I heard these *ahadith* from the Prophet, then I wrote them down and read them to him.'" The following derived *ahadith* from him in written form:... Abd Allah b. Dinar had a lengthy

---

[1] Azami, *Studies in Early Hadith*, pp. 40-42. In Azami's work, "b." stands for ibn or "son of."
[2] Azami, *Studies in Early Hadith*, pp. 45-46.

book from him... Ibrahim b. Hudbah had a
Nuskhah—book— from him...[1]

A fascinating example of a Companion is Abu
Hurairah. From his statement concerning Abdullah ibn Amr
ibn al-As it seems clear that he did not record hadith during the
time of the Prophet (peace be upon him) but from the
following narrations it is very clear that after the Prophet's
death he did record the hadith he knew or he had them
recorded. Amr ibn Umayya said, "I narrated a hadith in the
presence of Abu Hurairah and he rejected the hadith. I said, 'I
heard the hadith from you.' He said, 'If you had heard that
hadith from me you will find it recorded in my books.' He
took me by my hand to his house and I saw many books of the
Prophet's hadith and [in one of them] I found the hadith in
question."[2] Basheer ibn Naheek said, "I used to record what I
heard from Abu Hurairah. When I was to part from him, I
would take my book to him and read it to him and say, 'Is this
what I heard from you?' and he would say, 'Yes.'"[3] These
incidents prove that he had a written collection of his own
hadith and that he did not disapprove of others recording his
hadith.

Al-Azami also compiled a list, discussing each
personality individually, of forty-nine people of "the first
century successors" who recorded hadith.[4] One example from
that list is Abidah ibn Amr al-Salmaani who had many books
but out of fear that someone may make mistakes in dealing

---

[1] Azami, *Studies in Early Hadith*, p. 49.
[2] Quoted in Umar ibn Hasan Uthmaan al-Fullaatah, *al-Widha fi al-Hadeeth*
(Damascus: Maktabah al-Ghazzaali, 1981), vol. 2, p. 16. Some people reject this
narration because it seems to contradict the authentic report that Abu Hurairah
did not know how to read and write. However, ibn Hajr's explanation is plausible:
Ibn Hajr stated that these books must not have been written by Abu Hurairah
himself as it seems that he did not know how to write. However, they were
written on his behalf. (See *Fath al-Bari*, vol. 1, p. 207.)
[3] Fullaatah, vol. 2, p. 17.
[4] Al-Azami, *Early Hadith*, pp. 60-74.

with them, he willed for them to be burnt or erased.[1] Note here that his caution was not due to any Prophetic prohibition on recording hadith but only out of fear that people would make mistakes in narrating his hadith from his books.

Al-Azami goes on to list eighty-seven of "the scholars covering the late first and early second centuries" who recorded hadith.[2] Then he lists "from the early second century scholars" 251 people who collected and recorded hadith.[3] Thus al-Azami has produced a list of 437 scholars who had recorded hadith and all of them lived and died before the year 250 A. H. Many of them are from before the time of Umar ibn Abdul Azeez who is credited with having been the first person to ask for the collection of hadith. The story of Umar ibn Abdul Azeez has actually been misunderstood and it does not mean that no one collected hadith before him.[4]

To quote al-Azami, "Recent research has proved that almost all of the hadith of the Prophet was [*sic*] written down in the life of the companions, which stretched to the end of the first century."[5] This last statement is partially based on al-Azami's own research in which he has mentioned many Companions and Followers who possessed written hadith. Elsewhere, he himself writes,

> I have established in my doctoral thesis *Studies in Early Hadith Literature* that even in the first century of the Hijra many hundreds of booklets of hadith

---

[1] Ibid., p. 62.

[2] Ibid., pp. 74-106.

[3] Ibid., pp. 106-182.

[4] The story, as recorded by al-Bukhari, is that Umar (61-101) wrote to Abu Bakr ibn Muhammad (d. 100) saying, "Look for the knowledge of hadith and get it written, as I am afraid that religious knowledge will vanish and the religious learned men will pass away. Do not accept anything save the hadith of the Prophet." He also sent letters to Saad ibn Ibraaheem and al-Zuhri asking them to do the same. It has been incorrectly stated by some, for example, M. Z. Siddiqi, that it was this request of Umar's that led to the beginning of the collections of hadith.

[5] Al-Azami, *Methodology*, p. 30.

were in circulation. If we add another hundred years, it would be difficult to enumerate the quantity of booklets and books which were in circulation. Even by the most conservative estimate they were many thousands.[1]

But if there existed so many early writings and collections of hadith, as al-Azami demonstrated in his Ph.D. thesis, one may ask why is it that it seems that none or very few of them are still in existence today. Al-Azami also discussed what happened to these very early works. He wrote,

> These books were not destroyed nor did they perish, but [they] were absorbed into the work of later authors. When the encyclopedia-type books were produced, scholars did not feel the necessity to keep the early books or booklets, and so, slowly, they disappeared.[2]

Of the earliest works, one in particular deserves closer attention. This is the *Saheefah* of Hammaam ibn Munabbih. It is actually a written collection of hadith that the Companion Abu Hurairah dictated to his student Hammaam.[3] Since Abu Hurairah died around 58 A. H. (or some forty-eight years after the death of the Prophet), this collection must have been dictated to Hammaam sometime before that date.

Concerning the passing on of the *saheefah*, Hammaam (who died in 101 A. H.[4]) later read these hadith to his student Mamar (d. 113). Hamidullah writes,

> Many must have been the persons who received instructions in it [the *saheefah*], but by good fortune

---

[1] Ibid., p. 64.
[2] Ibid., p. 75. Al-Azami then goes on to prove his contention in great detail.
[3] For the text, translation and a study of this *saheefah*, see Muhammad Hamidullah, *Sahifah Hammam ibn Munabbih* (Paris: Centre Culturel Islamique, 1979), *passim*.
[4] Hamidullah, p. 64, n. 1.

he [Hammam] had among his pupils a man of distinction and enthusiasm, Mamar ibn Rashid, who without either addition or omission, transmitted it to his pupils. Mamar too was fortunate in having had a pupil universally esteemed, who distinguished himself by his learning, namely Abd ar-Razzaq ibn Hammam... Like his teacher Mamar, he decided not to amalgamate the *Saheefah* of Hammam in his own work, but preserve its integrity, and transmit to posterity in its original form as an independent work. Two of his pupils have become prominent in hadith lore, one Ahmad ibn Hanbal and the other Abu'l-Hasan Ahmad ibn Yusuf al-Sulami.[1]

Ahmad incorporated the entire work, save two hadith, into his famous *Musnad*. Al-Sulami, on the other hand, continued the passing on of this collection as an independent work. It was continually passed on until the 9th century which is the date of the Berlin manuscript, one of the four manuscripts of this work that is still in existence.[2]

Since the hadith in Ahmad's *Musnad* are arranged according to the Companion who narrated the hadith, it is very easy to find all of the hadith from Hammaam on the authority of Abu Hurairah in that collection. Other books, where the hadith are arranged according to *fiqh* topics, also incorporated a great deal of the *Saheefah*. A study of *Sahih al-Bukhari* and *Sahih Muslim* will demonstrate the following. Out of the 137 hadith in the *Saheefah* of Hammaam:

29 are recorded by both al-Bukhari and Muslim.

22 others are recorded only by al-Bukhari.

48 others are recorded only by Muslim.

Thus, 99 of the 137 hadith may be found in either *Sahih al-Bukhari* or *Sahih Muslim*. Furthermore, as Hamidullah writes,

---

[1] Hamidullah, pp. 66-7.

[2] For a discussion of the quality and *isnad*s of these manuscripts, see Hamidullah, pp. 88-97.

"As far as Muslim is concerned, it is worth pointing out that he cites these traditions generally in the following words: Mamar related hadith to us, on the authority of Hammam ibn Munabbih, who said: This is the hadith related to us by Abu Huraira from the Messenger of God—and he related a number of hadith of which is the following—and the Messenger of God said..."[1]

It is also interesting to note that all of the following works that contain many, if not all, of the hadith of this *saheefah* are now published: al-Bukhari's *al-Jaami al-Sahih*, Muslim's *Sahih*, Ahmad's *Musnad*, Abdul Razzaaq's *Musannaf*, Mamar's *Jaami* and even Hammaam's *Saheefah*. All of these collections may be studied to see that the meanings—actually the wordings—of the hadith have not been changed from the time of Abu Huraira to the time of al-Bukhari. Hamidullah commented,

> Supposing al-Bukhari cites a Hadith on the authority of the above chain of sources [Ahmad-Abdul Razzaq- Mamar- Hammam- Abu Huraira]. So long as these older sources were not available, a skeptic was certainly entitled to harbour doubts and say that perhaps al-Bukhari had not told the truth, but simply forged either the chain or the contents of both. But now that all the earlier sources are at our disposal, there is no possibility of imagining that al-Bukhari had mentioned anything by way of forging it, or narrating anything heard from forgerers... With the discovery in recent times of these earlier works, it is possible for us to verify the truthfulness of each. One is forced to recognize them all as solidly genuine.[2]

Ahmad's recording of these hadith is one of the most remarkable and interesting. He recorded the hadith of the

---

[1] Ibid., p. 79.
[2] Ibid., pp. 80-81.

Saheefah in his *Musnad* in almost exactly the same order as they are found in the *Saheefah*. His *Musnad* includes only one hadith that is not found in any of the manuscripts of the *Saheefah* while he is missing only two hadith from the *Saheefah*.

Hamidullah concludes,

> [E]ven after the lapse of more than 13 centuries there has not crept in a single alteration in the text of the collection... [S]ince these traditions have been transmitted not only by Abu Huraira, but, independently of him, by other Companions of the Prophet too, and in each case the chain or *isnad* has been different... If there had been no risk of boredom..., it would have been easy to show in proper detail, how, in addition to Abu Huraira, each of the traditions contained in the *Sahifah* of Hammam has been related by various other Companions... These traditions could never have been forged in the 3rd or 4th century...[1]

The *Isnaad* in the Early Years

Another important tool used in the preservation of hadith was the *isnaad* system that was developed uniquely by the Muslim nation. The *isnaad* system is where one states his sources of information, in turn tracing that narrative all the way back to the Prophet (peace be upon him).

The importance of the *isnaad* has been eloquently stated by Abdullah ibn al-Mubaarak who said, "The *isnaad* is part of the religion. If it were not for the *isnaad* anyone would say whatever he wishes to say."[2] Indeed, the *isnaad* has been

---

[1] Ibid., p. 87.
[2] Quoted by Imam Muslim in the introduction to his *Sahih* in the chapter entitled, "Expounding on the point that the *isnaad* is part of the religion."

essential in separating the authentic from the weak hadith and in identifying the fabricated hadith. Even today, no one can dare narrate a hadith without possibly being asked to provide the source of that hadith. Ibn al-Mubaarak continued and said, "If you ask the person where he got the hadith from he will [be forced to] become silent." The *isnaad* acted and acts as a type of guarantee or safeguard for the authenticity of the hadith. The early scholars of hadith would not even consider a hadith if it had no known *isnaad* to it.

Concerning the importance of the *isnaad*, Sufyaan al-Thauri (d. 161) said, "The *isnaad* is the sword of the believer. Without his sword with him with what will he fight?" By the use of the *isnaad*, the Muslim scholars were able to eradicate (or "fight") the innovations that people tried to bring into Islam. Muhammad ibn Seereen (d. 110), Anas ibn Seereen, Al-Dhuhaak and Uqba ibn Naafi have all been reported to have said, "This knowledge [of hadith] is the religion, therefore, look to see from whom you are taking your religion."[1] Since the sunnah forms an essential part of Islam, accepting hadith from a certain person is similar to taking one's religion from him. Hence, one must be careful only to take his religion from people who are trustworthy and who can trace what they have said back to the Prophet (peace be upon him) and this can only be done through the use of the *isnaad*.

This system was even more of a safeguard than today's system of publication and copyrighting. Hamidullah wrote,

> Modern scholars quote, in learned works, the sources of important statements of facts. But even in the most carefully documented works, there are two drawbacks: (a) In case of published works, there is little or no possibility of verifying whether there are any misprints or other inaccuracies— this would not

---

[1] Quoted in Fullaatah, vol. 2, p. 10.

happen if one were to depend on a work only after hearing [it] from the author himself, or obtaining a copy certified by the author, or— in case of old works— by those who have had the opportunity of hearing it from the author, or his authorized transmitter. (b) One is contented now-a-days with one's immediate source, without much caring to trace the preceding sources of that source, and mounting in seriatim up to the eye-witness of the event. In Hadith works the case has been different...[1]

In conclusion, one may state that the *isnaad* is an essential component of every hadith as without it there is no way for anyone to verify the authenticity of the narration. Abdullah ibn al-Mubaarak certainly spoke the truth when he said that without the *isnaad* anyone is free to say whatever he wishes to say and claim that it is part of the religion of Islam.[2] The importance of the *isnaad* is, in fact, very obvious and very few have ever questioned its importance. More important, therefore, is a discussion of when the *isnaad* began to be used for if it were not until a long time after the death of the Prophet (peace be upon him), it would, in fact, be useless.

There are basically three opinions concerning the beginning of the use of the *isnaad* proper. Each opinion is discussed separately below followed by Fulaatah's summary and conclusions on the topic.

The first opinion states that the use of the *isnaad* began after the *fitnah* ("Civil War" or great commotion). The

---

[1] Hamidullah, p. 83.

[2] One is reminded of the case of Paul and the origins of many Christian beliefs. Paul, of course, never met Jesus (peace be upon him). He could not trace his teachings back to Jesus (peace be upon him) and, in fact, he met opposition from many of Jesus' own companions who knew what Jesus (peace be upon him) had said. Unfortunately, the historical authenticity and tracing of claims back to the original teacher, Jesus, is something that did not truly develop in Christian thought. Hence, their religion became very distorted and distant from the true teachings of Jesus (peace be upon him).

proof for this opinion is the statement of ibn Seereen who said, "They did not use to ask about the *isnaad* but when the *fitnah* occurred, the people would say, 'State your authorities [for your hadith].' And they would look for the people of the sunnah and accept their hadith. And they would look for the people of innovations and reject their hadith." Dr. Akram Dhiya al-Umari states that it is not easy to determine exactly which *fitnah* ibn Seereen was referring to as the word may apply to any sort of battle, commotion or calamity. Most likely, though, it refers to the death of Uthmaan as ibn Seereen was referring back to the time when the *isnaad* began to be used and this interpretation is supported by external evidence.[1] Furthermore, that was definitely the most important and well-known "fitnah" and the first understanding that would come to a listener's mind upon hearing that word. This first opinion, therefore, states that the use of the *isnaad* began after the *fitnah*, most likely referring to the death of Uthmaan.

The second opinion states that the *isnaad* began to be used during the time of al-Zuhri (that is, the last quarter of the first century). The proof for this opinion is the statement of Imam Malik who said that al-Zuhri was the first person to use the *isnaad* in hadith.[2] (Note that the time of the Companions stretched until shortly after 100 A.H. Hence, there were still a number of Companions alive during the time of al-Zuhri who died in 124 A.H.)

The third opinion stems from a statement by Yahya ibn Saeed al-Qattaan who said that Amr al-Shabi (17-103) was the first to scrutinize the *isnaad*. Al-Rabi read a hadith to him and Amr al-Shabi told him, "Who narrated it to you?" He

---

[1] Akram Dhiyaa Al-Umari, *Buhooth fi Tareekh al-Sunnah al-Musharrifah* (Beirut: Muassasah al-Risaalah, 1975), pp. 49-50.

[2] In this author's opinion, Malik may have been referring to the first to use the *isnaad* in al-Sham as external evidence shows that the *isnaad* was in use before al-Zuhri. As an incident to be quoted indicates, al-Zuhri was very instrumental in convincing the people of al-Shaam (Greater Syria) that they must mention the *isnaad* with the hadith; perhaps this is what Imam Malik was referring to.

answered, "Amr ibn Maimun." And he asked Amr, "Who narrated it to you?" He answered, "Abu Ayyoob, the Companion of the Prophet."[1] Note that this incident (as well as the quote concerning al-Zuhri) could lend further support to the interpretation of the *fitnah* in Ibn Sireen's statement as being the death of Uthmaan.

Fullaatah, in his doctoral thesis, has done an excellent job of sorting through the various reports to discover the answer to the question of the beginning of the use of the *isnaad*. He states that the question must really be divided into three distinct questions: (a) When the *isnaad* was first used; (b) when narrators were forced by listeners to mention the *isnaad* for their narration; (c) when the narrators themselves began to insist on mentioning the *isnaad* of each hadith.

Concerning (a), when the *isnaad* was first used, he states that, by default, the Companions used to use *isnaad*s but since there was usually no intermediary between them and the Messenger of Allah (peace be upon him) it was not obvious that they were relating through the *isnaad*. The Companions would either narrate the hadith in a manner that made it clear that they heard it directly from the Prophet (peace be upon him), or in a manner that made it clear that they may not have heard that particular hadith directly from the Prophet (peace be upon him). Many of the younger Companions, such as Anas ibn Maalik and ibn Abbaas, did not hear the hadith they narrated directly from the Prophet (peace be upon him) but, instead, they heard it from another Companion who had heard it from the Prophet (peace be upon him). Fullaatah states, though, "this does not mean that every time the Companions or Followers narrated something they included the *isnaad* with it and would state clearly how they heard the hadith. Some of them would relate hadith from the Prophet (peace be upon him) although they did not hear it directly from him."[2]

---

[1] Quoted in al-Umari, p. 48.
[2] Fullaatah, vol. 2, p. 15.

Fullaatah then quoted Anas who said, "Not everything that we relate to you from the Messenger of Allah (peace be upon him) did we actually hear directly from him but our companions related it to us and we are a people who do not fib against one another."[1] He states that the vast majority of the hadith of the Companions were those hadith that they had heard directly from the Messenger of Allah (peace be upon him). Therefore, the *isnaad* was first used during the time of the Companions although, it may be said, that it was hardly noticeable. Going back to the statement from Malik about al-Zuhri, al-Umari wrote, "This does not mean that the *isnaad* did not exist before al-Zuhri. In fact, they began to ask about the *isnaad* during the time of the Companions and continued to do so during the time of the Major Followers. But during the time of al-Zuhri people began to greatly stress the mentioning of the *isnaad*."[2]

Concerning (b), when the narrators were forced by the listeners to mention their *isnaad*s, Fullaatah states that Abu Bakr was the first to make the narrator prove the authenticity of his narration as he sometimes would not accept a hadith unless the person presented a witness for his hadith. Umar also followed the same pattern. By doing so they made it clear if the person heard the hadith directly from the Messenger of Allah (peace be upon him) or through some intermediary source. Their goal was to confirm the correctness of the narration although they were, at the same time, inadvertently making the narrator state the *isnaad* for his hadith. Therefore, it was during their time (right after the death of the Prophet) that narrators were first being forced to state their *isnaad*s. Ali, the fourth caliph and the caliph during the *fitnah*, would sometimes take an oath from the person in which the person would swear that he heard the hadith directly from the Prophet (peace be upon him). Obviously, then, after the *fitnah*, the same process of requiring the narrator to state his sources

---

[1] Quoted in Ibid., vol. 2. p. 18 from *al-Kifaaya* by al-Khateeb al-Baghdaadi.
[2] Al-Umari, p. 49.

continued.[1] What ibn Seereen's statement simply means is that it became the regular practice of anyone interested in hadith, after the *fitnah*, to ask for the *isnaad* but this in no way contradicts what has been stated above concerning the use of the *isnaad* during the caliphates of Abu Bakr and Umar, before the *fitnah*.

Concerning (c), when the narrator himself began to insist on mentioning the *isnaad* of each hadith, Fullaatah states that the need for the *isnaad* really became apparent after weak narrators and immoral people began to relate hadith. During that time, the narrator himself made sure that he would mention the *isnaad* of the hadith he narrated. Al-Amash used to narrate hadith and then say, "Here is the head of the matter," and then he would mention the *isnaad*. Al-Waleed ibn Muslim of al-Shaam stated, "One day al-Zuhri said, 'What is wrong [with you people] that I see you narrating hadith without the critical or important part?' After that day our companions [that is, the people of al-Sham] made sure to mention the *isnaad*."[2] The scholars would blame their students for listening to hadith from teachers who would mention the hadith without the *isnaad*.[3] In fact they would reject any hadith which did not have an *isnaad* with it. Bahz ibn Asad said, "Do not accept a hadith from someone who does not say, 'He narrated to us..,'" that is, without an *isnaad*. The Muslims even began to insist on the use of the *isnaad* for people of disciplines other than hadith, for example, history, *tafseer*, poetry and so on.

Therefore, after discussing the question in detail, Fullaatah could soundly conclude the following:

1. The *isnaad* was first used during the time of the Companions.

2. Abu Bakr was the first to force narrators to mention the source for their hadith.

---

[1] Fullaatah, vol. 2, pp. 20-22.
[2] Quoted by Fullaatah, vol. 2, p. 28.
[3] Ibid., vol. 2, pp. 28-29. See the stories of al-Zuhri, Abdullah ibn al-Mubaarak and Sufyaan al-Thauri on those pages.

3. The narrator himself insisted on mentioning the *isnaad* of each hadith on the heels of (1) and (2) above.[1]

Another important point, made by al-Umari, is that just because some of the early scholars did not mention the *isnaad* of their hadith, that did not mean that they did not know the *isnaad* or that they had not mentioned it at some other time. (During the very early years they did not see the necessity of always mentioning the *isnaad*; when the liars appeared, obviously, the necessity was all too clear.) Al-Umari wrote,

> Qataadah (d. 118) used to narrate hadith in Basra without mentioning the *isnaad* in order to save time and to make things easy on his students. Sometimes his students would ask him for the *isnaad* and he would state it for them. Shuba ibn al-Hajjaaj used to ask him about the *isnaad* as did Mammar ibn Rasheed and other new people who had just started to attend his lectures. Others objected to them asking about the *isnaad* as, perhaps, they had been listening to him for a long time and were familiar with the *isnaad* and they blamed the others for wasting time.

Qataadah was not ignorant of the *isnaad*s and, in fact, later in his life he also insisted on mentioning the *isnaad* with the hadith.[2]

In conclusion, there was never any time that hadith narrations were completely void of mentioning the *isnaad*. During the time of the Companions the use of the *isnaad* was not so obvious as there was (usually) no intermediate narrator between the person mentioning the hadith and the Prophet (peace be upon him). (The period of the Companions "officially" ended in 110 A. H. with the death of the last Companion.) Abu Bakr and Umar were scrupulous in checking

---

[1] Fullaatah, vol. 2, p. 30.
[2] al-Umari, pp. 50-51.

the authenticity of hadith. Later people like al-Shabi and al-Zuhri appeared and they made the Muslims realize the importance of mentioning the *isnaad* with the hadith. This was especially manifest after major confrontations (such as the death of Uthmaan) which made the people realize that the hadith narrations were their religion and, therefore, they should look carefully at whom they were taking their religion from. After the early years, the *isnaad* and its proper use became standardized and its knowledge became an independent branch of hadith. This continued until the major collections of hadith were compiled in the third century.[1]

Allah has declared the Prophet Muhammad (peace be upon him) to be the seal of the Prophets who was sent for all of mankind. Thus it becomes necessary for the teachings of this last Prophet to be preserved in their pure form. This was not necessary in the case of the earlier prophets who were sent for a certain people and whose message was meant only for a specific time. Therefore, Allah blessed the nation of Muhammad with a unique way of preserving its original teachings: the *isnaad*. Muhammad ibn Haatim ibn al-Mudhaffar wrote,

> Verily Allah has honored and distinguished this nation and raised it above others by the use of the *isnaad*. None of the earlier or present nations have unbroken *isnaad*s. They have [ancient] pages in their possession but their books have been mixed with their historical reports and they are not able to distinguish between what was originally revealed as the Torah or the Gospel and what has been added

---

[1] In fact, the tradition of relating hadith by their *isnaad*s continued until the fifth century. After that time books were passed on, mostly by *ijaaza* (permission given to others to narrate one's books or hadith), although there are still some scholars today who can narrate hadith with a complete chain from themselves back to the Prophet (peace be upon him). Cf., Khaldoon al-Ahdab, *Asbaab Ikhtilaaf al-Muhaditheen* (Jeddah: al-Dar al-Saudiya, 1985), vol. 2, p. 707.

later of reports that have been taken from
untrustworthy [or, most likely, unknown] narrators.[1]

Travels For the Purpose of Seeking Hadith

Among all of the different religious communities of
the world it has been only the Islamic nation that has been
blessed with two particular characteristics that have saved it
from losing its original and pure teachings. These two unique
characteristics are the use of the *isnaad*, which has just been
discussed, and the journeying in search of hadith, that shall
presently be discussed. The great desire for religious
knowledge among the Muslims led individuals to travel, on
their own, for months at a time simply to collect or confirm
just one saying of the Prophet (peace be upon him). It was this
devotion to hadith and willingness to sacrifice any aspect of
this worldly life that greatly helped in the complete
preservation of the hadith of the Prophet (peace be upon him).
M. Zubayr Siddiqi has written,

> All these various generations of Traditionists
> displayed marvelous activity in the pursuit of hadith.
> Their love for the subject had been profound. Their
> enthusiasm for it knew no bounds. Their capacity to
> suffer for the sake of it had no limit. The rich among
> them sacrificed riches at its alter; and the poor among
> them devoted their lives to it in spite of their
> poverty.[2]

Why was this desire for knowledge so great among
these early Muslims? No one can answer this question

---

[1] Quoted in Abdul Wahaab Abdul Lateef, *Al-Mukhtasar fi Ilm Rijaal al-Athar*
(Dar al-Kutub al-Hadithiya, no date), p. 18.
[2] M. Z. Siddiqi, *Hadith Literature: Its Origin, Development, Special Features
and Criticism* (Calcutta: Calcutta University Press, 1961), p. 48.

completely but there must have been many reasons for this strong desire. These reasons must have included the following:

(a) The knowledge of hadith was known by these pious souls to lead them to the practice of the Prophet (peace be upon him) and, furthermore, they knew that by following his footsteps they would become closer to Allah.

(b) The Quran and the Prophet (peace be upon him) both stressed the virtues and importance of attaining knowledge. Allah says,

$$ قُلْ هَلْ يَسْتَوِي الَّذِينَ يَعْلَمُونَ وَالَّذِينَ لا يَعْلَمُونَ $$

"Say: Are those who are knowledgeable equal to those who are not knowledgeable?" (*al-Zumar* 9). Also,

$$ إِنَّمَا يَخْشَى اللَّهَ مِنْ عِبَادِهِ الْعُلَمَاءُ $$

"The erudite among His bondsmen fear Allah alone" (*Faatir* 28). Among the Prophet's many statements on this topic are:

$$ مَنْ سَلَكَ طَرِيقًا يَلْتَمِسُ فِيهِ عِلْمًا سَهَّلَ اللَّهُ بِهِ لَهُ طَرِيقًا إِلَى الْجَنَّةِ $$

"Whoever goes out along a path in search of knowledge, Allah makes a path to Paradise easy for him..." (Recorded by Muslim.) The Prophet (peace be upon him) also said,

$$ إِذَا مَاتَ الإِنْسَانُ انْقَطَعَ عَنْهُ عَمَلُهُ إِلاَّ مِنْ ثَلاَثَةٍ إِلاَّ مِنْ صَدَقَةٍ جَارِيَةٍ أَوْ عِلْمٍ يُنْتَفَعُ بِهِ أَوْ وَلَدٍ صَالِحٍ يَدْعُو لَهُ $$

"When the son of Adam dies all of his good deeds come to an end except three: a perpetual charity, beneficial knowledge [he left behind from which people gain some benefit] and a pious child who supplicates for him." (Recorded by Muslim.) The early scholars recognized the importance of attaining knowledge and they also recognized that no knowledge is better than knowledge about the Creator. Therefore, they did their best to learn the teachings of His Prophet (peace be upon him).

(c) Especially after the beginning of forgery in hadith, the scholars knew that the only way this nation could be saved from being misguided like the previous nations was to ensure that the pure teachings of the Prophet (peace be upon him) were kept in tact. It was partially through traveling that forgers, weak narrators and untrustworthy chains were spotted.

(d) The Prophet (peace be upon him) warned that anyone who falsely attributes something on his authority shall take his seat in the Hell fire. For the pious this warning was a great burden. Many of them would refrain from relating hadith unless they were absolutely certain that they were stating exactly what the Prophet (peace be upon him) had actually said. They would, therefore, travel great distances to confirm the words of the Messenger of Allah (peace be upon him).

Examples from the early years will give a clearer picture of these journeys in search of hadith. In reality, however, traveling in search of hadith can be said to have begun during the time of the Prophet (peace be upon him) himself. That is, even at that time, people would come from outside of Madinah to ask the Prophet (peace be upon him) about specific matters. In some cases, they would come to the Prophet (peace be upon him) to verify what has been reported by the Prophet's emissaries. In *al-Bukhari* and *Muslim* it can be seen that the other Companions looked forward to such an event. This was because, as Anas stated, they were prohibited from asking the Prophet (peace be upon him) too many questions, so they would look forward to the coming of an intelligent bedouin who traveled to come to the Prophet (peace be upon him) to ask him specific questions.

The following examples are of Companions who traveled in order to verify hadith that they themselves heard from the Prophet (peace be upon him).[1]

Imam al-Bukhari recorded in his *Sahih* that Jaabir ibn Abdullah traveled for one month to get a single hadith from Abdullah ibn Unais. In a version recorded by al-Tabaraani, it states that Jaabir said, "I used to hear a hadith on the authority of the Prophet (peace be upon him) about retribution and the one who narrated that hadith [directly from the Prophet (peace be upon him)] was in Egypt, so I bought a camel and traveled to Egypt..."[2]

The Companion Abu Ayyoob traveled all the way to Egypt to ask Uqba ibn Amr about one hadith. He told Uqba that only he and Uqba were left who had heard that particular hadith directly from the Prophet (peace be upon him). After hearing the hadith his business was completed in Egypt and he returned to Madinah.

One of the Companions traveled to visit Fadhala ibn Ubaid and told him that he came not to visit him but only to ask him about a hadith that they had both heard from the Prophet (peace be upon him) and the Companion was hoping that Fadhala had the complete wording of the hadith. (This incident was recorded by Abu Dawood.)

From the stories of the Companions one can conclude that they traveled in search of hadith for basically two reasons: (a) To hear a hadith from a fellow Companion concerning which they did not have the honor of hearing it themselves directly from the Prophet (peace be upon him), thereby adding to their knowledge of hadith. (b) To confirm the wording and/or meaning of a hadith that they and other Companions had heard directly from the Messenger of Allah (peace be upon him). Thus even the Companions were constantly checking,

---

[1] For more examples see al-Umari, pp. 203f.

[2] Ibn Hajr says that this version has a good chain. Cf., ibn Hajr, *Fath al-Baari*, vol. 1, p. 174.

rechecking and safeguarding the purity of the hadith that they narrated.

During the Followers' time the desire and willingness to travel in order only to hear or confirm a hadith of the Prophet (peace be upon him) did not diminish. Madinah, having been the home of the Prophet (peace be upon him) for many years, the home of the sunnah and the city where many of the Companions resided after the Prophet's death, was probably the main center of attraction, but, in fact, any place where it was known a particular hadith could be heard would attract "travelers."

Many examples could be given. Al-Khateeb al-Baghdadi has written an entire work on the subject of traveling in search of hadith. His work is entitled *Al-Rihla fi Talab al-Hadith* ("Travels in Search of Hadith"). What makes this work even more interesting is that it is not simply concerned with scholars travelling to learn hadith. This was done by almost every scholar in the history of Islam. Indeed, if a scholar did not travel that was usually pointed out as something strange, as the norm was to travel. However, this book, as pointed out by the editor of the work Noor al-Deen Itr, is about travels in search of just one hadith and not hadith in general.[1]

Early Hadith Criticism and Evaluation of Narrators

Another important aspect in the preservation of hadith was the early development of hadith criticism and evaluation of narrators. Even during the lifetime of the Messenger of Allah (peace be upon him), the Companions would often go to him to confirm some report that they had heard related on his authority. Professor Azami, referring to examples in the hadith collections of Ahmad, al-Bukhari, Muslim and al-Nasaai, writes,

---

[1] See Noor al-Deen Itr's introduction to al-Khateeb al-Baghdaadi, *al-Rihlah fi Talab al-Hadeeth* (Beirut: Daar al-Kutub al-Ilmiyyah, 1975), p. 10.

If criticism is the effort to distinguish between what is right and what is wrong, then we can say that it began in the life of the Prophet. But at this stage, it meant no more than going to the Prophet and verifying something he was reported to have said...

We find this sort of investigation or verification was carried [*sic*] out by Ali, Ubai ibn Kaab, Abdullah ibn Amr, Umar, Zainab wife of ibn Masud, and others. In the light of these events, it can be claimed that the investigation of hadith or, in other words, criticism of hadith began in a rudimentary form during the life of the Prophet.[1]

Obviously this practice of confirming reports directly with the Messenger of Allah (peace be upon him) had to cease with the death of the Prophet (peace be upon him). At that time the Companions, led by notables such as Abu Bakr, Umar, Ali, ibn Umar and others, used to confirm hadith with each other.

Umar, for example, was strict in safeguarding the proper dissemination of hadith. In *Sahih Muslim* one can find the example of Abu Moosa al-Ashari. Umar threatened to have him punished if he did not present a witness for a hadith that he had narrated to Umar. Commenting on this hadith, Abdul Hamid Siddiqi stated that Umar did not doubt Abu Moosa but he only meant to keep a strict supervision over the transmission of hadith.[2]

Many examples of this kind may be given. Abu Hurairah, Aishah, Umar and ibn Umar would verify hadith. Sometimes they would verify the hadith by "cross-reference" (like Umar and Abu Moosa above) and at other times they used what could be termed "time-series" checking. Imam Muslim records that Aishah heard a certain hadith narrated from Abdullah ibn Amr. A year later she had her servant go to

---

[1] Azami, *Methodology*, p. 48.
[2] Siddiqi, *Sahih Muslim*, vol. 3, pp. 1175-6.

Abdullah ibn Amr to hear the hadith again from him to make sure that he had narrated it exactly as he had heard it from the Prophet (peace be upon him) and that he had not made any mistakes or additions in its narration.[1]

The Beginnings of the Fabrication of Hadith

Another important question related to the preservation of hadith is the question of when the fabricating of hadith began. Due to the importance of this topic in relation to the overall question of the preservation of hadith, it shall be discussed in some detail here.

One of the most important teachings that the Prophet (peace be upon him) passed on to his followers was that of being sincere and honest. In fact, in Islam honesty is one of the signs of faith while dishonesty is one of the signs of hypocrisy. The Prophet (peace be upon him) said,

أَرْبَعٌ مَنْ كُنَّ فِيهِ كَانَ مُنَافِقًا خَالِصًا وَمَنْ كَانَتْ فِيهِ خَصْلَةٌ مِنْهُنَّ كَانَتْ فِيهِ خَصْلَةٌ مِنَ النِّفَاقِ حَتَّى يَدَعَهَا إِذَا حَدَّثَ كَذَبَ

"There are four characteristics that if someone possesses all of them, he is a pure hypocrite. If he possesses any of these characteristics, then he has a characteristic of hypocrisy until he leaves it. [They are:] if he speaks, he lies..." (Recorded by al-Bukhari and Muslim.) The Prophet's exhortations and warnings were enough to keep the Companions from lying. Beyond that, the Prophet (peace be upon him) also encouraged them to pass on the religion and he severely warned them about lying while attributing something to him. Besides the

---

[1] Ibid., vol. 4, p. 1405.

hadith quoted above, the Prophet (peace be upon him) also said,

$$
\text{إِنَّ كَذِبًا عَلَيَّ لَيْسَ كَكَذِبٍ عَلَى أَحَدٍ مَنْ كَذَبَ عَلَيَّ مُتَعَمِّدًا}
$$

$$
\text{فَلْيَتَبَوَّأْ مَقْعَدَهُ مِنَ النَّارِ}
$$

"Falsely attributing something to me is not like falsely attributing something to anybody else. Whoever falsely attributes something to me shall take his own seat in the hell-fire." (Recorded by al-Bukhari.)

With respect to the historical authenticity of hadith literature, the question of the beginning of the forging of hadith is a very important question. A number of opinions have been expressed on this topic. For the sake of brevity, the different opinions shall not be delved into in any detail.

Three of the myriad of opinions are:

(1) Fabricating began during the lifetime of the Messenger of Allah (peace be upon him) and that is why he made the statement, "Whoever falsely attributes anything to me shall take his seat in the hell-fire."

(2) Fabricating began during the latter part of Uthmaan's caliphate when many people were enraged with Uthmaan and ibn Udais ascended the pulpit and fabricated a statement against Uthmaan (although not in the form of a hadith of the Prophet).

(3) Fabricating began during the civil war that broke out upon Uthmaan's death by people such as ibn Saba, a heretical leader, and his followers.

Umar Fullaatah, in his doctoral dissertation, perceptively remarked,

> It is clear that all of these opinions [stated above] are theoretical and in need of actual direct evidence that some specific person fabricated specific hadith during that period and if that is established, then one

can say when the fabrication of hadith began. Just the establishment of the different groups after the death of Uthmaan does not necessitate that they should start fabricating hadith. It is very clear that [at the most] it would be the followers of these leaders and sects that would go to an extreme and fabricate hadith to support their group.[1]

He also says that references to historical events are not specific enough to prove that forging had actually begun during that time period. He then goes on to refute the different opinions stated above concerning the beginning of fabricated hadith.

Perhaps the following questions though should be addressed:

Is it possible that the forging of hadith may have started as early as during the life of the Prophet (peace be upon him)? This is inconceivable. If such did occur, it would have become well-known and brought to the attention of the Prophet (peace be upon him), perhaps via inspiration from Allah. No such case is known to exist and, without the existence of any report of this nature, no one can make the claim that fabrication began during the time of the Prophet (peace be upon him) himself.

Is it possible that some of the Companions may have forged hadith? It is inconceivable that any of the Companions should have fabricated hadith. In a number of places in the Quran, Allah has stated His pleasure with the Companions. For example, Allah has said,

وَالسَّابِقُونَ الْأَوَّلُونَ مِنْ الْمُهَاجِرِينَ وَالْأَنْصَارِ وَالَّذِينَ اتَّبَعُوهُمْ بِإِحْسَانٍ رَضِيَ اللَّهُ عَنْهُمْ وَرَضُوا عَنْهُ وَأَعَدَّ لَهُمْ جَنَّاتٍ تَجْرِي تَحْتَهَا الْأَنْهَارُ خَالِدِينَ فِيهَا أَبَدًا ذَلِكَ الْفَوْزُ الْعَظِيمُ

---

[1] Fullaatah, vol. 1, p. 182.

"And the first to lead the way, of the Emigrants and Helpers, and those who followed them in goodness—Allah is well pleased with them and they are well pleased with Him, and He has made ready for them gardens underneath which rivers flow, wherein they will abide forever. That is the supreme triumph" [*al-Taubah* 100]. It is inconceivable that Allah should declare His pleasure for a people who would fabricate hadith in the name of His Prophet (peace be upon him). Furthermore, the Companions were vary careful in their narrations of hadith in order to be certain that they were not making any mistakes in the words of the Prophet (peace be upon him).

The Companions sacrificed lives and wealth for the sake of Allah. The Companions showed how much they loved truth and justice. Mustafa al-Sibaa'ee gives many examples of how the Companions feared none except Allah. Abu Bakr, for example, held firm against the apostates and sent Usaamah on his military exposition despite the warnings from the other Companions. Ali corrected Umar on occasion and Umar's pride never kept him from accepting what was true. Abu Saeed told the caliph Marwaan to his face that he was violating the sunnah by giving the sermon before the *Eid* prayer. Ibn Umar defended al-Zubair in front of the tyrant al-Hajjaaj. These examples that al-Sibaa'ee presented, and many more like them, are proof that these noble individuals loved the truth and Allah above everything else. It is not believable that they would ever forge any words and declare them to be a hadith of their beloved Prophet (peace be upon him). Anas once related a hadith and he was asked, "Did you hear it from the Messenger of Allah?" He answered, "Yes or I heard it from one who does not lie. By Allah, we never lied nor did we even know what lying was."[1]

Fullaatah writes,

---

[1] Al-Sibaa'ee, pp. 76-78.

> What has become apparent to me, and Allah knows best, is that the fabricating of hadith—I mean falsely attributing something to the Messenger of Allah (peace be upon him)—began after that time [that is, after 41 A. H.]. It may be restricted to the last third of the first century. Evidence exists for the possible forging of statements of the Messenger of Allah (peace be upon him) during that time. There were some things that occurred after the nation split and fractionalized that laid the groundwork for this horrible deed that led to the end of the sanctity of the Messenger of Allah (peace be upon him) by forging reports of or from him that he did not do or say.[1]

Some of these phenomena that laid the groundwork for the forging of hadith were:

(1) The sanctity of the Companions who were the caliphs and led the nation was no longer honored. This can be seen in many events of that time. People began to openly criticize and attack these noble leaders. Ibn Udais ascended the Prophet's pulpit and verbally attacked Uthmaan. The Khawarij blamed Ali for his accepting of "human judgement" and called him a disbeliever. Of course, verbal abuse was not all there was as some of the caliphs were martyred.

(2) The Muslims split into different sects and each sect opposed the other. As is well known, there was even a civil war at that time.

(3) The effects of Abdullah ibn Saba, a rebel leader and heretic, began to be felt in the Muslim world. This also opened the way for other alien ideas from other parts of the world.

(4) Falsely attributing statements to the Companions occurred for the first time during that period, especially with respect to Ali ibn Abu Taalib.

---

[1] Fullaatah, vol. 1, p. 202.

All of these aspects were laying the groundwork for the beginning of the fabrication of hadith. Furthermore, and this is perhaps Fullaatah's strongest argument, Fullaatah states,

> In my research, I did not come across anyone who could confirm any case of fabricating a statement of the Messenger of Allah (peace be upon him) from the time of his death until the beginning of the last third of the first century—[in other words, I could not find] any incident that could, then, be considered the beginning of the forging of hadith.[1]

The first authentic incident—many authors use inauthentic reports to trace the begin of the forging of hadith—that points to any type of fabrication is the following story that was recorded by ibn al-Jauzi in *al-Maudhuaat* and by al-Bukhari in *al-Tareekh al-Sagheer*. Al-Mukhtaar asked al-Rabi al-Khuzai, who was alive during the time of the Prophet (peace be upon him), "O fellow, you have met the Prophet (peace be upon him) and you have not told a lie in what you have reported from him. Make some hadith of the Prophet for us and for you is seven hundred *deenaars*." He answered, "The fire is for the one who falsely attributes something to the Prophet (peace be upon him) and, therefore, I will not do it." Fullaatah writes, "It is clear that al-Mukhtaar wanted him to fabricate hadith for him in order to strengthen his claims. It is also related that he sought the same from Muhammad ibn Ammaar ibn Yaasir who refused and was killed for doing so."[2]

Fullaatah concludes,

> These reports make it clear that al-Mukhtaar al-Thaqafi tried to encourage the people to fabricate hadith of the Prophet (peace be upon him). Even though the narrations show that no one responded to

---

[1] Fullaatah, vol. 1, p. 212.
[2] Fullaatah, vol. 1, p. 213.

his plea they can be considered the beginning of the fabrication of hadith as they show that at that time fabrication was being considered. Since it is confirmed that there was no fabrication before that time, then it should be suspected that it occurred shortly after that time. Therefore, to me, the strongest opinion is that the attempts to fabricate hadith began during this last third of the first century when the greatest Companions had mostly passed away and only a small number of younger Companions were left and these had cut themselves off from society [in order to avoid the fighting and strife] and they did not possess prominent positions in the society during that period.[1]

Some people might object to this opinion because of what has been recorded from ibn Abbaas and ibn Seereen which make it seem like forging must have began at a much earlier time. Ibn Abbaas said, "We used to narrate on the authority of the Messenger of Allah (peace be upon him) and no one would falsely attribute anything to him and then when the people started riding wild and domesticated animals, we stopped narrating on his authority." Ibn Seereen said that after the civil war, they would not accept a hadith without its *isnaad*. Ibn Abbaas' statement seems to make it clear that lying began right after the civil war, this is what he refers to as "the people started riding wild and domesticated animals." Fullaatah also responds to these objections to his conclusions.

First, ibn Seereen's statement does not clearly state that people began to forge hadith during that time. He simply pointed out that the scholars began to be more careful in accepting hadith at that time in order to avoid the hadith of the innovators who were following a path other than that of the first generation of the Muslims. They were afraid to be

---

[1] Fullaatah, vol. 1, p. 214.

affected by their innovations by being soft on the innovators and by accepting their narrations.[1]

Ibn Abbaas' statement seems to come from near the end of his life as he died during the last third of the first century. This in no way contradicts the opinion stated above. This is proven by the expression he used which implies that the people had broken up into different sects and this was most prominent towards the end of ibn Abbaas' life. Furthermore, the statement from ibn Abbaas has been narrated in different manners. In one narration it states, "then the people started fabricating reports on the authority of the Prophet (peace be upon him)..." But this is simply the interpretation of the one who heard the statement of ibn Abbaas and it is not exactly what ibn Abbaas said.[2]

Therefore, it may be concluded that the fabricating of hadith may have occurred at the earliest during the last third of the first century. Anyone who claims otherwise must provide concrete evidence that it occurred before that time.

This recent research by Fullaatah is important as it shows that the fabricating of hadith occurred after the following events:

1. The people began to use the *isnaad* on a regular and scientific basis.

2. Many of the hadith of the Prophet (peace be upon him) were already recorded and preserved in written form.

3. The science of *jarh* and *tadeel* (critiquing and evaluating narrators) had already become somewhat commonplace.

Since this was the case, it shows that the fabrication of hadith did not, in any way, affect the preservation of the true and authentic hadith of the Prophet (peace be upon him). Some people claim that so many hadith were fabricated that there was no way for the scholars to distinguish between the true and

---

[1] Fullaatah, vol. 1, p. 215.
[2] Ibid., vol. 1, pp. 216-7.

false hadith. This statement is simply not true on two counts. First, the scholars had, for the most part, already instituted many of the principles of the sciences of hadith even before the fabrication of hadith began. Therefore, it was very easy for them to spot the fabricators and the fabricated hadith. Secondly, and this is beyond the scope of this work to prove, the number of hadith that the fabricators forged was not as great as believed.

Conclusion

In the following statement, M. Z. Siddiqi has done an excellent job of summing up the protection of the sunnah in the early years,

> The Hadith in this sense of the reports of the sayings and doings of Muhammad has been a subject of keen pursuit and constant study by the Muslims throughout the Muslim world since the very beginning of the history of Islam up to the present times. During the life-time of Muhammad many of the Companions tried to get by heart whatever he said, and observed keenly whatever he did; and they reported these things to one another. Some of them wrote down what he said in *Saheefah*s which were later on read by them to their students, and which were preserved in their families and also by the Followers. After the death of Muhammad, when his companions spread in various countries, some of them as well as their Followers undertook long arduous journeys, courted poverty and penury in order to collect them together... Their remarkable activity with regard to the preservation and propagation of hadith is unique in the literary history of the world... [And the excellence of their sciences

remains] unparalleled in the literary history of the world even to-day.[1]

The more one goes on to study the sciences of hadith, the more he will feel comfortable with the feeling that the sunnah of the Prophet Muhammad (peace be upon him) has been minutely preserved, just as Allah had promised in the Quran. When the scholars of hadith—who are the specialists in that field and who have spent their lifetime in mastering that discipline—agree upon the authenticity of a hadith, there should be no need for debate or question. The only thing left to do is to believe in it and do one's best to apply the meaning of that hadith in one's life.

---

[1] M. Z. Siddiqi, pp. 4-5.

Chapter Six:
The Ruling Concerning One
Who Rejects the Sunnah

Denying Anything Definitively Established as Part of the Religion

In this work, a number of important points have been proven. These include:

(1) The sunnah is a type of revelation from Allah.

(2) The place of the sunnah is confirmed in numerous verses of the Quran. If anyone claims to follow the Quran and yet he refuses to follow the sunnah, he is simply belying his claim to be following the Quran.

(3) The sunnah goes hand in hand with the Quran and is of equal status with respect to authority in Islamic law.

(4) The Quran itself cannot be understood without reference to the sunnah.

(5) All of these points have been established since the time of the Prophet (peace be upon him) and there is a unanimity of opinion among the scholars on these points.

The clear evidence for the authority of the sunnah puts it in the status of those things that unquestionably form part of the religion and that everyone should know about "by necessity." In other words, the scholars and commoners alike should be aware of these matters. Indeed, growing up an ideal Islamic environment, one could not but know about these essentials of the religion. Denying any of these parts of the religion is tantamount to disbelief and apostasy. Ibn Taimiyyah wrote,

> Belief in the obligatory nature of the clear, well-established obligations and belief in the forbidden nature of the clear, well-established prohibitions is one of the greatest foundations of faith and of the principles of the religion. The one who denies them is a disbeliever by the agreement [of the scholars].[1]

In a similar vein, Imam al-Nawawi wrote,

> As for today, the religion of Islam has spread. Spread among the Muslims has been the knowledge of the obligation of zakat, to the point that both the commoners and specialists know it, indeed even the scholars and the ignorant are all aware of it. No one is excused due to any type of reinterpretation that he may make to reject it. The same ruling holds true for whoever rejects any aspect of the religion which the [Muslim] community is agreed upon, if the knowledge of it has been spread. Such matters include the five daily prayers, fasting the month of Ramadhaan, making a full washing after become sexually defiled, forbiddance of fornication, forbiddance of alcohol, forbiddance of marrying close relatives... However, if the consensus is known only through the means of the specialists, such as the forbiddance of being married to both a woman and her paternal or maternal aunt, the fact that a murderer does not inherit [from the one he murdered], the fact that the grandmother gets one-sixth [of the inheritance] and similar other matters, then the one who rejects them is not considered a disbeliever. In fact, he is excused [until he is taught these matters]

---

[1] Ibn Taimiyyah, *Majmoo*, vol. 12, p. 497.

214

since the knowledge of such matters had not spread to the masses.[1]

Similar statements can be quoted from a number of scholars.[2] The conclusion of the scholars—that whoever denies what is firmly and unquestionably established as part of the religion is a disbeliever—is logical. In reality, when someone denies something of this nature, like the position of the sunnah or the five obligatory prayers, then, in reality, he is doing nothing other than denying the Quran itself and all of the individual verses that are related to those topics. Denying and belying the Quran is, obviously, disbelief and apostasy. Unfortunately, those who come from Western Jewish or Christian backgrounds can become very lackadaisical on this point. It is not uncommon for a Christian, for example, to reject what he wills of the Bible or to disbelieve in whatever he wants from Christian doctrine—yet at the same time, he considers himself a full and righteous Christian. This approach is not acceptable in Islam. Once a person converts to Islam, he must accept the entire Quran and sunnah as the absolute truth, without doubt.

Again, rejecting anything that is definitively established as part of the religion is tantamount to disbelief. This conclusion can be proven from verses in the Quran. In particular, one should note the following verses:

أَفَتُؤْمِنُونَ بِبَعْضِ الْكِتَابِ وَتَكْفُرُونَ بِبَعْضٍ فَمَا جَزَاءُ مَنْ يَفْعَلُ ذَلِكَ مِنْكُمْ إِلاَّ خِزْيٌ فِي الْحَيَاةِ الدُّنْيَا وَيَوْمَ الْقِيَامَةِ يُرَدُّونَ إِلَى أَشَدِّ الْعَذَابِ وَمَا اللَّهُ بِغَافِلٍ عَمَّا تَعْمَلُونَ

---

[1] Quoted in Abdul Azeez al Abdul Lateef, *Nawaaqidh al-Imaan al-Qauliyyah wa al-Amaliyyah* (Riyadh: Daar al-Watan, 1414 A.H.), p. 244.
[2] Cf., al-Abdul Lateef, pp. 242ff; Muhammad al-Wuhaibi, *Nawaaqidh al-Imaan al-Itiqaadiyyah wa Dhawaabit al-Takfeer ind al-Salaf* (Riyadh: Daar al-Muslim, 1996), vol. 2, pp. 57-59.

"Then is it only a part of the Book that you believe in, and do you reject the rest? But what is the reward for those among you who behave like this but disgrace in this life? And on the Day of Judgment they shall be consigned to the most grievous penalty. For Allah is not unmindful of what you do" (*al-Baqarah* 85).

Allah describes those who will be thrown into the Hell-fire with the following words,

فَلَا صَدَّقَ وَلَا صَلَّى وَلَكِنْ كَذَّبَ وَتَوَلَّى

"So he gave nothing in charity, nor did he pray. But on the contrary, he rejected [the truth] and turned away" (*al-Qiyaamah* 31-32).

Allah also says,

وَمَنْ أَظْلَمُ مِمَّنِ افْتَرَى عَلَى اللَّهِ كَذِبًا أَوْ كَذَّبَ بِآيَاتِهِ إِنَّهُ لَا يُفْلِحُ الظَّالِمُونَ

"Who does more wrong than he who invents a lie against Allah or rejects His Signs (*ayaat*)? But verily the wrongdoers never shall prosper" (*al-Anaam* 21; *Yoonus* 17 is virtually the same).

Again, Allah says,

إِنَّ الَّذِينَ كَذَّبُوا بِآيَاتِنَا وَاسْتَكْبَرُوا عَنْهَا لَا تُفَتَّحُ لَهُمْ أَبْوَابُ السَّمَاءِ وَلَا يَدْخُلُونَ الْجَنَّةَ حَتَّى يَلِجَ الْجَمَلُ فِي سَمِّ الْخِيَاطِ وَكَذَلِكَ نَجْزِي الْمُجْرِمِينَ

"To those who reject Our Signs and treat them with arrogance, no opening will there be of the gates of heaven, nor will they enter the Garden, until the camel can pass through the eye of the needle: such is Our reward for those in sin" (*al-Araaf* 40).

Finally—although numerous other relevant verses could be quoted here—Allah says,

وَمَا يَجْحَدُ بِآيَاتِنَا إِلَّا الْكَافِرُونَ

"None but unbelievers reject Our Signs" (*al-Ankaboot* 47).

Statements From Various Scholars Concerning One Who Rejects the Sunnah

The scholars of Islam who have discussed what distinguishes a Muslim from a non-Muslim are in agreement that whoever refuses to accept the Prophet's sunnah as a binding perfect example becomes an apostate. Ibn Hazm wrote, "If a person says, 'We only follow what we find in the Quran,' then he has become an unbeliever according to the consensus of this nation [of Islam]."[1]

Al-Shaukaani said, "The stand of the sunnah and its being an independent source of law is part of the knowledge that is known to every Muslim and no one differs from this point except for those people who have nothing to do with Islam."[2]

Shaikh al-Dausiri was asked about the ruling concerning a person who rejects the sunnah and lives only according to the Quran. He said that

> this is the claim of the *zandiqa*[3] and heretics who deny half of the faith and fool the people by claiming that they are honoring the Quran. They are liars, as the Quran itself orders the obedience to the Messenger (peace be upon him) and this can only be done by following his sunnah... There is no difference of opinion on this point except from those

---

[1] Quoted in Abdul Rahmaan Itr, *Maalim al-Sunnah al-Nabawiyya* (Jordan: Maktabah al Manaar, 1986), p. 32.

[2] Muhammad Ali al-Shaukaani, *Irshaad al-Fahool* (Beirut: Daar al-Marifa, 1979), p. 33.

[3] The *zandiqa* are those people who entered into Islam without a sincere belief; in fact, their only intention was to destroy Islam from within.

people who have no relationship to the religion of Islam whatsoever.[1]

Abdul Azeez ibn Baaz has written,

The denial of the sunnah... and rendering it inapplicable is an act of *kufr* and apostasy due to the fact that whoever denies the sunnah actually denies the Quran and whoever denies either or both of them is a disbeliever according to all of the schools of thought in Islam.[2]

Al-Suyooti stated,

You should know, may Allah have mercy on all of you, that whosoever rejects the fact that the hadith of the Prophet (peace be upon him), being a report of his statement or action that meets the well-known conditions, is an authority has become an unbeliever and he shall be gathered with the Jews and Christians or with whomsoever Allah wishes to gather him with of the non-believing groups [on the Day of Judgment].[3]

Note that the disbelief of one who denies the sunnah is not simply the conclusion of human scholars that is open to dispute. Nor is it just the consensus of the scholars, which would be even more difficult to dispute. Actually, a number of verses that were already presented clearly indicate that one who refuses to accept the authority of the sunnah is one who is void of faith and is among the disbelievers. In particular, one

---

[1] Abdul Rahmaan al-Dausiri, *Al-Ajwiba al-Mufeedah limuhimmat al-Aqeedah* (Beirut: Maktabah Daar al-Arqam, 1982), pp. 62-63.

[2] *In Defence of the Quran and Sunnah* (Majlis of al-Haq Publication Society, S. Burnaby, Canada), p. 5. Cf., Abdul Azeez ibn Baaz, *Wujoob al-Amal bisunnat al-Rasool wa kufr man inkaaraha* (Riyadh: Shaarikah al-Taba al-Arabiya al-Saudiya, 1400 A. H.), pp. 13-14.

[3] Ibn Baaz, ibid., p. 30, quoting from *Miftah al-Jannah*.

should note the following the verses, which have been discussed earlier:[1]

فَلَا وَرَبِّكَ لَا يُؤْمِنُونَ حَتَّى يُحَكِّمُوكَ فِيمَا شَجَرَ بَيْنَهُمْ ثُمَّ لَا يَجِدُوا فِي أَنفُسِهِمْ حَرَجًا مِمَّا قَضَيْتَ وَيُسَلِّمُوا تَسْلِيمًا

"But no, by your Lord, they will not actually believe until they make you the judge of what is in dispute between them and find within themselves no dislike of that which you decide and they submit with full submission" (*al-Nisaa* 65).

وَإِذَا قِيلَ لَهُمْ تَعَالَوْا إِلَى مَا أَنزَلَ اللَّهُ وَإِلَى الرَّسُولِ رَأَيْتَ الْمُنَافِقِينَ يَصُدُّونَ عَنكَ صُدُودًا

"When it is said to them, 'Come to what Allah has revealed, and to the Messenger,' you see the hypocrites avert their faces from you in disgust" (*al-Nisaa* 61).

قل أطيعوا الله والرسول فإن تولوا فإن الله لا يحب الكافرين

"Say: Obey Allah and the Messenger. And if you turn away [know that] verily Allah does not love the unbelievers" (*ali-Imraan* 32).

In fact, this disbelief extends not only to denying the sunnah as a whole, but it extends to denying anything that one hears from the Prophet (peace be upon him) while the person is convinced that the statement did actually come from the Prophet (peace be upon him). Sulaimaan ibn Sahmaan wrote, "There is no difference of opinion among the scholars that if a person believes in the Prophet (peace be upon him) in some matters and belies him in another matter, he does not enter into Islam; he is like one who rejects an obligatory or mandatory act..."[2] Ibn Battah stated, "If a person believes in everything that the Messenger brought except for one thing, and he rejects that thing, then he is a disbeliever according to all of the

---

[1] Cf., Shawaat, pp. 282-283.
[2] Quoted in al-Wuhaibi, p. 57.

scholars."[1] Again, the person does not have the right to choose between what he wants to believe of the Prophet's statements and what he does not want to believe. His belief in the Prophet (peace be upon him) mandates that he believes in everything that the Prophet (peace be upon him) stated.

In order for the intent here not to be misunderstood or misapplied, three important points must also be mentioned. First, there is a difference between doubting whether or not a hadith is authentic and accepting that the hadith is an actual statement of the Prophet (peace be upon him) while denying its truthfulness. The latter case is like one saying, "I know the Prophet (peace be upon him) said it, but I do not believe it." This is the disbelief described in the statements above from Sahmaan and ibn Battah. The former case, where one doubts the authenticity of the hadith, may not be a case of disbelief, depending however on how well established is the particular hadith. In any case, judging the authenticity of hadith is the job of hadith experts. A non-scholar or non-specialist is not free to make his own judgment about hadith. Second, ignorance concerning the sunnah, even though it is well-established in the Quran, may be excused for a new convert, for example, who has not been exposed to those evidences from the Quran or who has only been exposed to those people who deny the sunnah. Once the proofs are shown to him, then he has no choice but to believe in them. Finally, to declare anyone a disbeliever is a grave matter. It should not be taken lightly. Numerous conditions must be met before anyone would be declared a disbeliever.

Another point that should not be forgotten is that the door to repentance is always open. Allah is very pleased with the repentance of anyone who returns to Him sincerely and sorrowfully. Allah alone knows the many reasons why someone may be pulled into denying the sunnah or specific hadith of the Prophet (peace be upon him)—especially in this

---

[1] Quoted in al-Abdul Lateef, p. 250.

day and age wherein the sunnah has been under attack by both unbelievers and, sadly, Muslims themselves. It could have been the case that a Muslim never had the fortune of reading in detail about the place of the sunnah. It could have also been the case that a Muslim was surrounded by those who refused to follow the sunnah or admit its authority in Islam. Whatever the case may be, repenting to Allah and having the strong will and intention to adhere to the sunnah may wipe away all the sins that one did in the past and allow the person to gain Allah's pleasure and enter into Paradise.

Conclusions

To deny the place of the sunnah in Islam, to deny that it is obligatory to believe in what the Prophet (peace be upon him) said, to deny that it is obligatory to obey his commands and prohibitions or to deny that he is the example that every Muslim must follow are all acts of *kufr* (disbelief). If a person willingly and knowingly continues to hold such beliefs after the clear proofs have been shown and explain to him, he falls outside of the fold of Islam and is a disbeliever. In this world, he is to be treated as a disbeliever. He is not deserving of the love and respect that one must give to one's brother in faith. Unless he repents before he dies, all of his deeds will be of no avail to him and in the Hereafter he will be in the Hell-fire forever.

This is not meant to be an exhortation to quickly call others disbelievers. One always has to be careful about such matters and make sure that the proofs have been clearly presented to those who holds blasphemous beliefs. (Indeed, such matters are best left in the hands of the well-grounded scholars.) However, the proofs of the Quran and sunnah are clear. They must be abided by and they must be stated. Emotions must play no part in this type of matter. No one has the right to declare another person a disbeliever unless he has clear and definitive evidence from the Quran and sunnah that such a person is to be considered a disbeliever and there are no impediments to that judgment. Similarly, no one should consider another person a Muslim unless he has evidence based on the Quran and sunnah that such a person is a Muslim. If a person denies the obligation to believe in and follow the sunnah after the clear and definitive evidence has been presented to him, he has given up that right to be considered as or treated like a Muslim. This is the declaration of the Quran, sunnah and consensus of the scholars.

Chapter Seven:
The Way of the Sunnah Is the Way of Islam

A person enters into Islam by testifying that none is worthy of worship except Allah and that Muhammad is the Messenger of Allah (peace be upon him). When he makes the testimony of faith, he is attesting to its truthfulness. Furthermore, he is making a commitment that he will, to the best of his ability, abide by the requirements of that statement.

In reality, the first portion of this statement of faith actually means that the person will not take as a God or object of worship anything or anyone other than Allah. His acts will be for the sake of pleasing Allah alone. The second portion is where the person accepts that the proper fashion to worship Allah is according to the teachings of the Prophet Muhammad (peace be upon him). If a person refuses to abide by the standards set by the Prophet (peace be upon him), his deeds will not be acceptable to Allah, no matter how much he may claim that he believes in the one God. Imam al-Nawawi wrote,

> It is clear that Allah does not accept a deed from any human if the one who performed that deed did not do so according to the pattern set by the Messenger of Allah (peace be upon him), regardless of whether it be a statement [belief] or an action. The only deeds that may be accepted by Allah are those in which its doer has done them purely for the sake of Allah and in following the Messenger (peace be upon him) via his guidance to the straight path, the path of Allah. Allah has said, "And verily you (O Muhammad) do guide (men) to the straight way— the Way of Allah

to whom belongs whatever is in the heavens and whatever is on earth. Behold how all affairs tend towards Allah" (*al-Shoora* 52-53). And Allah has also said, "And they have been commanded no more than this: to worship Allah alone, offering Him sincere devotion, being true (in faith); to establish regular prayer; and to give the zakaat; and that is the religion right and straight" (*al-Bayyinah* 5).[1]

Hence, it is part of the implication of a person's testimony of faith that he emulate and follow the Messenger of Allah (peace be upon him). In fact, the Prophet's sunnah is Islam. Not because it is not in need of the Quran but because it is the concrete actualization of the teachings of the Quran.

Furthermore, this way of Islam—the way of the sunnah—is the only valid and authentic expression of Islam. It is not the case that there are many paths and they all lead to Allah's pleasure. The Prophet (peace be upon him) showed that such is not true, as is demonstrated in the following hadith:

عَنْ عَبْدِ اللَّهِ بْنِ مَسْعُودٍ قَالَ خَطَّ لَنَا رَسُولُ اللَّهِ صَلَّى اللَّهم عَلَيْهِ وَسَلَّمَ خَطًّا ثُمَّ قَالَ هَذَا سَبِيلُ اللَّهِ ثُمَّ خَطَّ خُطُوطًا عَنْ يَمِينِهِ وَعَنْ شِمَالِهِ ثُمَّ قَالَ هَذِهِ سُبُلٌ مُتَفَرِّقَةٌ عَلَى كُلِّ سَبِيلٍ مِنْهَا شَيْطَانٌ يَدْعُو إِلَيْهِ ثُمَّ قَرَأَ (إِنَّ هَذَا صِرَاطِي مُسْتَقِيمًا فَاتَّبِعُوهُ وَلَا تَتَّبِعُوا السُّبُلَ فَتَفَرَّقَ بِكُمْ عَنْ سَبِيلِهِ)

On the authority of Abdullah ibn Masood who said, "The Messenger of Allah (peace be upon him) drew a straight line

---

[1] Yahya al-Nawawi, *Sharh Matin al-Arbaeen al-Nawawiya* (Muhammad Rasheed Ridha, ed., Maktabah al-Salaam al-Aalimiyyah, n.d.), p. 85.

for us. Then he said, 'This is the path of Allah.' Then he drew lines to the left of it and to the right of it. He then said, 'These are divergent paths. Upon each of those paths is a devil calling to that path.' Then he recited [the verse], 'Verily, this is My Way leading straight. Follow it and do not follow (other) paths. They [the other paths] will scatter you about from His path' [*al-Anaam* 153]."[1]

Allah's straight path is undoubtedly the path of the sunnah of the Prophet (peace be upon him). Allah said about the Prophet (peace be upon him),

$$\text{فَاسْتَمْسِكْ بِالَّذِي أُوحِيَ إِلَيْكَ إِنَّكَ عَلَى صِرَاطٍ مُسْتَقِيمٍ}$$

"So hold you fast to the Revelation sent down to you. Verily you are on a straight path" (*al-Zukhruf* 43). Allah also said about the Prophet's guidance, that is, his sunnah,

$$\text{وَإِنَّكَ لَتَهْدِي إِلَى صِرَاطٍ مُسْتَقِيمٍ}$$

"You certainly guide to a path which is straight" (*al-Shoora* 52).

If anyone claims that the way of the sunnah of the Prophet (peace be upon him) is not the straight path, he is contradicting what Allah has said in the Quran. Furthermore, if anyone claims that his way is just one of many paths that a

---

[1] Recorded by Ahmad and ibn Maajah. According to al-Albaani, this hadith is *sahih*. See Muhammad Naasir al-Deen al-Albaani, footnotes to Umar ibn Abi al-Asim al-Shaibaani, *Kitaab al-Sunnah* (Beirut: al-Maktab al-Islaami, 1985), vol. 1, p. 13. Al-Teebi (vol. 2, p. 635) notes that part of the implication of this hadith is that there are paths which go to different extremes, "to the left and right of the straight path." All of these extremes are wrong and they may be with respect to different parts of the religion. For example, overzealousness and going beyond the sunnah of the Messenger of Allah (peace be upon him) is one extreme. The opposite extreme to that is where one downplays the ordinances of the Quran and sunnah, claiming that belief is in the heart and need not manifest itself in the proper deeds that the Prophet (peace be upon him) established. Separate from those extremes is the way of the Prophet (peace be upon him) and his true followers, in the middle, along Allah's straight path. Cf., Muhammad Ba-Abdullah, *Waasitiyyah Ahl al-Sunnah Bain al-Firaq* (Riyadh: Daar al-Raayah, 1994), *passim*.

Muslim is free to follow, he is once again contradicting what Allah has said in the Quran. The correct path to Allah's pleasure and paradise is one path and one path only and that is the path of the sunnah, the practical embodiment of the Quran. The Prophet (peace be upon him) also said,

إِنَّ بَنِي إِسْرَائِيلَ تَفَرَّقَتْ عَلَى ثِنْتَيْنِ وَسَبْعِينَ مِلَّةً وَتَفْتَرِقُ أُمَّتِي عَلَى ثَلاثٍ وَسَبْعِينَ مِلَّةً كُلُّهُمْ فِي النَّارِ إِلاَّ مِلَّةً وَاحِدَةً قَالُوا وَمَنْ هِيَ يَا رَسُولَ اللَّهِ قَالَ مَا أَنَا عَلَيْهِ وَأَصْحَابِي

"The Tribes of Israel divided into seventy two religious sects. My nation will divide into seventy-three sects. All of them will be in the Fire except one." They said, "And who is that one, O Messenger of Allah (peace be upon him)?" He replied, "[The one following] what I and my Companions are upon."[1] The Prophet (peace be upon him) still described those other groups as being part of his "nation". This implies that they do not fall outside of the fold of Islam. However, the hadith also implies that they will have to taste some of the torment of Hell due to their straying from the clear and straight path of what the Prophet (peace be upon him) established and passed on to his Companions—unless Allah wills to forgive them. Thus, punishment in the Hell-fire is the horrendous result of straying from the way of the sunnah..

In this hadith, the Prophet (peace be upon him) prophesized that there would be straying from the path that he (peace be upon him) had established and which his Companions had earnestly followed. Yet, at the same time, in a number of other hadith, the Prophet (peace be upon him) gave the glad tidings that there will always be a sector of

---

[1] Recorded by al-Tirmidhi. According to al-Albaani, this hadith is *hasan*. See al-Albaani, *Saheeh al-Jaami al-Sagheer*, vol. 2, p. 944.

Muslims who will be along that straight path. For example, in one hadith the Prophet (peace be upon him) said,

لَا تَزَالُ طَائِفَةٌ مِنْ أُمَّتِي ظَاهِرِينَ عَلَى الْحَقِّ لَا يَضُرُّهُمْ مَنْ خَذَلَهُمْ حَتَّى يَأْتِيَ أَمْرُ اللَّهِ وَهُمْ كَذَلِكَ

"A group of my nation will continue to be victorious upon the truth and those who abandon them will not harm them. [They will continue in that state] until the command comes and they are still in that state." (Recorded by Muslim.)

Every Muslim should desire to be a member of that group which is the saved sect and which will be following the truth until the Day of Judgment. The first question, therefore, is how to identify that group. This question can be answered by referring to the other hadith and verses mentioned above. This group is definitely that group which adheres to the sunnah. If the answer is anything other than that, it implies that the Prophet (peace be upon him) and his Companions were not from among that saved sect and that group which continued to fight for the truth. This answer is inconceivable in the light of the Quran and sunnah.

Therefore, that saved sect and party which will continue to be victorious is none other than those who cling steadfastly and unswervingly to the sunnah or the hadith of the Messenger of Allah (peace be upon him). After recording the hadith about the saved sect, al-Tirmidhi recorded that Ali ibn al-Madeeni (al-Bukhari's teacher) said, "They are the followers and adherents of the hadith (*ahl al-hadith*)." Imam Ahmad said, "If they are not the people of hadith, I have no idea who they might be."[1] Abdullah ibn al-Mubaarak also said, "In my opinion this group could only be the people of hadith."[2] The meaning of the expression, *ahl al-hadith* or "the

---

[1] Both quoted in al-Salafi, p. 70.
[2] Quoted in al-Suyooti, *Miftah al-Jannah*, p. 119.

people of hadith," is those people who learn and apply the sunnah, hadith and guidance that the Prophet (peace be upon him) brought and passed on to his Companions.

Ibn Taimiyyah noted that what is meant by the people of the sunnah and hadith are not those who simply read hadith, write them or pass them on. What is meant by the people of the hadith are those who truly preserve them by understanding them properly, their apparent and deeper meanings, and those who follow such hadith exoterically and esoterically. The same kind of statement, he said, can be made for what is meant by the "people of the Quran." That is, they are not those who simply memorize the Quran but they are those who learn it and apply it in the way it is meant to be applied. The least that can be said about such people is that they love the Quran and hadith. They seek to understand the correct meaning of the Quran and hadith and to apply them in their lives.[1]

In a very important passage, ibn Taimiyyah speaks about the identification of that saved sect and victorious group. He says that many people claim that a specific sect is the saved group, but they have no true evidence for what they say. They are simply basing their claims on conjecture or their own personal desires. They claim that they are from the people of the sunnah and everyone who opposes them is from the heretics. But if their beliefs are from anyone other than the Prophet (peace be upon him) or the leader of their group is anyone other than the Prophet (peace be upon him), their claim cannot be accepted. This is because there is no one who is to be totally believed and totally obeyed except the Prophet (peace be upon him). As for anyone else, some of his statements will be accepted and some may be rejected—they

---

[1] Ibn Taimiyyah, *Majmoo*, vol. 4, p. 95. Historically, one of the criticisms of some people who called themselves "the people of hadith" is that they would simply pass on hadith without understanding the meaning of the hadith they were passing on. Although that may have been true in the case of some of the later narrators of hadith, ibn Taimiyyah is saying that in essence these are not the real people of hadith.

must be judged in the light of the Quran and sunnah. Some groups take a person or persons other than the Prophet (peace be upon him), be they Imams, scholars, pious men or whatever, as the standard for what is truth. They claim that whoever follows their leader is on the straight path and whoever goes against him is deviant. They love each other based on their adherence to that leader and hate others due to their view of that leader.[1] In reality, what they are doing is not

---

[1] Unfortunately, this practice, which ibn Taimiyyah condemns in a number of his writings, even occurs among those who seem to be adhering to the way of the Prophet (peace be upon him). They set up three or four scholars and state that these are the "leading scholars," which they very well may be. (Sometimes it is even just one scholar around whom, to his followers, all truth revolves.) But then they take these scholars' *ijtihaad* (personal judgment) or rulings as the basis for truth and loyalty. If anyone disagrees with their conclusions, they are then labeled as deviant. (Even if a person differs as to which opinion he follows concerning what to do with his right index finger during the sitting of the prayer, he may be labeled a deviant.) Again, as ibn Taimiyyah noted, this type of loyalty and branding is the practice of the heretics and not that of the people of the sunnah. The kind of loyalty that they exhibit must, in reality, be expressed only to the Prophet (peace be upon him), and not to any other scholar or scholars no matter how excellent they may be. Even if those three or four are the leading scholars, that does not mean that their conclusion is a type of consensus that all others must fall in line with. It also does not mean that no other scholar has the right to voice his opinion on matters of *ijtihaad*, on matters of applying the texts of the Quran and sunnah to new or different situations. Even if those leading scholars are absolutely correct in their conclusion, this does not mean that anyone who comes to a differing conclusion must be a deviant. A person does not automatically become a deviant simply because he has some difference of opinion in a matter of *ijtihaad*. Allah says in the Quran, "O you who believe, obey Allah and obey the Messenger and those in authority among you. And if you are in dispute over any matter, refer it to Allah and His Messenger if you are actually believers in Allah and the Last Day. That is better for you and more seemly in the end" (*al-Nisaa* 59). This verse says that all disputes must be taken to the Quran and sunnah. This was the practice of the Companions. The verse also implies that if a matter is taken back to the Quran and sunnah and it is found that it is a matter that is clear in the Quran and sunnah, there is no room for any difference of opinion. Any straying in such a matter would in fact be deviance. On the other hand, if a matter is taken back to the Quran and sunnah and it is found that that matter is one open to *ijtihaad*, then one cannot force his conclusion on others. This was the way of the Companions that they had learned directly from the Prophet (peace be upon him). [For example, no blame was placed on either of the two groups who differed about when to perform the *Asr* Prayer when the

from the practice of the people who correctly adhere to the Prophet's teachings. Instead, such was the practice of all of the heretical groups in the history of Islam. This is further verification of the correctness of the way of the people of the sunnah. True loyalty must be only for the sake of Allah. Furthermore, no one is deserving of the status of "standard for the truth" except the Messenger of Allah (peace be upon him). These are the two pillars—loyalty for the sake of Allah and the Messenger (peace be upon him) being the only infallible standard of truth—upon which revolve the practices of the people of the sunnah. If something can be proven from what the Prophet (peace be upon him) presented in either the Quran or the sunnah, they accept it and follow it. As part of their love for Allah, they love those people who follow what he brought. Out of their love for Allah, they also oppose anyone who opposes what the Prophet (peace be upon him) taught. They are the only ones who can make the claim that their leader is infallible. They are the only ones who can make the claim that Allah has commanded absolute obedience and belief in their leader. Hence, they are the only ones truly on the true straight path.[1]

Furthermore, when one thinks about those who study, understand and adhere to the sunnah and hadith in detail, one will conclude that they have some characteristics that set them

---

Prophet (peace be upon him) had sent them to the Tribe of Quraidah.] The Companions differed on a number of issues of *ijtihaad*, yet they never allowed those acceptable differences to cause their hearts to divide. They continued to love each other and support each other fully despite differences in *ijtihaad* on those matters which were not definitively covered in either the Quran or sunnah. They had mutual respect for each other and they understood that each was doing his best to worship Allah alone. They also understood that it was not their job to condemn others simply because they may come to a different conclusion. To divide the Muslims based on *ijtihaad* or loyalty to specific scholars is from the means of Satan and the result of personal desires, all of which the true adherents to the sunnah must be free of. Cf., Abu al-Mudhafar al-Samaani's passage quoted in Muhammad Bazamool, *Al-Intisaar li-Ahl al-Hadeeth* (al-Khobar, Saudi Arabia: Daar al-Hijrah, 1997), pp. 67-72.

[1] Cf., ibn Taimiyyah, *Majmoo*, vol. 3, pp. 346-347.

apart from all others. For example, they should be the ones who understand the Quran best. This is because they are studying the real source of *tafseer* (Quranic commentary). Upon reading Quranic commentaries, one can note that some commentators rely much more on hadith and the statements of the Companions (those who learned directly from the Prophet) than others. Although it is beyond the scope of this work to prove this point here, it can be rightly said that those commentators with the largest amount of errors and heretical thoughts in their commentaries are those who relied the least on the sunnah and the Companions. This is because they had to rely on their own personal intellect and understanding, which is very limited when it comes to understanding the great guidance that Allah has revealed in the Quran. Due to their lack of reliance on the teachings of the Prophet (peace be upon him), they had no way to grasp the correct meanings of the verses and were forced to interpret the Quran based merely on their intellect without having a real understanding of who the Quran was first revealed to and to what exactly it was referring. A basic understanding of hermeneutics demonstrates that one has to have a firm grasp of the environment and persona of the time of the revelation to truly have a feel for what the revelation is speaking about.

In addition, those who study, understand and adhere to the sunnah and hadith in detail are the people who are most familiar with the life, goals and directives of the Prophet (peace be upon him). They become specialists in the life and deeds of the Prophet (peace be upon him). They study the Prophet's life in such detail that upon hearing anything about the Prophet (peace be upon him), they can immediately recognize if that fits what is known about the Prophet (peace be upon him) or not. They know the Prophet (peace be upon him) very well and, therefore, they know how to behave like the Prophet (peace be upon him). The goal of their in-depth and detailed study is to learn from the Prophet (peace be upon him) and implement his teachings in their lives. This is what

Imam al-Shafiee said, "When I see one of the people of hadith, it is as if I am seeing the Messenger of Allah (peace be upon him) alive."[1]

The adherents and students of hadith are also much more aware of the Prophet's message than those who only rarely turn to his sayings. To make a modern-day type of analogy, they are like those who are specialists in the music of Beethoven or the paintings of Picasso. Such experts can almost immediately tell when a piece of music is or is not Beethoven's or when a painting claimed to be one of Picasso's is a forgery. This is because they are so much into their works that they have encompassed everything that is known to come from them and, based on that definitive knowledge, they can identify when something must not have come from them. The scholars of hadith and strong adherents to the sunnah reached a similar position with respect to the Prophet (peace be upon him). When heretical ideas or new issues appear among the people, due to their deep knowledge of the sunnah, these scholars can immediately recognize that those ideas are not consistent with what they know of the Prophet (peace be upon him). Hence, they are saved from straying from the straight path, by the will and mercy of Allah. Furthermore, people spend their time reading and learning the works of others—even if indirectly they think it will lead them to know about Allah and His Messenger (peace be upon him)—while the people of the hadith spend their time and efforts reading and learning directly about Allah and His Messenger (peace be upon him).

Finally, the people of the sunnah and hadith are the people of stability, tranquility and unity. They are the people of stability because they are following something that is the truth, that will never change, coming directly from Allah. When it comes to matters of faith and belief, they restrict the

---

[1] Quoted in Rabee al-Madkhali, *Makaanah Ahl al-Hadeeth* (Bahrain: Daar al-Arqam, 1985), p. 54.

use of personal reasoning because many of those matters are beyond the realm of human perception. In the history of Islam, one of the greatest sources of confusion has been turning to the very limited human intellect to determine the aspects of faith. Even though the proponents of such schools of thought claim that their approach is based on the most definitive of rational proofs, one can find that they are the people who differ the most and, beyond that, one can find them moving from one opinion to the other, endlessly at a loss. In fact, some of their leaders continued to be perplexed until finally they turned to the way of the sunnah, hadith and Companions. It was only then that they truly realized the truth and discovered that they did not have to waver from this firm belief anymore. Their hearts finally come to a rest and they were finally able to experience true tranquility, the tranquility of belief that the Companions of the Prophet (peace be upon him), following in his footsteps, had.[1]

It follows from this that the people of hadith are the real people of unity. One reason for this is that when it comes to the fundamentals of their faith, they are not followers of personal opinions, which are bound to be various and conflicting. Their book is one, the Quran. Their leader is one, the Prophet Muhammad (peace be upon him). This is what they adhere to. Others may claim to adhere to the same but the reality is different. In reality, the others adhere to the Quran

---

[1] Cf., quote from al-Samaani in Bazamool, pp. 70-72. Uthmaan ibn Hasan notes how it has never been known for a follower of the sunnah to give up on his beliefs or become disenchanted with them. No matter what trials he had to face, he would remain patient. Indeed, such was the way of the Prophets throughout the ages. On the other hand, those who turned away from the sunnah and followed man-made theories or philosophy often repented from their false ideologies. For example, al-Raazi lamented that all he had acquired through the years was, "It is said and they said..." Al-Juwaini stated that if he had it all to do over again, he would not study philosophy and theology, as it led him to nothing. Instead, he would adhere strictly to the wordings of the Quran and sunnah. Al-Shahristaani is another famous scholar of the *ahl al-kalaam* (scholastic theology) who regretted his past efforts which led him to no certainty whatsoever. Cf., Uthmaan ibn Hasan, vol. 2, pp. 739-742.

and the Prophet (peace be upon him) only when such is in conformity with what their scholar, Imam or shaikh has said. On the other hand, the people of hadith and the sunnah apply the following Quranic verse to put an end to their disputes:

يَاأَيُّهَا الَّذِينَ آمَنُوا أَطِيعُوا اللَّهَ وَأَطِيعُوا الرَّسُولَ وَأُوْلِي الأَمْرِ مِنْكُمْ

فَإِنْ تَنَازَعْتُمْ فِي شَيْءٍ فَرُدُّوهُ إِلَى اللَّهِ وَالرَّسُولِ إِنْ كُنْتُمْ تُؤْمِنُونَ

بِاللَّهِ وَالْيَوْمِ الآخِرِ ذَلِكَ خَيْرٌ وَأَحْسَنُ تَأْوِيلاً

"O you who believe, obey Allah and obey the Messenger and those in authority among you. And if you are in dispute over any matter, refer it to Allah and His Messenger if you are actually believers in Allah and the Last Day. That is better for you and more seemly in the end" (*al-Nisaa* 59). They do not follow their desires or personal opinions but they resort to the Quran and sunnah. Al-Shaatibi notes that it is the Quran and sunnah that will be able to bring an end to their disputes, otherwise the command in this verse would be folly.[1] In fact, it is only the people of hadith who apply—and who can apply—the verse of the Quran,

وَاعْتَصِمُوا بِحَبْلِ اللَّهِ جَمِيعًا وَلا تَفَرَّقُوا

"Adhere to the rope of Allah and be not divided" (*ali-Imraan* 103). The rope of Allah is Allah's revelation in the Quran and sunnah. Hence, the people of the sunnah and hadith are the only ones who are truly adhering to that and, therefore, they are the only ones who can have any hope of not being divided.

---

[1] Al-Shaatibi, *al-Muwaafaqaat*, vol. 5, p. 60. As noted in a previous footnote, the Quran and sunnah will also show them wherein they may differ and wherein it is not allowed to differ. In other words, some disputes are allowed to be left open as long as they do not reach the person's heart and cause division among the Muslims. On some other issues, such difference of opinion is not acceptable. It is the Quran and sunnah that will show the Muslims wherein it is acceptable, to some extent, to differ and wherein it is not allowed to differ.

What It Means to Be From the People of the Sunnah and Hadith

The following of the sunnah and hadith is a very serious and comprehensive commitment. When done properly, it permeates every facet of one's life. Uthmaan Dhumairiyyah wrote,

> Some people restrict their following of the Prophet (peace be upon him) to one particular area—the outward aspects—and they neglect all of the other aspects. They say, "So and so is upon the sunnah" because he lets his beard grow or he shortens the length of his garment. While we do not belittle the importance of these aspects in any way, as there is a direct relationship between the outward appearance or shape and the driving force behind it, but they are forgetting the other aspects which are of utmost importance, such as proper belief, religious knowledge, manners and behavior and so forth.[1]

In particular, one must do his best to make sure that his beliefs, his outward actions and his morals and characters are in accord with the example and sunnah of the Prophet Muhammad (peace be upon him). Each of these areas is deserving of some discussion:

(1) With respect to beliefs: This is one of the most important aspects of what the Prophet (peace be upon him) brought and passed on to his Companions. There is no question that this is part of the essence of following the sunnah of the Prophet (peace be upon him). Allah says,

---

[1] Dhumairiyyah, p. 93.

فَإِنْ آمَنُوا بِمِثْلِ مَا آمَنْتُمْ بِهِ فَقَدِ اهْتَدَوْا وَإِنْ تَوَلَّوْا فَإِنَّمَا هُمْ فِي شِقَاقٍ فَسَيَكْفِيكَهُمُ اللَّهُ وَهُوَ السَّمِيعُ الْعَلِيمُ

"So if they believe as you believe, they are indeed on the right path; but if they turn back, it is they who are in schism; but Allah will suffice you against them, and He is the All-Hearing, the All-Knowing" (*al-Baqarah* 137). This verse is, in particular, in reference to the People of the Book. However, its meaning is general and is as ibn Abbaas explained it, "If they believe in what you believe in, they will be rightly guided."[1] Indeed, one's beliefs are definitely one of the distinguishing features of the followers of the sunnah. This is why, ibn Taimiya, for example, stated,

> What is meant by "the pure people of the hadith and sunnah" (*ahl al-hadeeth wa al-sunnah*) is the exclusion of everyone except those who affirm Allah's attributes, say that the Quran is not created, say that Allah will be seen in the Hereafter, affirm predestination and other well-known principles and foundations among the people of the hadith and sunnah.[2]

The Muslim should believe without doubt or suspicion in anything which came from the Prophet (peace be upon him), in the Quran or authentic hadith. If the Prophet (peace be upon him) said, for example, that something will happen on the Day of Judgment, the Muslim believes that such will definitely occur just as the Prophet (peace be upon him) stated it.

---

[1] Quoted in al-Tabari by the well-known chain of Muaawiyyah ibn Saalih on the authority of Ali ibn Abi Talha on the authority of ibn Abbaas. Muhammad ibn Jareer al-Tabari, *Jaami al-Bayaan an Taweel Ayi al-Quran* (Beirut: Daar al-Fikr, 1988), vol. 1, p. 571.

[2] Ahmad Ibn Taimiyyah, *Minhaaj al-Sunnah* (Riyadh: Jaamiat al-Imaam, 1986), vol. 2, p. 221.

Some of the principle beliefs that are held by this group in their following of the Prophet (peace be upon him) and what he passed on to his Companions include, among many other aspects, the following:

(a) Belief in Allah as the one Lord, Creator and God: This also includes belief in all the names and attributes that Allah has affirmed of Himself or that the Prophet (peace be upon him) has attributed to Allah. Those attributes are neither denied nor interpreted in such a way as to deny any real existence to them. At the same time, though, any similarity between the attributes of Allah and the attributes of His creation are denied. None can delve into the exact nature of those attributes as they are unique to Allah and beyond the realm of human experience.

(b) Belief in all of the previous prophets and belief in the Prophet Muhammad (peace be upon him) as the final prophet: This includes believing that the Prophet Muhammad (peace be upon him) conveyed all of the message and he was protected by Allah from committing any error in that conveyance. His teachings are final for all of mankind until the Day of Judgment. This also includes believing that everything the Messenger of Allah (peace be upon him) said is the absolute truth.

(c) Belief in all of the books revealed by Allah and belief in the Quran as the final revelation: This includes believing that the Quran is the uncreated word of Allah.

(d) Belief in the concept of faith as described by Allah and His Messenger (peace be upon him); this includes recognizing that: Faith is composed of beliefs in the heart, statement of the tongue and actions by the physical being. A person's faith can increase or decrease. A person does not become a disbeliever due to a sin—less than committing *shirk* (associating partners with Allah); however, at the same time, his faith is affected by his sin and he may even be sent to the Hell-fire for some period due to the enormous sins he has committed. The Prophet (peace be upon him) has reserved his

237

intercession for those of his nation who committed the major sins.

(e) Belief in the nobility and virtuousness of all of the noble Companions of the Prophet Muhammad (peace be upon him).

(f) Belief in life after death and all related aspects that are mentioned in either the Quran or the authentic hadith: This includes the signs of the Day of Judgment, the bridge that people will have to pass over, the weighing of all the deeds, the intercession of the Prophet (peace be upon him) and so forth. Note that many of these aspects are not mentioned at all or in detail in the Quran; that fact, however, should not affect a person's belief in them.

(g) Belief that the goal and purpose of one's life is to worship and please Allah: One cannot be considered to be following the pattern set by the Prophet (peace be upon him) if his goals and aspirations are merely for this life, even if on the outside it looks like he is following the sunnah.

If one does not believe in these principles that are firmly rooted in the Quran and sunnah and that form part of the teachings that the Prophet (peace be upon him) passed on, then he cannot rightly claim to be adhering to the sunnah in its entirety.

(2) With respect to outward deeds, including rites of worship: The deeds that a person performs is one of the quintessential aspects of his religion or *deen*. The deeds are so important that some of the early scholars identified the correct path and the way of the sunnah by specific deeds. For example, Sufyaan al-Auzaaee said, "The Companions of the Messenger of Allah and those who followed them in good deeds based their lives on five [principles]: sticking to the community, following the sunnah, building [and attending] the mosques, reciting the Quran and jihad in the way of Allah."[1]

---

[1] Quoted in al-Suyooti, *Mitfah*, p. 112.

In order to be a true adherent of the sunnah, one must practice the essential pillars of the faith: perform the five daily prayers, fast the month of Ramadhaan, give the zakaat when required and make the pilgrimage once in a lifetime when one has the means. Beyond these pillars are numerous other deeds, such as those just mentioned in the quote from Sufyaan al-Auzaaee.

The adherent to the sunnah recognizes that he must worship Allah in the manner that Allah has prescribed for him via the example and teachings of the Prophet Muhammad (peace be upon him). This means that he should be extremely cautious when it comes to any type of innovation or heresy in the religion. He should realize that innovated deeds will not be accepted by Allah. The Prophet (peace be upon him) said,

$$ \text{مَنْ عَمِلَ عَمَلاً لَيْسَ عَلَيْهِ أَمْرُنَا فَهُوَ رَدٌّ} $$

"Whoever does an act that is not in accord with our matter will have it rejected." (Reported by al-Bukhari and Muslim.) He will avoid any practice that supposedly takes one closer to Allah upon realizing that said practice was not sanctioned or followed by the Prophet (peace be upon him) himself.

With respect to "worldly deeds," one must be certain that he is abiding by the laws of the Quran and sunnah. Islamic law touches upon every aspect of life. Before a person does an action, he should first be certain that it is permissible according to Islamic law. If a person is running a business, he should make sure that his business is not violating any tenets of the law. If a person is getting married, he must make sure that he is getting married in the proper way. Within a marriage, both the husband and the wife have to make sure that they are behaving in the correct way, fulfilling each others' rights. The laws of divorce and child custody are covered by Islamic law. Hence, when it comes to divorce, one must divorce in the proper way and not allow one's emotions to drive one beyond the limits of the law. When it comes to jihad, one must know the laws of Islam and the guidance of the Prophet (peace be upon him). Jihad in no way implies a justification for attacking the enemy in any way shape or form; instead, it has very strict and important regulations by which one must abide.

When a person violates these laws and rules of Islam, he cannot claim to be following the sunnah. Indeed, he is not following the sunnah in those acts. The ultimate goal is to be following the sunnah in all aspects of one's life, such that one's life becomes a complete and true worship of Allah.

(3) One must also adhere to the sunnah with respect to manners, morals and behavior. This is one aspect of the sunnah that is most overlooked by many who believe that they are following the sunnah. As the quote earlier from Dhumairiyyah noted, to be a true follower of the sunnah, it is not sufficient to outwardly display oneself as a follower of the sunnah. Even abiding by the legal rules of Islam is not sufficient. A person can avoid all sorts of vices and can make sure that he is meeting the letter of the law in his deeds and transactions, but he will still fall short of adhering to the sunnah if his behavior and morals are not according to the guidance of the sunnah.

It is amazing for someone to have bad character while he claims to be a follower of the sunnah. Proper behavior and conduct is one of the most essential aspects of adhering to the sunnah. This is one of the aspects that Allah specifically pointed out about the Prophet (peace be upon him):

$$وَإِنَّكَ لَعَلَى خُلُقٍ عَظِيمٍ$$

"You [O Muhammad] are indeed on an exalted standard of character" (*al-Qalam* 4). The Prophet (peace be upon him) described part of his mission when he said,

$$إِنَّمَا بُعِثْتُ لِأَتَمِّمَ صَالِحَ الْأَخْلَاقِ$$

240

"I have been sent for the purpose of perfecting good morals."[1]
The Prophet (peace be upon him) also said,

$$\text{الْبِرُّ حُسْنُ الْخُلُقِ}$$

"Piety and righteousness is being of good character."
(Recorded by Muslim.) That this is one of the most important
aspects of the sunnah to the Prophet (peace be upon him)
himself can be seen in the following hadith:

$$\text{إِنَّ مِنْ أَحَبِّكُمْ إِلَيَّ وَأَقْرَبِكُمْ مِنِّي مَجْلِسًا يَوْمَ الْقِيَامَةِ}$$
$$\text{أَحَاسِنَكُمْ أَخْلَاقًا}$$

"Those who will be most beloved to me and seated the closest
to me on the Day of Judgment are those of you who are of the
best conduct."[2]

The adherent to the sunnah must study the Prophet's
character and manners. Then he must work on himself to
change himself to become like the Prophet (peace be upon
him). He should take note of hadith like the following and then
do his best to make sure that it becomes a description of
himself:

$$\text{عَنْ أَنَسِ بْنِ مَالِكٍ رَضِيَ اللَّهُم عَنْهم قَالَ لَمْ يَكُنِ النَّبِيُّ صَلَّى}$$
$$\text{اللَّهُم عَلَيْهِ وَسَلَّمَ سَبَّابًا وَلَا فَحَّاشًا وَلَا لَعَّانًا كَانَ يَقُولُ}$$
$$\text{لِأَحَدِنَا عِنْدَ الْمَعْتِبَةِ مَا لَهُ تَرِبَ جَبِينُه}$$

[1] Recorded by al-Haakim and others. Graded *sahih* by al-Albaani in *Saheeh al-Jaami*, vol. 1, p. 464.

[2] Recorded by al-Tirmidhi. According to al-Albaani, it is *sahih*. See Muhammad Naasir al-Deen al-Albaani, *Saheeh Sunan al-Tirmihdi* (Riyadh: Maktab al-Tarbiyyah al-Arabi li-Duwal al-Khaleej, 1988), vol. 2, pp. 196-197.

Anas ibn Maalik narrated that the Messenger of Allah (peace be upon him) was neither one who abuses others, one who had a bad tongue nor one who cursed others. If he wanted to reproach someone, the most he would say is, "What is wrong with him? May dust be on his forehead." (Recorded by al-Bukhari.)

It is incomprehensible for someone to claim to be a true follower of the sunnah and then he backbites this person, spreads tales about another person, makes innuendoes about a third person and so on. It is incomprehensible for someone who claims to be an adherent of the sunnah to have envy in his heart for another brother or to have undue suspicions which he actually acts upon. It is incomprehensible for someone to claim to be an adherent of the sunnah and then to call others names and label them as disbelievers, heretics, deviants and evildoers while he has no proof from Allah or the sunnah of the Prophet (peace be upon him) for such a claim. It is incomprehensible for someone to claim to be an adherent of the sunnah and then he goes to his home and verbally abuses and beats his wife without any due cause. Even if a person has a long beard, a short mustache, a *miswak* in his mouth, a lower gown well above his ankles and a copy of *Sahih al-Bukhari* in his hand, he is still not a true adherent to the sunnah until he changes his ways, and his manners and behavior become like that of the Prophet (peace be upon him).

In sum, the true adherence to the sunnah requires that all of one's life be lived in the shade of the revelations from Allah, the Quran and sunnah.

Following the Sunnah Requires True Commitment

Once a person realizes that he must do his best to emulate the Prophet (peace be upon him) in all aspects of his life, he should also realize that this requires a real commitment on his part. This is especially true today when people have strayed far from the beautiful and excellent example of the Prophet (peace be upon him). The person who turns to the sunnah and begins to apply it in his life will most likely—if not definitely—be met with scorn and ridicule from those around him, even the Muslims. Those who are closest to him, his family and loved ones, might even be the harshest upon him. They may be the first to try to convince him not to take the sunnah so seriously. They might even argue that as long as he lives by the general rules of the Quran, he should be fine. They may argue that he should live like all the other Muslims today—after all, they all claim to be Muslims. In fact, other Muslims may accuse him of setting himself apart from the others and insinuating that the others are not true Muslims because he is patterning his life after the example of the Prophet (peace be upon him) and not in the manner that most live their lives today.

A person must be ready for all of these onslaughts when he turns to follow the true path of the sunnah. For example, if he applies the hadith,

$$مَا تَحْتَ الْكَعْبَيْنِ مِنَ الإِزَارِ فَفِي النَّارِ$$

"What falls below the ankles of the waistcloth [garment over the lower portion of a body] is in the Hell-fire,"[1] he will be ridiculed by those who consider that unfashionable. One might think that the length of a person's clothing is his own personal choice that should not be of much concern to others but one may be very surprised at how even the length of one's clothing can be so bothersome to others.

Take the following hadith as another example:

$$كن في الدنيا كأنك، غريب أو عابر سبيل$$

---

[1] Recorded by al-Nasaai, Ahmad and others. According to al-Albaani, it is *sahih*. See al-Albaani, *Saheeh al-Jaami*, vol. 2, p. 979.

"Be in the world as if you were a stranger or a traveler along a path." (Recorded by al-Bukhari.) In this world with such great concern for materialism and status, even among the Muslims, one faces great opposition when trying to follow this ever important advice of the Prophet (peace be upon him). When a Muslim is not overly concerned with profit and loss, when he is not overly concerned with status or degrees, when he is not concerned with the luxuries of this life and he wants to lead a simple life, he is looked upon in a very strange manner nowadays. Many times a true adherent of the sunnah will take a lesser paying job because it is better from an Islamic point of view. He is not concerned with amassing more money than he needs because he does not consider this world his real home and final resting place. He is trying to work for the Hereafter and not this life, as the wisdom of this hadith shows him. First and foremost, his parents might object to this type of behavior. His parents may be upset with him because he is not getting the highest paying job that he can get given his education—and this is an embarrassment to them among their materialistic friends. They may tell him that they struggled to get him a good education and now he is wasting it on a small paying job. They cannot fathom that, although they are all Muslims, their son has chosen a very different path than the path that is followed by most Muslims today. He is making certain life choices because he is truly trying to follow the path of the Prophet Muhammad (peace be upon him).

One of the most glaring examples today revolves around the hadith of the Prophet (peace be upon him):

$$\text{مَنْ تَشَبَّهَ بِقَوْمٍ فَهُوَ مِنْهُمْ}$$

"Whoever appears like a people is one of them."[1] Perhaps there is nothing more glaring than the Muslims' neglect of this

---

[1] Recorded by Abu Dawood. According to al-Albaani, it is *sahih*. See al-Albaani, *Saheeh al-Jaami*, vol. 2, p. 1059.

hadith. Today, throughout the Muslim world, the disbelievers are looked upon as models of dress and behavior rather than being look upon as people whom Muslims should do their best to avoid imitating. The fads and fashions of the West spread quickly through the Muslim world. The latest designer dresses and perfumes go directly from the fashion centers in Europe to the Muslim world. In the Western countries, a very strange phenomena today is that if one consciously decides not to appear like the disbelievers by intentionally dressing with loose clothing, a long shirt, headdress, beard, garment not below the ankles and other aspects that have been traditionally associated with Muslim dress, he will find himself also not looking like most of the other Muslims. When he enters a mosque, he will look like an outsider to many of the people in the mosque who cannot fathom why he insists on dressing in that fashion.

Numerous other examples can be given concerning different hadith of the Prophet (peace be upon him). It is hoped, though, that the point is made clear: Once a person has made the conscientious choice to truly follow the way of the sunnah, he should be ready for the onslaught. He should realize that he is going to become a stranger in the midst of millions of Muslims who have no real understanding of what it truly means to follow the sunnah. He may be so bombarded with attacks that Satan will make him doubt whether or not he has made the right choice in following the sunnah.

However, he should not be deceived by the fact that so many Muslims seem to be going in the opposite direction of where he has decided to turn. The Prophet (peace be upon him), by the grace and mercy of Allah, warned the Muslims that these types of things would happen. He also gave them the clue as to what they should do during such times. And he also gave them the glad tidings of the results of their righteous deeds. For example, the Prophet (peace be upon him) said,

أُوصِيكُمْ بِتَقْوَى اللهِ وَ السَّمْعِ وَالطَّاعَةِ وَإِنْ تَأَمَّرَ عَلَيْكم عَبْدٌ
فَإِنَّهُ مَنْ يَعِشْ مِنْكُمْ فَسَيَرَى اخْتِلافًا كَثِيرًا فَعَلَيْكُمْ بِسُنَّتِي
وَسُنَّةِ الْخُلَفَاءِ الرَّاشِدِينَ الْمَهْدِيِّينَ عَضُّوا عَلَيْهَا بِالنَّوَاجِذِ
وَإِيَّاكُمْ وَمُحْدَثَاتِ الأُمُورِ فَإِنَّ كُلَّ بِدْعَةٍ ضَلالَةٌ

"I advise you to have *taqwa* of Allah and to listen and obey
even if a slave is a leader over you. Certainly, the one who will
live among you will see lots of differences. So stick to my
sunnah and the sunnah of the right-principled and rightly-
guided successors. Bite onto that with your molar teeth. And
avoid newly-introduced matters. Verily, every heresy is a
going astray."[1]

During times when people have strayed away from the
example set by the Prophet (peace be upon him), the follower
of the sunnah becomes a stranger. He may find very few who
act and behave in the same way he does. This loneliness can be
a very heavy burden along the path. However, the Prophet's
words should inspire the person to bear his hardships with
patience. The Prophet (peace be upon him) said,

بَدَأَ الإِسْلامُ غَرِيبًا وَسَيَعُودُ كَمَا بَدَأَ غَرِيبًا فَطُوبَى لِلْغُرَبَاءِ

"Islam began as something strange and it will return as it
began [that is, as being something strange]. So glad tidings of
Tooba [a tree in Paradise] for the strangers." (Recorded by
Muslim.) Another narration describes those "strangers" as:

---

[1] Recorded by Abu Daawood and by al-Tirmidhi who said, "It is a *hasan sahih*
hadith." According to ibn Muhammad, al-Albaani, al-Bazzaar, al-Tirmidhi, al-
Haakim, ibn Abdul Barr, Abu Nuaim and numerous others, this is an authentic
hadith. For particular references, see Fauzi ibn Abdullah ibn Muhammad, *al-
Adhwaa al-Samaawiyyah fi Takhreej al-Ahadeeth al-Arbaeen al-Nawawiya*
(Amman: al-Maktabah al-Islamiyya, 1413 A.H.), p. 171.

أُنَاسٌ صَالِحُونَ فِي أُنَاسٍ سُوءٍ كَثِيرٍ مَنْ يَعْصِيهِمْ أَكْثَرُ مِمَّنْ يُطِيعُهُمْ

"Pious people among evil people. Those who disobey them are more than those who obey them."[1] What a Muslim is facing today could not be worse than what the Prophet (peace be upon him) faced in Makkah. When the Prophet (peace be upon him) received his first revelation, it meant a life that was completely opposed to the society around him. When he began, he was with just a handful of followers and the society around him thought him insane or possessed.

Thus, even when it comes to the feeling of strangeness, the Prophet (peace be upon him) set the example. When Muslims today feel that feeling of strangeness due to their adherence to the sunnah, they should complete their adherence to the sunnah by observing how the Prophet (peace be upon him) faced his strangeness. He faced it with patience and struggle. He was never daunted because he knew that what he was following was the truth from Allah. He knew that his behavior was pleasing to Allah. That was his main concern. So he never gave up hope and he never gave up his mission. The "stranger" today must follow the same path. He must realize that he has chosen that path in order to please Allah. Allah will not let his struggle and patience go to waste. Instead, if he is truly sincere to Allah, Allah will help him in this life and He will reward him with the tree of *Tooba* in the Hereafter.

Ibn al-Qayyim states that the strangers are the true "people of Allah." They do not turn to anyone other than Allah and they do not ascribe themselves to anyone other than the Prophet (peace be upon him). They do not call anyone to other than what the Prophet (peace be upon him) brought. When the people follow their gods and leaders on the Day of Judgment,

---

[1] Recorded by Ahmad. According to al-Albaani, this narration is *sahih*. See al-Albaani, *Saheeh al-Jaami*, vol. 2, p. 728.

they will be waiting for the true Lord to arrive. In reality, this stranger is not alone or fearful because he has the company of Allah. His friends are Allah, the Messenger (peace be upon him) and the true believers.

Ibn al-Qayyim continues by saying that the strangers whom the Prophet (peace be upon him) gave glad tidings to are the people who adhere to the sunnah and avoid what the people have innovated, even though what they have innovated has become the norm and the accepted practice. They have a pure *tauheed* (monotheism) and worship of Allah, although the others may object to it. They do not ascribe or align themselves with any shaikh, *tareeqah* (Sufi order) or *madhhab* (school of fiqh or thought); they only align themselves with Allah, His Messenger (peace be upon him) and whatever is in accord with that.

Ibn al-Qayyim states that these are the people the Messenger of Allah (peace be upon him) was speaking of when he said,

$$ يَأْتِي عَلَى النَّاسِ زَمَانٌ زَمَانٌ الصَّابِرُ فِيهِمْ عَلَى دِينِهِ كَالْقَابِضِ عَلَى الْجَمْرِ $$

"There will come a time upon the people in which the one who perseveres with his religion is like a person grasping a burning coal."[1] In other words, as ibn al-Qayyim, most of the people blame the person for the path that he has chosen to follow. So he must persevere and remain patient along that path.

Writing in the Eighth Century of the Hijrah, ibn al-Qayyim wrote that the true Islam—that which the Prophet (peace be upon him) and his Companions were following—was something strange during his time. Though the outward signs of Islam were apparent everywhere, the true

---

[1] Recorded by al-Tirmidhi. According to al-Albaani, it is *sahih*. See al-Albaani, *Saheeh al-Jaami*, vol. 2, p. 1326.

Islam and the true followers were in an extreme state of "strangeness." He says that it is not unexpected that the followers of the true Islam are small in number, given that they are just one group of the seventy-three groups into which this nation will divide. It is not surprising that humans follow their desires and personal opinions, thus making those who stick to the straight path small in number.[1]

The interesting thing is that the "strangers" are actually not alone. They have the example of the Prophet (peace be upon him) in front of them, as mentioned above. They also have the example of many scholars throughout the history of Islam. One particular moving example is the experience of Imam al-Shaatibi as he recounted it in his work *al-Itisaam*. Like ibn al-Qayyim, al-Shaatibi lived in the Eighth Century of the Hijrah. He writes that when he made the decision to follow the straight path of the Prophet Muhammad (peace be upon him), free of all heresies and innovations, he found himself to be a stranger among the people of his time. The customs and practices of his people—even though the customs and practices were not based on the guidance of Allah and even though all of those people were ascribing themselves to Islam—had so overcome them that they could not recognize or accept the true Islam anymore.

Al-Shaatibi notes that a decision had to be made. He could follow the sunnah in opposition to what the people were doing. This meant that he had to face a lot of opposition for going against their customs, especially since the people ignorantly believed that their customs were in fact the sunnah. This meant a heavy burden but, as he pointed out, a great reward in the end. Or he could follow the people's ways in opposition to the sunnah and the practice of the early pious generations of Muslims. This would land him in misguidance.

---

[1] Cf., Muhammad ibn al-Qayyim, *Madaarij al-Saalikeen bain Manaazil Iyyaaka Nabudu wa Iyyaaka Nastaeen* (Beirut: Daar al-Kitaab al-Arabi, n.d.), vol. 3, pp. 196-210.

He, by the grace and mercy of Allah, recognized that "being destroyed" by following the sunnah was, in reality, the true salvation. He realized that none of the people would be able to avail him at all when he stands before Allah on the Day of Judgment.

Upon making that decision, he had to face the wrath of the people. (No doubt he understood that it is better to face the wrath of the people than to face the wrath of Allah.) The name-calling and the insults began. They called him a heretic and an astray person, considering him among the ignorant and the foolish. His opinions were scrutinized and it was claimed that he was from this or that heretical group. For example, the people claimed that he was one of those who believed that there was no benefit to supplications. They made this claim against him because he did not participate in the innovational group supplications with the Imam after the prayers. Some claimed that he was from the Shiah and he hated the Companions. They said this because he said it was not necessary to mention and pray for the rightly-guided caliphs in the Friday speech (*khutbah*). He said that such was not the practice of the early generations in their *khutbah*s and that is why he did not follow that practice. They claimed that he opposed the devoted servants of Allah. They made this claim against him because, as he said, he did oppose those innovational *fuqaraa* (impoverished Sufis) who were going against the sunnah. Since they opposed the sunnah, they were not from the devoted servants of Allah. Some claimed that he was going against the *ahl al-Sunnah wa al-Jamaah* (the people of the sunnah and congregation) because such was represented by what the majority (*jamaah*) follow. Al-Shaatibi replied to this by saying that the people did not even realize that the *Jamaah* referred to in the hadith is the congregation of the Prophet (peace be upon him), his Companions and those who followed along their paths. He says that all of those were lies and innuendoes made against him.

Al-Shaatibi then recounts the story of ibn Battah, a renowned scholar. Ibn Battah said that his adventures were truly stupefying. He traveled far and wide and met with many people. If he agreed with the people's views, he was in fine shape. If he disagreed in any way, he was then branded.[1] If he commented that an opinion seem to contradict the Quran and sunnah, they would call him one of the Khawaraij (those extremists who broke off from the early Muslim community). If he read to them hadith about *tauheed*, they would claim he believes in anthropomorphism. If the hadith were about faith, they would call him a Murjiite (those who separate actions from the concept of faith). If the hadith were about the virtues of Abu Bakr and Umar, they would call him a Nasabite (those who cursed the Companion Ali). If the hadith were about the virtues of the Prophet's family, they would call him a Raafidhi (Shiite). If he was silent about the interpretation of a verse or hadith and would just respond with the verse or hadith itself, they would call him a Dhaahiri (literalist). If he responded with some explanation, they would call him a Baatini (esotericist). If he gave an interpretation, they would call him an Ashari (the followers of Abu al-Hasan al-Ashari who gave allegoric interpretations to many of Allah's attributes). If he rejected the apparent meaning of the text, they would call him a Mutazili. (those who put reason above revelation). If he demonstrated to them what was the strongest opinion based on the reports from the Prophet (peace be upon him), they would say that he is doubting their scholars' trustworthiness. After all this, ibn Battah concluded that there was no escape. The only thing he could do was to cling to the Book and the sunnah and seek forgiveness from Allah.

---

[1] Today the name calling and branding continues. Upon turning to the sunnah, one may be called anything from being "backwards" to a "fundamentalist" to a "Wahabi" to a "terrorist." (Although the person will have nothing to do with terrorism, the Western inspired media has done an excellent job of portraying those who follow the sunnah in the same manner that they portray terrorists. Hence, the term is applied to the followers of the sunnah.)

After recounting his story, al-Shaatibi says that it were as if ibn Battah was speaking through everyone's tongue. That is, there is no scholar or virtuous person who adheres to the sunnah except that he has to put up with this kind of onslaught from those who are not truly following the Quran and sunnah. This is because the others are actually following personal desires and likes and they are ignorant of what is best and true.[1]

All of that and more can fall upon a person after he makes the conscious and wise decision to adhere strictly to the sunnah of the Prophet (peace be upon him). At no time, though, should the person lose hope and faith. Those who are following paths other than that shown by the Prophet (peace be upon him) are doing so by their own choice and at their own loss. The one who decides to obey the Prophet (peace be upon him) and follow his sunnah will be the one who will earn Allah's pleasure and be entered into Paradise. As the Prophet (peace be upon him) said,

كُلُّ أُمَّتِي يَدْخُلُونَ الْجَنَّةَ إلاَّ مَنْ أَبَى

"All of the people of my nation will enter paradise except those who refuse." His companions asked, "Who would refuse?" He answered,

مَنْ أَطَاعَنِي دَخَلَ الْجَنَّةَ وَمَنْ عَصَانِي فَقَدْ أَبَى

"Those who obey me will enter paradise; those who disobey me have refused (to enter paradise)." (Recorded by al-Bukhari and others.)

---

[1] Cf., Ibraaheem al-Shaatibi, *Al-Itisaam* (Al-Khobar, Saudi Arabia: Daar ibn Affaan, 1992), vol. 1, pp. 33-39.

Conclusions

The straight path leading to Allah's pleasure, the path of Islam, is none other than the path followed by the Prophet Muhammad (peace be upon him). That is the only true "version" of Islam. The Prophet (peace be upon him) made it clear that all other paths have devils upon them calling people towards them. The astute person must realize this fact and cling stubbornly to the sunnah of the Prophet (peace be upon him), as if biting onto it with his molar teeth.

But this following of the Prophet (peace be upon him) must be the correct type of following. It is not by repeating some articles of faith day and night. Nor is it by simply showing oneself in public as a follower of the sunnah. Instead, the true following of the sunnah must be a comprehensive one, encompassing every facet of one's life. One's beliefs, one's deeds and one's behavior all must be in accord with the sunnah of the Messenger of Allah (peace be upon him).

In this day and age, this goal may not be that easy to achieve. Few people may be willing to assist a person along that path. Those who tread along the path of the sunnah are bound to experience the kind of strangeness that the Prophet (peace be upon him) himself experienced and spoke about. However, the glad tidings of Paradise are for the strangers. In the Hereafter, Allah willing, they will realize that they made the right choice when they opted for trying to please Allah instead of pleasing the people in this world.

Final Words

There is no need to reiterate the conclusions of the different chapters. The authority and importance of the sunnah is established without question. The matter is clear and bright, like a shining light. The Muslim should realize this fact. By the grace and mercy of Allah, Allah has provided Muslims with two perfect and sufficient guides: the Quran and the sunnah of the Messenger of Allah (peace be upon him). The Muslim just has to believe completely in them and desire to apply them to the best of his ability. If he does so, Allah willing, he can look forward to Allah's forgiveness, mercy and pleasure. If a person refuses that, then he is only sending himself to his own destruction. The Messenger of Allah (peace be upon him) said,

قَدْ تَرَكْتُكُمْ عَلَى الْبَيْضَاءِ لَيْلُهَا كَنَهَارِهَا لا يَزِيغُ عَنْهَا بَعْدِي
إِلاَّ هَالِكٌ

"I have left you upon a very clear, serious matter, whose night is like its day. No one strays from it after me except a destroyed person."[1]

---

[1] Recorded by Ahmad, ibn Maajah and al-Haakim. According to al-Albaani, it is *sahih*. See Muhammad Naasir al-Deen al-Albaani, *Silsilat al-Ahaadeeth al-Saheehah* (Damascus: al-Maktab al-Islaami, 1979), vol. 2, pp. 647-8. Note that in many non-hadith works, this hadith is quoted with the words, "I have left you on a clear proof (المحجة البيضاء)." However, to this author's knowledge, such is not found in any of the books of hadith. The correct wording is that presented in the text above. Allah knows best.

Appendix:
Selected Verses of the Quran Indicating the Authority and Importance of the Sunnah[1]

No.	Verse	Text
1	*al-Baqarah* 129	رَبَّنَا وَابْعَثْ فِيهِمْ رَسُولاً مِنْهُمْ يَتْلُو عَلَيْهِمْ آيَاتِكَ وَيُعَلِّمُهُمُ الْكِتَابَ وَالْحِكْمَةَ وَيُزَكِّيهِمْ "O our Lord! Raise up in their midst a Messenger from among them who shall recite unto them Your revelations and shall instruct them in the scripture and in the *Hikmah* and shall make them grow."
2	*al-Baqarah* 151	كَمَا أَرْسَلْنَا فِيكُمْ رَسُولاً مِنْكُمْ يَتْلُو عَلَيْكُمْ آيَاتِنَا وَيُزَكِّيكُمْ وَيُعَلِّمُكُمُ الْكِتَابَ وَالْحِكْمَةَ وَيُعَلِّمُكُمْ مَا لَمْ تَكُونُوا تَعْلَمُونَ "Even as We have sent unto you a messenger from among you, who recites to you Our revelations and causes you to grow, and teaches you the scripture and the

---

[1] The verses are presented according to the order of the Quran. Verses obliging the belief in the Messenger of Allah (peace be upon him) are not included in this table. Some scholars mention them as proofs for the authority of the sunnah, but for the purposes here, they are considered not explicit enough to be considered proofs for the authority of the sunnah. The verses are numbered in order to emphasize the large number of such verses. Finally, this lengthy list makes no claims to be exhaustive.

No.	Verse	Text
		Hikmah and teaches you what which you knew not."
3	al-Baqarah 231	وَاذْكُرُوا نِعْمَةَ اللّهِ عَلَيْكُمْ وَمَا أَنزَلَ عَلَيْكُمْ مِنْ الْكِتَابِ وَالْحِكْمَةِ يَعِظُكُم بِهِ وَاتَّقُوا اللّهَ وَاعْلَمُوا أَنَّ اللّهَ بِكُلِّ شَيْءٍ عَلِيمٌ "Solemnly recall Allah's favors on you, and the fact that He sent down to you the Book and the *Hikmah* for your instruction. And fear Allah, and know that Allah is well-acquainted with all things."
4	ali-Imraan 31	قُلْ إِن كُنتُمْ تُحِبُّونَ اللّهَ فَاتَّبِعُونِي يُحْبِبْكُمُ اللّهُ وَيَغْفِرْ لَكُمْ ذُنُوبَكُمْ وَاللّهُ غَفُورٌ رَحِيمٌ "Say (O Muhammad): If you truly love Allah then follow me and Allah will love you and forgive your sins. Allah is the Forgiving, the Merciful."
5	ali-Imraan 32	قُلْ أَطِيعُوا اللّهَ وَالرَّسُولَ فَإِن تَوَلَّوْا فَإِنَّ اللّهَ لا يُحِبُّ الْكَافِرِينَ "Say: Obey Allah and the Messenger. And if you turn away [know that] verily Allah does not love the unbelievers."
6	ali-Imraan 132	وَأَطِيعُوا اللّهَ وَالرَّسُولَ لَعَلَّكُمْ تُرْحَمُونَ "O you who believe, obey Allah and the Messenger that you may attain mercy."

No.	Verse	Text
7	ali-Imraan 164	لَقَدْ مَنَّ اللَّهُ عَلَى الْمُؤْمِنِينَ إِذْ بَعَثَ فِيهِمْ رَسُولاً مِنْ أَنْفُسِهِمْ يَتْلُوا عَلَيْهِمْ آيَاتِهِ وَيُزَكِّيهِمْ وَيُعَلِّمُهُمُ الْكِتَابَ وَالْحِكْمَةَ وَإِنْ كَانُوا مِنْ قَبْلُ لَفِي ضَلالٍ مُبِينٍ "Allah has clearly shown grace to the believers by sending unto them a Messenger of their own who recites unto them His revelations, and causes them to grow and teaches them the Book and the *Hikmah*, although before they were in flagrant error."
8	al-Nisaa 13	وَمَنْ يُطِعْ اللَّهَ وَرَسُولَهُ يُدْخِلْهُ جَنَّاتٍ تَجْرِي مِنْ تَحْتِهَا الأَنْهَارُ خَالِدِينَ فِيهَا وَذَلِكَ الْفَوْزُ الْعَظِيمُ "Those who obey Allah and His Messenger will be admitted to Gardens with rivers flowing beneath, to abide therein (forever) and that will be the Supreme achievement."
9	Al-Nisaa 14	وَمَنْ يَعْصِ اللَّهَ وَرَسُولَهُ وَيَتَعَدَّ حُدُودَهُ يُدْخِلْهُ نَارًا خَالِدًا فِيهَا وَلَهُ عَذَابٌ مُهِينٌ "But those who disobey Allah and His Messenger and transgress His limits will be admitted to a Fire, to abide therein: and they shall have a humiliating punishment."
10	al-Nisaa 42	يَوْمَئِذٍ يَوَدُّ الَّذِينَ كَفَرُوا وَعَصَوْا الرَّسُولَ لَوْ تُسَوَّى بِهِمُ الأَرْضُ وَلا يَكْتُمُونَ اللَّهَ حَدِيثًا "On that day those who reject faith and

No.	Verse	Text
		disobey the Messenger will wish that the earth were made one with them [so they may escape punishment]. But never will they hide a single fact from Allah."
11	*al-Nisaa* 59	يَاأَيُّهَا الَّذِينَ آمَنُوا أَطِيعُوا اللَّهَ وَأَطِيعُوا الرَّسُولَ وَأُوْلِي الْأَمْرِ مِنْكُمْ فَإِنْ تَنَازَعْتُمْ فِي شَيْءٍ فَرُدُّوهُ إِلَى اللَّهِ وَالرَّسُولِ إِنْ كُنْتُمْ تُؤْمِنُونَ بِاللَّهِ وَالْيَوْمِ الآخِرِ ذَلِكَ خَيْرٌ وَأَحْسَنُ تَأْوِيلاً "O you who believe, obey Allah and obey the Messenger and those in authority among you. And if you are in dispute over any matter, refer it to Allah and His Messenger if you are actually believers in Allah and the Last Day. That is better for you and more seemly in the end."
12	*Al-Nisaa* 61	وَإِذَا قِيلَ لَهُمْ تَعَالَوْا إِلَى مَا أَنْزَلَ اللَّهُ وَإِلَى الرَّسُولِ رَأَيْتَ الْمُنَافِقِينَ يَصُدُّونَ عَنْكَ صُدُودًا "When it is said to them, 'Come to what Allah has revealed, and to the Messenger,' you see the hypocrites avert their faces from you in disgust."
13	*al-Nisaa* 64	وَمَا أَرْسَلْنَا مِنْ رَسُولٍ إِلاَّ لِيُطَاعَ بِإِذْنِ اللَّهِ "We never sent any messenger except for him to be obeyed, by Allah's leave."

No.	Verse	Text
14	al-Nisaa 65	فَلَا وَرَبِّكَ لَا يُؤْمِنُونَ حَتَّى يُحَكِّمُوكَ فِيمَا شَجَرَ بَيْنَهُمْ ثُمَّ لَا يَجِدُوا فِي أَنفُسِهِمْ حَرَجًا مِمَّا قَضَيْتَ وَيُسَلِّمُوا تَسْلِيمًا "But nay, by thy Lord, they will not actually believe until they make you the judge of what is in dispute between them and find within themselves no dislike of that which you decide and they submit with full submission."
15	Al-Nisaa 69	وَمَنْ يُطِعْ اللَّهَ وَالرَّسُولَ فَأُولَئِكَ مَعَ الَّذِينَ أَنْعَمَ اللَّهُ عَلَيْهِمْ مِنْ النَّبِيِّينَ وَالصِّدِّيقِينَ وَالشُّهَدَاءِ وَالصَّالِحِينَ وَحَسُنَ أُولَئِكَ رَفِيقًا "All who obey Allah and the Messenger are in the company of those on whom is the Grace of Allah, of the Prophets, the sincere, the martyrs, and the righteous. Ah! What a beautiful fellowship."
16	Al-Nisaa 80	مَنْ يُطِعْ الرَّسُولَ فَقَدْ أَطَاعَ اللَّهَ وَمَنْ تَوَلَّى فَمَا أَرْسَلْنَاكَ عَلَيْهِمْ حَفِيظًا "Whoever obeys the Messenger verily obeys Allah; but if any turn away, We have not sent you to watch over their (evil deeds)."
17	al-Nisaa 113	وَأَنزَلَ اللَّهُ عَلَيْكَ الْكِتَابَ وَالْحِكْمَةَ وَعَلَّمَكَ مَا لَمْ تَكُنْ تَعْلَمُ وَكَانَ فَضْلُ اللَّهِ عَلَيْكَ عَظِيمًا "Allah has revealed to you the Book and

No.	Verse	Text
		the *Hikmah* and taught you what you knew not (before): and great is the Grace of Allah unto you."
18	*Al-Nisaa* 115	وَمَنْ يُشَاقِقِ الرَّسُولَ مِنْ بَعْدِ مَا تَبَيَّنَ لَهُ الْهُدَى وَيَتَّبِعْ غَيْرَ سَبِيلِ الْمُؤْمِنِينَ نُوَلِّهِ مَا تَوَلَّى وَنُصْلِهِ جَهَنَّمَ وَسَاءَتْ مَصِيرًا "If anyone contends with the Messenger even after guidance has been plainly conveyed to him, and follows a path other than that becoming to men of Faith, We shall leave him in the path he has chosen, and land him in Hell, what an evil refuge."
19	*Al-Maaidah* 92	وَأَطِيعُوا اللَّهَ وَأَطِيعُوا الرَّسُولَ وَاحْذَرُوا فَإِنْ تَوَلَّيْتُمْ فَاعْلَمُوا أَنَّمَا عَلَى رَسُولِنَا الْبَلَاغُ الْمُبِينُ "Obey Allah, and obey the Messenger, and beware (of evil). If you do turn back, know that it is Our Messenger's duty to proclaim (the Message) in the clearest manner."
20	*al-Araaf* 157	يَأْمُرُهُمْ بِالْمَعْرُوفِ وَيَنْهَاهُمْ عَنِ الْمُنْكَرِ وَيُحِلُّ لَهُمُ الطَّيِّبَاتِ وَيُحَرِّمُ عَلَيْهِمُ الْخَبَائِثَ وَيَضَعُ عَنْهُمْ إِصْرَهُمْ وَالْأَغْلَالَ الَّتِي كَانَتْ عَلَيْهِمْ فَالَّذِينَ آمَنُوا بِهِ وَعَزَّرُوهُ وَنَصَرُوهُ وَاتَّبَعُوا النُّورَ الَّذِي أُنزِلَ مَعَهُ أُولَئِكَ هُمُ الْمُفْلِحُونَ "For he [the Prophet (peace be upon him)] commands them what is just and forbids them what is evil; He allows them as

No.	Verse	Text
		lawful what is good and pure and prohibits them from what is bad and impure. He releases them from their heavy burdens and from the yokes that are upon them. So it is those who believe in him, honor him, help him, and follow the Light which is sent down with him, it is they who will prosper."
21	*al-Araaf* 158	قُلْ يَاأَيُّهَا النَّاسُ إِنِّي رَسُولُ اللَّهِ إِلَيْكُمْ جَمِيعًا الَّذِي لَهُ مُلْكُ السَّمَاوَاتِ وَالأَرْضِ لا إِلَهَ إِلاَّ هُوَ يُحْيِي وَيُمِيتُ فَآمِنُوا بِاللَّهِ وَرَسُولِهِ النَّبِيِّ الأُمِّيِّ الَّذِي يُؤْمِنُ بِاللَّهِ وَكَلِمَاتِهِ وَاتَّبِعُوهُ لَعَلَّكُمْ تَهْتَدُونَ "Say: O mankind! I am sent unto you all, as the Messenger of Allah, to Whom belongs the dominion of the heavens and the earth: there is no god but He. It is He who gives both life and death. So believe in Allah and His Messenger, the unlettered Prophet, who believed in Allah and His Words. Follow him that (so) you may be guided."
22	*al-Anfaal* 12-13	إِذْ يُوحِي رَبُّكَ إِلَى الْمَلائِكَةِ أَنِّي مَعَكُمْ فَثَبِّتُوا الَّذِينَ آمَنُوا سَأُلْقِي فِي قُلُوبِ الَّذِينَ كَفَرُوا الرُّعْبَ فَاضْرِبُوا فَوْقَ الأَعْنَاقِ وَاضْرِبُوا مِنْهُمْ كُلَّ بَنَانٍ ذَلِكَ بِأَنَّهُمْ شَاقُّوا اللَّهَ وَرَسُولَهُ وَمَنْ يُشَاقِقِ اللَّهَ وَرَسُولَهُ فَإِنَّ اللَّهَ شَدِيدُ الْعِقَابِ

No.	Verse	Text
		"Remember your Lord inspired the angels (with the message), 'I am with you. Give firmness to the believers. I will strike terror into the hearts of the Unbelievers. Smite above their necks and smite all their finger tips off them.' This because they defied and disobeyed Allah and His Messenger: if any defy and disobey Allah and His Messenger, Allah is strict in punishment."
23	*al-Anfaal* 20	يَاأَيُّهَا الَّذِينَ آمَنُوا أَطِيعُوا اللَّهَ وَرَسُولَهُ وَلا تَوَلَّوْا عَنْهُ وَأَنْتُمْ تَسْمَعُونَ "O you who believe! Obey Allah and His Messenger, and turn not away from him while you hear (what he spoke)."
24	*al-Anfaal* 24	يَاأَيُّهَا الَّذِينَ آمَنُوا اسْتَجِيبُوا لِلَّهِ وَلِلرَّسُولِ إِذَا دَعَاكُمْ لِمَا يُحْيِيكُمْ "O you who believe, respond to Allah and His Messenger when they call you to that which gives you life."
25	*al-Taubah* 71	وَالْمُؤْمِنُونَ وَالْمُؤْمِنَاتُ بَعْضُهُمْ أَوْلِيَاءُ بَعْضٍ يَأْمُرُونَ بِالْمَعْرُوفِ وَيَنْهَوْنَ عَنِ الْمُنْكَرِ وَيُقِيمُونَ الصَّلاةَ وَيُؤْتُونَ الزَّكَاةَ وَيُطِيعُونَ اللَّهَ وَرَسُولَهُ أُوْلَئِكَ سَيَرْحَمُهُمُ اللَّهُ إِنَّ اللَّهَ عَزِيزٌ حَكِيمٌ "The believers, men and women, are protectors one of another. They enjoin what is right and forbid what is evil. They establish the prayers, give the zakaat, and

No.	Verse	Text
		obey Allah and His Messenger. On them will Allah pour His Mercy, for Allah is Exalted in power, Wise."
26	*al-Nahl* 44	وَأَنزَلْنَا إِلَيْكَ الذِّكْرَ لِتُبَيِّنَ لِلنَّاسِ مَا نُزِّلَ إِلَيْهِمْ وَلَعَلَّهُمْ يَتَفَكَّرُونَ "And We have revealed unto you (Muhammad) the reminder so you may expound unto all of mankind that which has been revealed for them. So perchance they may ponder."
27	*Al-Noor* 48-52	وَإِذَا دُعُوا إِلَى اللَّهِ وَرَسُولِهِ لِيَحْكُمَ بَيْنَهُمْ إِذَا فَرِيقٌ مِنْهُمْ مُعْرِضُونَ وَإِنْ يَكُنْ لَهُمُ الْحَقُّ يَأْتُوا إِلَيْهِ مُذْعِنِينَ أَفِي قُلُوبِهِمْ مَرَضٌ أَمِ ارْتَابُوا أَمْ يَخَافُونَ أَنْ يَحِيفَ اللَّهُ عَلَيْهِمْ وَرَسُولُهُ بَلْ أُولَئِكَ هُمُ الظَّالِمُونَ إِنَّمَا كَانَ قَوْلَ الْمُؤْمِنِينَ إِذَا دُعُوا إِلَى اللَّهِ وَرَسُولِهِ لِيَحْكُمَ بَيْنَهُمْ أَنْ يَقُولُوا سَمِعْنَا وَأَطَعْنَا وَأُولَئِكَ هُمُ الْمُفْلِحُونَ وَمَنْ يُطِعِ اللَّهَ وَرَسُولَهُ وَيَخْشَ اللَّهَ وَيَتَّقِيهِ فَأُولَئِكَ هُمُ الْفَائِزُونَ "When they are summoned to Allah and His Messenger, in order that he [the Prophet (peace be upon him)] may judge between them, behold, some of them decline (to come). But if the right is on their side, they come to him with all

No.	Verse	Text
		submission. Is it that there is a disease in their hearts? Or do they doubt, or are they in fear, that Allah and His Messenger will deal unjustly with them? Nay, it is they themselves who do wrong. The answer of the believers, when summoned to Allah and His Messenger, in order that he may judge between them, is no other than this: they say, 'We hear and we obey.' It is such as these who will attain felicity. It is such as obey Allah and His Messenger, and fear Allah and do right, that will win (in the end)."
28	Al-Noor 54	قُلْ أَطِيعُوا اللَّهَ وَأَطِيعُوا الرَّسُولَ فَإِنْ تَوَلَّوْا فَإِنَّمَا عَلَيْهِ مَا حُمِّلَ وَعَلَيْكُمْ مَا حُمِّلْتُمْ وَإِنْ تُطِيعُوهُ تَهْتَدُوا وَمَا عَلَى الرَّسُولِ إِلاَّ الْبَلاغُ الْمُبِينُ "Say: Obey Allah, and obey the Messenger. But if you turn away, he is only responsible for the duty placed on him and you for that placed on you. If you obey him, you shall be on right guidance. The Messenger's duty is only to preach the clear (Message)."
29	Al-Noor 56	وَأَقِيمُوا الصَّلاةَ وَآتُوا الزَّكَاةَ وَأَطِيعُوا الرَّسُولَ لَعَلَّكُمْ تُرْحَمُونَ "So establish regular prayer and give the zakaat; and obey the Messenger; that you may receive mercy."

No.	Verse	Text
30	al-Noor 62	إِنَّمَا الْمُؤْمِنُونَ الَّذِينَ آمَنُوا بِاللَّهِ وَرَسُولِهِ وَإِذَا كَانُوا مَعَهُ عَلَى أَمْرٍ جَامِعٍ لَمْ يَذْهَبُوا حَتَّى يَسْتَأْذِنُوهُ "Only those are believers, who believe in Allah and His Messenger and when they are with him on some common matter, they do not depart until they have asked for his leave."
31	al-Noor 63	فَلْيَحْذَرِ الَّذِينَ يُخَالِفُونَ عَنْ أَمْرِهِ أَنْ تُصِيبَهُمْ فِتْنَةٌ أَوْ يُصِيبَهُمْ عَذَابٌ أَلِيمٌ "Let those who conspire to evade orders beware lest a calamity or painful punishment should befall them."
32	al-Naml 79	فَتَوَكَّلْ عَلَى اللَّهِ إِنَّكَ عَلَى الْحَقِّ الْمُبِينِ "So put your trust and reliance in Allah. You are upon the clear truth."
33	al-Ahzaab 21	لَقَدْ كَانَ لَكُمْ فِي رَسُولِ اللَّهِ أُسْوَةٌ حَسَنَةٌ لِمَنْ كَانَ يَرْجُو اللَّهَ وَالْيَوْمَ الْآخِرَ وَذَكَرَ اللَّهَ كَثِيرًا "Verily in the Messenger of Allah you have an excellent example for him who looks unto Allah and the Last Day and remembers Allah much."
34	al-Ahzaab 34	وَاذْكُرْنَ مَا يُتْلَى فِي بُيُوتِكُنَّ مِنْ آيَاتِ اللَّهِ وَالْحِكْمَةِ "And recite that which is rehearsed in your houses of the revelations of Allah and the

No.	Verse	Text
		Hikmah."
35	*al-Ahzaab* 36	وَمَا كَانَ لِمُؤْمِنٍ وَلَا مُؤْمِنَةٍ إِذَا قَضَى اللَّهُ وَرَسُولُهُ أَمْرًا أَنْ يَكُونَ لَهُمُ الْخِيَرَةُ مِنْ أَمْرِهِمْ وَمَنْ يَعْصِ اللَّهَ وَرَسُولَهُ فَقَدْ ضَلَّ ضَلَالاً مُبِينًا "It does not become a believing man or believing woman, when Allah and His Messenger have decided an matter that they should (after that) claim any say in their affair; and whoever is disobedient to Allah and His Messenger has certainly gone astray in manifest error."
36	*al-Ahzaab* 66	يَوْمَ تُقَلَّبُ وُجُوهُهُمْ فِي النَّارِ يَقُولُونَ يَالَيْتَنَا أَطَعْنَا اللَّهَ وَأَطَعْنَا الرَّسُولَ "The Day that their faces will be turned upside down in the Fire, they will say: 'Woe to us! Would that we had obeyed Allah and obeyed the Messenger.'"
37	*al-Ahzaab* 71	وَمَنْ يُطِعْ اللَّهَ وَرَسُولَهُ فَقَدْ فَازَ فَوْزًا عَظِيمًا "He who obeys Allah and His Messenger, has already attained the highest achievement."
38	*Ya Seen* 3-4	إِنَّكَ لَمِنَ الْمُرْسَلِينَ عَلَى صِرَاطٍ مُسْتَقِيمٍ "Verily, you are from among the messengers upon a straight path."

No.	Verse	Text
39	*al-Shoora* 52-53	وَإِنَّكَ لَتَهْدِي إِلَى صِرَاطٍ مُسْتَقِيمٍ صِرَاطِ اللَّهِ الَّذِي لَهُ مَا فِي السَّمَاوَاتِ وَمَا فِي الْأَرْضِ أَلَا إِلَى اللَّهِ تَصِيرُ الْأُمُورُ "And verily you (O Muhammad) do guide (men) to the straight way— the Way of Allah to whom belongs whatever is in the heavens and whatever is on earth. Behold how all affairs tend towards Allah."
40	*Muhammad* 33	يَا أَيُّهَا الَّذِينَ آمَنُوا أَطِيعُوا اللَّهَ وَأَطِيعُوا الرَّسُولَ وَلَا تُبْطِلُوا أَعْمَالَكُمْ "O you who believe, obey Allah and obey the Messenger and do not make your deeds vain."
41	*al-Fath* 10	إِنَّ الَّذِينَ يُبَايِعُونَكَ إِنَّمَا يُبَايِعُونَ اللَّهَ يَدُ اللَّهِ فَوْقَ أَيْدِيهِمْ فَمَنْ نَكَثَ فَإِنَّمَا يَنْكُثُ عَلَى نَفْسِهِ وَمَنْ أَوْفَى بِمَا عَاهَدَ عَلَيْهُ اللَّهَ فَسَيُؤْتِيهِ أَجْرًا عَظِيمًا "Lo those who swear allegiance to you (Muhammad), swear allegiance only unto Allah. The Hand of Allah is above their hands. So whosoever breaks his oath, breaks it only to his soul's hurt; while whosoever keeps his covenant with Allah, on him will He bestow immense reward."
42	*Al-Fath* 17	وَمَنْ يُطِعِ اللَّهَ وَرَسُولَهُ يُدْخِلْهُ جَنَّاتٍ تَجْرِي مِنْ تَحْتِهَا الْأَنْهَارُ وَمَنْ يَتَوَلَّ يُعَذِّبْهُ عَذَابًا أَلِيمًا "But for he who obeys Allah and His

No.	Verse	Text
		Messenger, (Allah) will admit him to Gardens beneath which rivers flow; and he who turns back, (Allah) will punish him with a grievous penalty."
43	*al-Hujur-aat 1-2*	يَاأَيُّهَا الَّذِينَ آمَنُوا لَا تُقَدِّمُوا بَيْنَ يَدَيِ اللَّهِ وَرَسُولِهِ وَاتَّقُوا اللَّهَ إِنَّ اللَّهَ سَمِيعٌ عَلِيمٌ يَاأَيُّهَا الَّذِينَ آمَنُوا لَا تَرْفَعُوا أَصْوَاتَكُمْ فَوْقَ صَوْتِ النَّبِيِّ وَلَا تَجْهَرُوا لَهُ بِالْقَوْلِ كَجَهْرِ بَعْضِكُمْ لِبَعْضٍ أَنْ تَحْبَطَ أَعْمَالُكُمْ وَأَنْتُمْ لَا تَشْعُرُونَ "O you who believe, be not forward in the presence of Allah and His Messenger. O you who believe, lift not up your voices above the voice of the Prophet, nor speak aloud to him in talk as you speak loudly one to another, lest your works be rendered vain while you perceive not."
44	*al-Najm 2-4*	مَا ضَلَّ صَاحِبُكُمْ وَمَا غَوَى وَمَا يَنْطِقُ عَنِ الْهَوَى إِنْ هُوَ إِلَّا وَحْيٌ يُوحَى "Your companion errs not nor is he deceived. Nor does he speak out of his own desires. It is only an inspiration that is being revealed to him."
45	*al-Mujaa-dalah 5*	إِنَّ الَّذِينَ يُحَادُّونَ اللَّهَ وَرَسُولَهُ كُبِتُوا كَمَا كُبِتَ الَّذِينَ مِنْ قَبْلِهِمْ وَقَدْ أَنْزَلْنَا آيَاتٍ بَيِّنَاتٍ وَلِلْكَافِرِينَ عَذَابٌ مُهِينٌ "Those who resist Allah and His

No.	Verse	Text
		Messenger will be humbled to dust, as were those before them: for We have already sent down clear signs. And the unbelievers (will have) a humiliating penalty."
46	*al-Mujaadalah* 9	يَاأَيُّهَا الَّذِينَ آمَنُوا إِذَا تَنَاجَيْتُمْ فَلَا تَتَنَاجَوْا بِالْإِثْمِ وَالْعُدْوَانِ وَمَعْصِيَةِ الرَّسُولِ وَتَنَاجَوْا بِالْبِرِّ وَالتَّقْوَى وَاتَّقُوا اللَّهَ الَّذِي إِلَيْهِ تُحْشَرُونَ "O you who believe! When you hold secret counsel, do it not for iniquity and hostility, and disobedience to the Messenger; but do it for righteousness and self-restraint; and fear Allah, to whom you shall be brought back."
47	*Al-Hashr* 7	وَمَا آتَاكُمُ الرَّسُولُ فَخُذُوهُ وَمَا نَهَاكُمْ عَنْهُ فَانْتَهُوا وَاتَّقُوا اللَّهَ إِنَّ اللَّهَ شَدِيدُ الْعِقَابِ "Whatsoever the Messenger gives you, take it; and whatsoever he forbids for you, abstain from it. And be aware of Allah. Verily, Allah is sever in punishment."
48	*al-Jumuah* 2	هُوَ الَّذِي بَعَثَ فِي الْأُمِّيِّينَ رَسُولًا مِنْهُمْ يَتْلُو عَلَيْهِمْ آيَاتِهِ وَيُزَكِّيهِمْ وَيُعَلِّمُهُمُ الْكِتَابَ وَالْحِكْمَةَ وَإِنْ كَانُوا مِنْ قَبْلُ لَفِي ضَلَالٍ مُبِينٍ "He it is who has sent among the unlettered ones a messenger of their own to recite to them His revelations and to make them grow. And to teach them the Book and the *Hikmah*, though heretofore they were

No.	Verse	Text
		indeed in error manifest."
49	*Al-Taghaa-bun* 12	وَأَطِيعُوا اللَّهَ وَأَطِيعُوا الرَّسُولَ فَإِنْ تَوَلَّيْتُمْ فَإِنَّمَا عَلَى رَسُولِنَا الْبَلَاغُ الْمُبِينُ "So obey Allah, and obey His Messenger: but if you turn back, the duty of Our Messenger is but to proclaim (the message) clearly and openly."
50	*al-Jinn* 23	وَمَنْ يَعْصِ اللَّهَ وَرَسُولَهُ فَإِنَّ لَهُ نَارَ جَهَنَّمَ خَالِدِينَ فِيهَا أَبَدًا "For any who disobeys Allah and His Messenger, for them is Hell: they shall dwell therein forever."

References

al-Abbaad, Abdul Muhsin. [عبـــد المحســـن العبـــاد]. *Diraasat Hadeeth Nadhara Allahu imraan Sama Muqaalati...: Riwaayah wa Diraayah* [دراسة حديث نضر الله امرأ سمع مقالتي..: رواية ودراية]. No publication information given.

Abdul Kareem, Fathi [فتحي عبد الكريم]. *Al-Sunnah: Tashree Laazim... Wa Daaim* [السنة تشريع لازم ودائم]. Maktabah Wahbah. 1985.

Abdul Khaaliq, Abdul Ghani [عبد الغني عبد الخالق]. *Hujjiyah al-Sunnah* [حجية السنة]. Beirut: Daar al-Quran al-Kareem. 1986.

al-Abdul Lateef, Abdul Azeez. [عبد العزيز العبد اللطيف]. *Nawaaqidh al-Imaan al-Qauliyyah wa al-Amaliyyah* [نواقض الإيمان القوليــة والعملية]. Riyadh: Daar al-Watn. 1414 A.H.

Abdul Lateef, Abdul Wahaab [عبد الوهاب عبد اللطيف]. *Al-Mukhtasar fi Ilm Rijaal al-Athar* [المختصر في علم رجال الأثر]. Daar al-Kutub al-Hadeethiyyah. no date.

Abdul Raheem, Abdul Jaleel [عبد الرحيم عبد الجليل]. *Lughat al-Quran al-Kareem* [لغة القرآن الكــريم]. Amman, Jordan: Maktabah al-Risaalah al-Hadeethah. 1981.

Abu Jaib, Saadi [سعدي أبو جيب]. *Mausooah al-Ijmaa fi al-Fiqh al-Islaami* [موسوعة الإجمــاع في الفقـه الإســلامي]. Beirut: Daar al-Arabiyyah. n.d.

Abu Zahra, Muhammad [محمد أبو زهــرة]. *Usool al-Fiqh* [أصول الفقه]. Cairo: Daar al-Fikr al-Arabi. n.d.

al-Adhami, Muhammad Dhiyaa al-Rahmaan [محمد ضياء الرحمان الأعظمي]. *Mujam Mustalahaat al-Hadeeth wa Lataaif al-Asaaneed* [معجم مصطلحات الحديث ولطائف الأســانيد]. Riyadh: Adhwaa al-Salaf. 1999.

Al-Ahdab, Khaldoon. [خلــدون الأحـــدب]. *Asbaab Ikhtilaaf al-Muhaditheen* [أســباب اعتــلاف المحدثـين]. Jeddah: al-Daar al-Saudiyah. 1985.

al-Albaani, Muhammad Naasir al-Deen [محمد ناصر الدين الألباني]. *Dhaeef Sunan al-Nasaai* [ضعيف سنن النسائي]. Beirut: al-Maktab al-Islaami. 1990.

-----*Irwaa al-Ghaleel fi Takhreej Ahaadeeth Manaar al-Sabeel* [إرواء الغليل في تخريج أحاديث منار السبيل]. Beirut: al-Maktab al-Islaami. 1979.

-----*Manzalat al-Sunnah fi al-Islaam* [منزلة السنة في الإسلام]. Kuwait: al-Daar al-Salafiyyah. 1980.

-----*Saheeh al-Jaami al-Sagheer* [صحيح الجامع الصغير]. Beirut: al-Maktab al-Islaami. 1986.

-----*Saheeh Sunan Abi Dawood* [صحيح سنن أبي داود]. Riyadh: Maktab al-Tarbiyyah al-Arabi li-Duwal al-Khaleej. 1989.

-----*Saheeh Sunan al-Tirmidhi* [صحيح سنن الترمذي]. Riyadh: Maktab al-Tarbiyyah al-Arabi Li-Duwal al-Khaleej. 1988.

-----*Saheeh al-Targheb wa al-Tarheeb* [صحيح الترغيب والترهيب]. Riyadh: Maktabah al-Maarif. 1988.

-----*Silsilat al-Ahaadeeth al-Dhaeefah* [سلسلة الأحاديث الضعيفة]. Beirut: al-Maktab al-Islaami. 1978.

-----*Silsilat al-Ahaadeeth al-Saheehah* [سلسلة الأحاديث الصحيحة]. Kuwait: al-Daar al-Salafiyyah. 1983.

----- Footnotes to Amr ibn al-Aasim [عمرو بن العاصم]. *Kitaab al-Sunnah* [كتاب السنة]. Beirut: al-Maktab al-Islaami. 1985.

Al-Ameen, al-Ameen al-Saadiq [الأمين الصادق الأمين]. *Mauqaf al-Madrasah al-Aqliyyah min al-Sunnah al-Nabawiyyah* [موقف المدرسة العقلية من السنة النبوية]. Riyadh: Maktabah al-Rushd. 1998.

Al-Aql, Naasir [ناصر العقل]. *Mabaahith fi Aqeedah Ahl al-Sunnah wa al-Jamaah wa Muwaqif al-Harakaat al-Islaamiyyah al-Muaasirah Minha* [مباحث في عقيدة أهل السنة والجماعة وموقف الحركات الإسلامية المعاصرة منها]. Riyadh: Daar al-Watan. n.d.

-----*Mafhoom Ahl al-Sunnah wa al-Jamaah Ind Ahl al-Sunnah wa al-Jamaah* [مفهوم أهل السنة والجماعة عند أهل السنة والجماعة]. Riyadh: Daar al-Watan. n.d.

al-Arnaoot, Abdul Qaadir [عبد القادر الأرناؤوط]. Footnotes to al-Mubaarak ibn al-Atheer [مبارك بن الأثير]. *Jaami al-Usool fi al-*

Ahadeeth al-Rasool [جامع الأصول في الأحاديث الرسول]. Maktaba al-Hilwaani. 1972.

al-Arnaoot, Shuaib [شعيب الأرناؤوط], *et al.* Footnotes to Ahmad ibn Hanbal [أحمد بن حنبـــل]. *Musnad al-Imam Ahmad* [مسند الإمام أحمد]. Beirut: Muassasat al-Risaalah. 1997.

al-Asbahaani, Abu al-Qaasim Ismaaeel [أبو القاسم إسماعيل الأصبحاني]. *al-Hujjah fi Bayaan al-Muhijjah wa Sharh Aqeedah Ahl al-Sunnah* [الحجة في بيان المحجة وشرح عقيدة أهل السنة]. Riyadh: Daar al-Raayah. 1990.

al-Ashqar, Umar [عمر الأشقر]. *Thalaath Sha'aair* [ثلاث شعائر]. Kuwait: al-Daar al-Salafiyyah. 1985.

Azami, Habib-ur-Rahman. *The Sunnah in Islam: The Eternal Relevance of the Teaching and Example of the Prophet Muhammad.* Leicester, United Kingdom: UK Islamic Academy. 1989.

Al-Azami, Muhammad Mustafa. *On Schacht's Origins of Muhammadan Jurisprudence.* New York: John Wiley and Sons, Inc. 1985.

-----*Studies in Early Hadith Literature.* Indianapolis, IN: American Trust Publications. 1978.

-----*Studies in Hadith Methodology and Literature.* Indianapolis, IN: American Trust Publications. 1977.

Ba-Abdullah, Muhammad [محمد با عبدالله]. *Wasitiyyah Ahl al-Sunnah Bain al-Firaq* [وسطية أهل السنة بـــين الفـــرق]. Riyadh: Daar al-Raayah. 1994.

al-Baghawi, Al-Husain [الحسين البغوي]. *Tafseer al-Baghawi: Maalim al-Tanzeel* [تفسير البغوي: معـــالم التـــنزيل]. Riyadh: Daar Taiba. 1989.

Bakhsh, Khaadim Husain Ilaahi [خادم حسين إلهي بخش]. *Al-Quraaniyoon wa Shubahaatuhum Haul al-Sunnah* [القرأنيون وشبهاقم حول السنة]. Al-Taif, Saudi Arabia: Maktabah al-Sideeq. 1989.

al-Bayaanooni, Muhammad Abu al-Fath [محمد أبو الفتح البيـــانوني]. *Al-Hukum al-Takleefi fi al-Shareeah al-Islaamiyyah* [الحكـــم التكليفي في الشريعة الإسلامية]. Damascus: Dar al-Qalam. 1988.

275

Bazamool, Muhammad [محمد بـــازمول]. *Al-Intisaar li-Ahl al-Hadeeth* [الانتصـــار لأهـــل الحديـــث]. al-Khobar, Saudi Arabia: Daar al-Hijrah. 1997.

Al-Birr, Abdul Rahmaan [عبد الرحمـــن الـــبر]. *Manaahij wa Adaab al-Sahaabah fi al-Taallum wa al-Taleem* [مناهج وأداب الصحابة في التعلم والتعليم]. Al-Mansoorah, Egypt: Daar al-Yaqeen. 1999.

Al-Buqaawi, Saalih [صالح البقاوي]. *al-Talaazim Bain al-Kitaab wa al-Sunnah min Khilaal al-Kutub al-Sittah* [التلازم بين الكتاب والسنة من خلال الكتب الستة]. Riyadh: Daar al-Maarij al-Dauliyyah lil-Nashr. 1416 A.H.

al-Dausiri, Abdul Rahmaan [عبـــد الرحمـــن الدوســـري]. *Al-Ajwiba al-Mufeedah limuhimmat al-Aqeedah* [الأجوبة المفيـــدة لمهمـــة العقيدة]. Beirut: Maktabah Daar al-Arqam. 1982.

Dhumairiyyah, Uthmaan ibn Jumuah [عثمان بن جمعة ضميرية]. *Madkhal li-Diraasah al-Aqeedah al-Islaamiyyah* [مدخل لدراسة العقيدة الإسلامية]. Jeddah: Maktabah al-Suwaari. 1993.

al-Fairoozabaadi, Majud al-Deen [محمد الفيروزابادي]. *Basaair Dhawai al-Tamyeez fi Lataaif al-Kitaab al-Azeez* [بصائر ذوى التمييز في لطائف الكتاب العزيز]. Beirut: Al-Maktabah al-Ilmiyyah. N.d.

al-Fulaani, Saalih [صالح الفلاني]. *Eeqaadh Himam Ooli-l-Absaar* [إيقاظ همم أولى الأبصار]. Taif, Saudi Arabia: Maktabah al-Maarif. n.d.

al-Fullaatah, Umar ibn Hasan Uthmaan [عمر بن حسن عثمان الفلاتة]. *al-Widha fi al-Hadeeth* [الوضع في الحديث]. Damascus: Maktabah al-Ghazzaali. 1981.

al-Hamad, Muhammad [محمد الحمـــد]. *Aqeedah Ahl al-Sunnah wa al-Jamaah: Mafhoomuhaa, Khasaaisuhaa, Khasaais Ahluhaa* [عقيدة أهل السنة والجماعة: مفهومها خصائصها خصائص أهلها]. Riyadh: Dar al-Watan. 1416 A.H.

Hamidullah, Muhammad. *Sahifah Hammam ibn Munabbih*. Paris: Centre Culturel Islamique. 1979.

Hasan, Ahmad. *Principles of Islamic Jurisprudence*. Islamabad, Pakistan: Islamic Research Institute. 1993.

ibn Abdul Barr, Yoosuf [يوسف بن عبد البر]. *Jaami Bayaan al-Ilm wa Fadhlihi* [جامع بيان العلم وفضلـــه]. Al-Damaam, Saudi Arabia: Daar ibn al-Jauzi. 1996.

ibn Abu Amuh, Al-Sayyid Ibraaheem [السيد إبراهيم بن أبو عمــه]. *Al-Saheeh al-Musnad min al-Tafseer al-Nabawi li-l-Quran al-Kareem* [الصحيح المسند من التفسير النبوي للقــــرآن الكـــريم]. Tanta, Egypt: Daar al-Sahaabah lil-Turaath. 1990.

ibn Baaz, Abdul Azeez [عبد العزيز بن باز]. *Wujoob al-Amal bisunnat al-Rasool wa kufr man Ankaaraha* [وجوب العمل بسنة الرسول] [وكفـــر مـــن أنكارهـــا]. Riyadh: Shaarikah al-Taba al-Arabiya al-Saudiya. 1400 A. H.

ibn Battah al-Akbari, Ubaidullah [عبيدالله بن بطة العكبري]. *al-Ibaanah an Shareeah al-Firq al-Naajiah* [الإبانة عن شريعة الفرق الناجــــة]. Riyadh: Daar al-Raayah. 1988.

ibn Hajr, Ahmad. [أحمد بن حجر]. *Fath al-Baari bi-Sharh Saheeh al-Bukhaari* [فتح الباري بشرح صحيح البخاري]. Makkah: Maktabah Daar al-Baaz. 1989.

-----*Tahdheeb al-Tahdheeb* [تهذيـــب التـــهذيب] Beirut: Muassasat al-Risaalah. 1996.

ibn Hasan, Uthmaan [عثمان بن علي بن الحســـن]. *Minhaj al-Istidlaal ala Masaail al-Itiqaad Ind Ahl al-Sunnah wa al-Jamaah* [منهج الاستدلال على مسائل الاعتقاد عنـــد أهـــل الســـنة والجماعـــة]. Riyadh: Maktaba al-Rushd. 1992.

ibn Hazm, Ali [علي بن حزم]. *Al-Ihkaam fi Usool al-Ahkaam* [الإحكام في أصول الأحكام]. Zakariyyah Ali Yoosuf publisher. n.d.

ibn al-Jauzi, Abdul Rahmaan [عبد الرحمن بن الجوزي]. *Zaad al-Maseer fi Ilm al-Tafseer* [زاد المسير في علم التفســـير]. Beirut: Daar al-Fikr. 1987.

Ibn Katheer, Ismaaeel [إسماعيل بن كثير]. *Tafseer al-Quran al-Adheem al-Maroof bi Tafseer ibn Katheer* [تفسير القرآن العظيم المعروف بتفسير ابن كثير]. Riyadh: Maktabah Daar al-Salaam. 1998.

ibn Muhammad, Fauzi [فوزي بن محمد]. *al-Adhwaa al-Samaawiyyah fi Takhreej Ahadeeth al-Arbaeen al-Nawaiyah* [الأضواء السماوية في تخرج أحاديث الأربعين النووية]. Amman, Jordan: al-Maktabah al-Islamiyyah. 1413 A.H.

ibn al-Qattaan, Ali ibn Muhammad [علي بن محمد بن القطان]. *Bayaan al-Wahm wa al-Eehaam al-Waqi'een fi Kitaab al-Ahkaam* [بيان الوهم والإيهام الوقعين في كتـــاب الأحكـــام]. Riyadh: Daar Taibah. 1997.

Ibn al-Qayyim, Muhammad [محمد بن القيم]. *Ilaam al-Muwaqqieen an Rabb al-Alameen* [إعلام الموقعين عـــن رب العـــالمين]. Beirut: al-Maktabah al-Asriyyah. 1987.

-----*Madaarij al-Saalikeen bain Manaazil Iyyaaka Nabudu wa Iyyaaka Nastaeen* [مدارج السالكين بين منازل إياك نعبد وإياك نستعين]. Beirut: Daar al-Kitaab al-Arabi. n.d.

Ibn Taimiyyah, Ahmad [أحمد بن تيمية]. *Majmooat al-Fataawa Shaikh al-Islaam ibn Taimiyyah* [مجموعة الفتاوى شيخ الإسلام ابن تيمية]. Collected by Abdul Rahmaan ibn Qasim and his son Muhammad. Riyadh: Daar al-Ifta. 1978.

----- *Minhaaj al-Sunnah* [منــهاج السـنة]. Riyadh: Jaamiat al-Imaam. 1986.

ibn Tooloon al-Dimishqi, Muhammad [محمد بن طولون الدمشقي]. *Ilaam al-Saaileen an Kutub Sayyid al-Mursaleen* [إعلام السائلين عن كتب سيد المرسلين]. Beirut: Muassasah al-Risaalah. 1987.

Itr, Abdul Rahmaan [عبد الرحمن عتر]. *Maalim al-Sunnah al-Nabawiyya* [معالم السنة النبوية]. Jordan: Maktabah al-Manaar. 1986.

Itr, Noor al-Deen [نــور الديــن عــتر]. Introduction to al-Khateeb al-Baghdaadi [الخطيب البغــدادي]. *al-Rihlah fi Talab al-Hadeeth* [الرحلة في طلــب الحديــث]. Beirut: Daar al-Kutub al-Ilmiyyah. 1975.

Kamali, Mohammad Hashim. *Principles of Islamic Jurisprudence.* Selangor, Malaysia: Pelanduk Publications. 1989.

Khadduri, Majid. *Islamic Jurisprudence: Shafi'i's Risala.* Baltimore: Johns Hopkins Press. 1961.

al-Khairabaadi, Muhammad [محمد الخير آبادي]. Footnotes to Hunaad ibn al-Sirri [هناد بــــن السـري]. *Al-Zuhd* [الزهد]. Published by the Ameer of Qatar. n.d.

Kuwaiti Ministry of Religious Endowments and Religious Affairs. *Al-Mausooah al-Fiqhiyyah* [موسوعة الفقهية]. Kuwait: 1992.

Lane, E. W. *Arabic-English Lexicon.* Cambridge, England: Islamic Texts Society. 1984.

al-Madkhali, Rabee [ربيع المدخلي]. *Makaanah Ahl al-Hadeeth* [مكانة أهل الحديث]. Bahrain: Daar al-Arqam. 1985.

Majlis of al-Haq Publication Society. *In Defence of the Quran and Sunnah.* S. Burnaby, Canada.

al-Manshaawi, Muhammad [محمد المنشاوي]. *Qaamoos Mustalahaat al-Hadeeth al-Nabawi* [قاموس مصطلحات الحديث النبـــوي]. Cairo: Daar al-Fadheelah. n.d.

Maudoodi, Abul Ala. *An Introduction to Understanding the Quran*. Riyadh: WAMY. 1990.

al-Nadwi, Sulaimaan [سليمان النـــدوي]. *Tahqeeq Mana al-Sunnah wa Bayaan al-Haajah Ilaihaa* [تحقيق معنى السنة وبيان الحاجة إليــها]. Beirut: al-Maktab al-Islaami. 1994.

al-Nawawi, Yahya [يحيى النووي]. *Sharh Matin al-Arbaeen al-Nawawiya* [شرح مـــتن الأربعــين النوويــة]. Muhammad Rasheed Ridha, ed. Maktabah al-Salaam al-Aalimiyyah. n.d.

-----*Sharh Saheeh Muslim* [شرح صحيح مسلم]. Beirut: Daar al-Marifah. 1996.

al-Qaasimi, Jamaal al-Deen [جمال الدين القاسمي]. *Mahaasan al-Ta'weel* [محاسن التأويل]. Beirut: Daar al-Fikr. 1978.

al-Qurtubi, Abu Abdullah [أبو عبـــد الله القرطـــي]. *al-Jaami li-Ahkaam al-Quran* [الجامع لأحكام القـــرآن]. Beirut: Daar Ihya al-Turaath al-Arabi.

Philips, Bilal. *The Evolution of Fiqh*. Riyadh: International Islamic Publishing House. 1995.

al-Raazi, Fakhr al-Deen [فخر الدين الـــرازي]. *Tafseer al-Kabeer* [التفسير الكبير]. Beirut: Daar Ihyaa al-Turaath al-Arabi.

al-Saadi, Abdul-Rahmaan [عبد الرحمـــن الســـعدي]. *Taiseer al-Kareem al-Rahmaan fi Tafseer Kalaam al-Mannaan* [تيسير الكريم الرحمن في تفسير كلام المنان]. Riyadh: Al-Muasassah al-Saeediyyah.

al-Saalihi, Ali [علي الصالحي]. *Al-Dhau al-Muneer ala al-Tafseer* [الضوء المنير على التفسير]. Riyadh: Maktabah Daar al-Salaam. n.d.

al-Saayis, Muhammad Ali [محمد علي السايس]. *Tafseer Ayaat al-Ahkaam* [تفسير آيات الأحكام]. Kulliyat al-Shareeah. Azhar.

Salaamah, Mustafa [مصطفـــى ســـلامة]. *Al-Tasees fi Usool al-Fiqh ala Dhau al-Kitaab wa al-Sunnah* [التأسيس في أصول الفقه على ضوء الكتاب والســـنة]. Cairo: Maktabah al-Haramain li-l-Uloom al-Naafiah. 1415 A.H.

Al-Salafi, Muhammad Luqmaan [محمد لقمـــان الســـلفي]. *Al-Sunnah: Hujiyyatuhaa wa Makaanatuhaa fi-l-Islaam wa al-Radd ala*

Munkireehaa [السنة: حجيتها ومكانتها في الإسلام والرد على منكريها]. Madinah: Maktabah al-Imaan. 1989.

Salmaan, Mashoor Hasan [مشهور حسن سلمان]. Footnotes to Ibraaheem al-Shaatibi [إبراهيم الشـــاطبي]. *Al-Muwaafaqaat* [الموافقات]. Al-Khobar, Saudi Arabia: Daar ibn Affaan. 1997.

al-Shaafi'ee- See Khadduri.

al-Shaatibi, Ibraaheem [إبراهيـــم الشـــاطبي]. *Al-Itisaam* [الاعتصام]. Al-Khobar, Saudi Arabia: Daar ibn Affaan. 1992.

-----*Al-Muwaafaqaat* [الموافقـــات]. Al-Khobar, Saudi Arabia: Daar ibn Affaan. 1997.

al-Shaukaani, Muhammad ibn Ali [محمد بـــن علـــي الشوكـــاني]. *Fath al-Qadeer* [فتح القدير]. Mustafa al-Babi al-Halabi. 1964.

-----*Irshad al-Fahool* [ارشاد الفحول]. Beirut: Daar al-Marifa. 1979.

Shawaat, al-Husain [الحسين شـــواط]. *Hujiyyat al-Sunnah* [حجية السنة]. Falls Church, VA: American Open University. n.d.

al-Sibaa'ee, Mustafa [مصطفى السباعي]. *Al-Sunnah wa Makaanatuhaa fi al-Tashree al-Islaami* [السنة ومكانتها في التشريع الإسلامي]. Beirut: al-Maktab al-Islaami. 1982.

Al-Sid, Muhammad. "The Hermeneutical Problem of the Quran in Islamic History." Ph.D. Dissertation. Temple University. 1975.

Siddiqi, M. Z. *Hadith Literature: Its Origin, Development, Special Features and Criticism.* Calcutta: Calcutta University Press. 1961.

Siddiqui, Abdul Hamid, trans. and commentator. *Sahih Muslim.* Lahore, Pakistan: Sh. Muhammad Ashraf. 1972.

al-Sihaibaani, Abdul Qayyoom [عبد القيـــوم الصحيبـــاني]. *Tadheem al-Sunnah wa Muwaqaf al-Salaf miman Aaridhuhaa au Istahza bi-Shain Minhaa* [تعظيم السنة وموقف السلف ممن عارضها أو استهزاء بشيء منها]. Madinah: Maktabah ibn al-Qayyim. 1414 A.H.

al-Subki, Ali. "*Mana Qaul al-Imaam al-Mutalibi Idha Sah al-Hadeeth Fahuwa Madhhabi* [معنى قول الإمام المطلبي إذا صح الحديث فـــهو مذهـــي]." In *Majmooah Rasaail al-Munairiyyah* [مجموعة رسائل المنيرية]. Riyadh: Maktabah Taibah. n.d.

al-Suyooti, Jalaal al-Deen [جلال الدين السيوطي]. *al-Itqaan fi Uloom al-Quran* [الإتقان في علوم القرآن]. Beirut: Daar al-Marifah. 1978.

-----*Lubaab al-Naqool fi Asbaab al-Nuzool* [الباب النقول في أسباب التزول].
Beirut: Daar Ihya al-Uloom. 1980.

-----*Miftaah al-Jannah fi al-Ihtijaaj bi al-Sunnah* [مفتـاح الجنــة في
الاحتجـــاج بالســنة]. Badr al-Badr, ed. Kuwait: Daar al-Huda
al-Nubuwwa.

al-Tabaraani, Sulaimaan [ســليمان الطـــبراني]. *Turuq Hadeeth Man
Kadhaba Alayya Mutamadan* [طرق الحديث من كذب علي متعمدا].
Beirut: al-Maktab al-Islaami. 1990.

al-Tabari, Muhammad ibn Jareer [محمد بن جريـــر الطـــبري]. *Jaami al-
Bayaan an Taweel Ayi al-Quran* [جامع البيان عن تأويل أي القرآن].
Beirut: Daar al-Fikr. 1988.

al-Tartoori, Husain [حسين الـــترتوري]. *"Mabaahith al-Sunnah ind al-
Usooliyeen* [مباحث السنة عند الأســـوليين].*" Majallat al-Buhooth
al-Islaamiyyah* [مجلـة البحـــوث الإســـلامية]. No. 20, Dhul-
Qaadah/Dhul-Hijjah 1407 A.H./Muharram/Safar 1408 A.H.

Al-Teeby, al-Husain [الحسين الطيــي]. *Sharh al-Teebi ala Mishkaat al-
Masaabeeh* [شرح الطيي على مشكاة المصابيح]. Makkah: Maktaba
Nazaar Mustafa al-Baaz.1997.

al-Turki, Abdullah [عبد الله التركي]. *Usool al-Imaam Ahmad* [أصول الإمام
أحمد]. Riyadh: Maktabah al-Riyaadh al-Hadeethah. 1977.

Al-Umrai, Akram Dhiyaa [أكرم ضياء العمري]. *Buhooth fi Tareekh al-
Sunnah al-Musharrifah* [بحوث في تاريخ السنة المشرفـــة]. Beirut:
Muassasah al-Risaalah. 1975.

Uqailaan, Ahmad [أحمـــد عقيـــلان]. *Min Lataaif al-Tafseer* [من لطائف
التفسير]. Al-Mansoorah, Egypt: Daar al-Yaqeen. 1998.

Usmani, Muhammad Taqi. *The Authority of Sunnah.* New Delhi,
India: Kitab Bhavan. 1991.

von Denffer, Ahmad. *Ulum al-Quran: An Introduction to the
Sciences of the Quran.* Leicester, England: The Islamic
Foundation. 1983.

al-Wuhaibi, Muhammad [محمـــد الوهيــي]. *Nawaaqidh al-Imaan al-
Itiqaadiyyah wa Dhawaabit al-Takfeer ind al-Salaf* [نواقض
الإيمان الاعتقادية وضوابط التكفـــير عنــد الســـلف]. Riyadh: Daar al-
Muslim. 1996.

Yusuf, S. M. *An Essay on the Sunnah: Its Importance, Transmission, Development and Revision.* Lahore, Pakistan: Institute of Islamic Culture. 1966.

Zarabozo, Jamaal al-Din. *Commentary on the Forty Hadith of al-Nawawi.* Boulder, CO: Al-Basheer Company for Publications and Translations. 1999.

-----*The Friday Prayer: Part I: The Fiqh.* Ann Arbor, MI: Islamic Assembly of North America. 1998.

-----*The Methodology of the Quranic Commentators.* Falls Church, VA: American Open University. 1997.

-----"Sahih Hadith." *al-Basheer.* Vol. 3, No. 4, Nov.-Dec. 1989.

al-Zuhairi, Abu al-Ashbaal [أبو الأشبال الزهيري]. Footnotes to Yoosuf ibn Abdul Barr [يوسف بن عبد البر]. *Jaami Bayaan al-Ilm wa Fadhlihi* [جامع بيان العلم وفضله]. Al-Damaam, Saudi Arabia: Daar ibn al-Jauzi. 1996.

Quranic Verses Cited

General Index

Notes

Notes

Notes